WITHDRAWN

HARVARD LIBRARY

WITHDRAWN

Nicholas Rescher
(1983, age 55)

ONGOING JOURNEY

Nicholas Rescher

UNIVERSITY
PRESS OF
AMERICA

LANHAM • NEW YORK • LONDON

Copyright © 1986 by

Nicholas Rescher

University Press of America,® Inc.

4720 Boston Way
Lanham, MD 20706

3 Henrietta Street
London WC2E 8LU England

All rights reserved

Printed in the United States of America

Library of Congress Cataloging in Publication Data

Rescher, Nicholas.
  Ongoing journey.

  Rev. and updated ed. of: Mid-journey, © 1983.
  Bibliography: p.
  Includes index.
  1. Rescher, Nicholas.   2. Philosophers—United States
—Biography.   I. Rescher, Nicholas, Mid-journey.
II. Title.
B945.R45A3   1986   191   86-15847
ISBN 0-8191-5590-X (alk. paper)
ISBN 0-8191-5591-8 (pbk. : alk. paper)

All University Press of America books are produced on acid-free
paper which exceeds the minimum standards set by the National
Historical Publications and Records Commission.

FOR MY CHILDREN

Contents

Introduction ix

Part I
MID-JOURNEY (1975)

One	Family Background	3
Two	A German Childhood—Hagen: 1928-1938	19
Three	An Immigrant Boy—Beechhurst: 1938-1942	27
Four	High School Days: 1942-1946 (Age 13-17)	37
Five	Queens College; 1946-1949 (Age 17-21)	51
Six	Princeton University: 1949-1952 (Age 21-23)	61
Seven	U.S.M.C.: 1949-1952 (Age 23-25)	79
Eight	The Rand Corporation: 1954-1956 (Age 25-28)	95
Nine	Lehigh University: 1957-1961 (Age 28-32)	109
Ten	Pittsburgh—The First Years: 1961-1966 (Age 32-38)	125
Eleven	Pittsburgh—The Years of Change: 1966-1971 (Age 38-42)	139
Twelve	Pittsburgh and Oxford: 1971-1974 (Age 42-46)	155
Thirteen	Retrospect: 1975 (Age 47)	175

Part II
ONGOING JOURNEY (1985)

Transition (1985) 189

Fourteen	Squirrel Hill: 1975-1980 (Age 47-52)	191
Fifteen	Wanderings: 1981-1985 (Age 53-57)	201
Sixteen	Retrospect: 1985 (Age 57)	215

NOTES AND INDEX

Notes 219
Index of Names 227

Introduction

I TOOK up my first teaching post at the age of 23 at Princeton, ending the years of academic apprenticeship and setting out on a professional career. I shall—God willing—in due course be rusticated at the age of 70, the long-established retirement age at the University of Pittsburgh. Thus at the time when this biographical material is being written—in 1974-1975, when I am 46/47 years of age—I stand at the exact mid-point of my professional life.

Autobiographies are generally produced by septuagenarians reviewing the course of their lives in distant and detached retrospect. It is a matter of looking back with seemly pride at one's achievements, offering plausible excuses for one's failures, and perhaps settling a few old scores. One shortcoming of this procedure is that whatever wisdom might come from such a scrutiny of one's self and one's doings can no longer be put to active use. The hour is late, the sun is setting, the work of the day is done—it is too late to do or undo. In writing the present book too early, as it were, I hope to avoid this shortcoming. This premature autobiographical exercise will, I trust, enable me to obtain whatever useful lessons of self-knowledge can be extracted at a stage when some profit can still be drawn from its deliberations.

In retrospect things always look simple: we know with the wisdom of hindsight just where the twists and turns lead. But at the time, when much is unknown and undecided, there is an uncertainty and anxiety that yields some element of suspense. And so, it seems fitting to take stock of the journey I have travelled, and to peer—however myopically—down the road that lies ahead.

I believe, moreover, that some special interest attaches to such an essay written *in medias res*, before all the returns are in and one confronts settled issues with the wisdom of hindsight. The course is not yet run, so that it is a genuinely open question how things will eventuate—whether with fondest hopes exceeded or with reasonable aspirations blighted. Some element of suspense still hovers about the picture of a life that is yet unfinished and has to face the yet unissued rulings of the goddess Fortuna whose stern decrees permeate all human contingencies.

This autobiography began in an endeavor to record for the benefit of my children some information about their own antecedents and parentage—information which would otherwise go to the grave with me, leaving them virtually pastless. Gradually, however, a sea-change came upon the work. It took on a life of its own and became an endeavor in self-definition and self-comprehension.

The reader who looks here for "the life and times" will be disappointed in the latter regard. For one thing, I am too small a fish in too large a pond for this sort of thing. For another, it has been my practice to go my own way insofar as possible and let the times go hang. By temperament I am not a joiner or promoter of causes. I have generally found my own allotted share of the world's work quite enough to handle. Without hiding my head in the sand as to the great issues and developments of the day, I have concentrated on the tasks that confronted me on the agenda of my personal and professional life, and have been disinclined to expend time and energy on things I deemed impervious to such feeble efforts as I could muster.

Ideally, a "life"—be it written or lived—should have a certain plan, a plot that endows it with some coherent structure. It should have a tale to tell—a rise to riches or power, a failure to realize great expectations, a story of tragic decline and unmerited degradation, perhaps an overcoming of great obstacles by sheer force of character. In my own case, there is indeed such a plot, although one that lacks the great drama of the preceding sketches. Its story-line revolves about my finding myself in the career of a philosopher and especially as an author of philosophical books. In reviewing one of my publications, a German scholar once spoke of my "*beängstigender Autorenfleiss*"—fearsome diligence in authorship or *scriptomania*, to put it less kindly. It is this aspect of my makeup—the gradual emergence of an inveterate writer of philosophical books—that is the recurrent *Leitmotiv* of these pages. Paradoxically, the book is my *Apologia pro libris suis*.

In the Preface to his *Autobiography*, the English philosopher R. G. Collingwood wrote that "The autobiography of a man whose business is thinking should be the story of his thought." I do not believe this for a moment—any more than I believe that the autobiography of a painter should be the story of his pictures. An autobiography should tell the story of a *life*, and man lives neither by nor in his work alone. Moreover, an author should not have to speak for his books—they should speak for themselves. I have tried to write here the biography of a person who happens to be an "intellectual" of sorts, but not to produce an intellectual autobiography.

At this point, more that sixty thousand copies of my two dozen books are knocking about in the world. By best-seller standards this is infinitesimal, but for an academic author of professionally technical material it represents a respectable production. And it seems plausible to suppose that occasionally here or there someone who encounters one of my books should wonder about the person who brought it into being. After all, as one wanders down the library shelves among all those products of brains long stilled, one cannot wholly suppress one's curiosity about the people who produced these books—about their personalities and characteristics, their hopes and fears, their successes and failures, and their management of the business of living. Moreover, viewed at close range no active human life can be altogether withoug interest for a fellow human being. This circumstance, which assures immortality to the character of a gossip, also gives the autobiographer some comfort when faced with the otherwise daunting question: "But why on earth should you presume that *your* doings are of the least interest to anybody?" After all, even the most commonplace life of one generation is destined to appear strange and extraordinary to the distant retrospect of its eventual successors.

No man is a hero to his valet, no man a villain to his autobiographer. Yet everyone's life involves some episodes that occasion subsequent regret—transactions from which he does not emerge as the sort of person he would wish to be. The reader can scarcely expect to find all of them chronicled and detailed in an autobiography. The amazing Pepys aside—for in human affairs every rule has its exception—the autobiographer whose candor knows no limits has a boor for a subject. This said, I think it nevertheless fair to add I have endeavored to produce an honest work, one that portrays a real and thus an imperfect person, endowed with an ample quota of human shortcomings and failings. I am persuaded that a reasonably accurate picture—not necessarily of the sort of person I would ideally like to be, but of the sort of person I actually am—can be drawn from the data presented here. The watchful reader will find that I have pictured myself as Cromwell wished to be painted, "with the warts on."

Still, a biographical work is bound to wear a somewhat unrealistic aspect. Its subject is constantly at center-stage. Such exclusive focus upon ourselves suggests a false importance and centrality. Life, of couse, is not like that. Almost always and everywhere we are but one among numerous others who feature no less prominently in the scheme of things. Because this distortion is unavoidable, the reader should be generous enough not to impute automatically to an autobiographer a narcissism that is not necessarily there.

In a work of this autobiographical nature perhaps a word about the writing of it is not out of order. I must say that I have found it harder to write than anything else I have produced. For I am a person who is naturally reticent about his personal affairs almost to the point of secretiveness, and the idea of admitting others into the inner precincts of my life is antipathetic to me. But having embarked on the project as a matter of obligation I have pressed ahead. However, I have found this sort of writing possible only in very short bursts, usually lasting for only a paragraph or two, as a particular mood conducive to this sort of candor was transiently upon me. For me, this writing project was a harder-won victory over blank pages than most.

ADDENDUM: 1985

Initially written in 1974-75, this book remained a typescript in a drawer until 1982. At that point, the University Press of America was about to launch a series of reprints of books of mine, and Jed Lyons, its excellent editor, asked me if I might have something of a more personal nature to form part of this project to give it an "added touch" of sorts. After thought and hesitation I concluded that there was no cogent reason for declining to "go public" with this book, which thus appeared in 1983 under the title *Mid-Journey*. For reasons explained on page 189, I eventually decided to update the book to 1985, adding the three additional chapters that differentiate this book from its predecessor. (Apart from the explicitly designated addenda there are only a few minor corrections and additions to the earlier text.) The title under which the book now appears, *Ongoing Journey*, seemed an obvious choice in indicating the relationship to its predecessor.

PART I
Mid-Journey (1975)

One

Family Background

A. Rescher Forefathers

THE GENERAL consensus of opinion and the universal practice of biographers agree that a person is to be viewed against the background of his family antecedents. As a traditionalist, I find no difficulty in yielding to the pressure of this tradition. Few people are wholly self-made. For most, at least some facet of *what sort* of a person one is will turn on *who* one is. And here the motley throng of people who provide one's ancestral heritage becomes significant.

The basic name-pattern *R-scher* has many dialect variations through the multiplicity of spoken German forms. It can occur with *A*, or *E*, or *O*, or *Ö* (that is, OE). But all of these go back to *Rascher* as their common original. However, two distinct etymological routes lead to this common destination: one via the Anglo-Saxon *rasch* = swift, active, lively, hasty,[1] the other via *rasch* from Arras, the medieval tapestry center, with *r-scher* = *r-schner* = a weaver of tapestry.[2] The name would thus have two distinct English equivalents: *Rusher*, one who hastens, and an approximation to the far more common *Weaver*. I have sometimes thought fleetingly of anglicizing the name in the former way.

Raschers were active in Franconia in the 13th century.[3] The Roschers are an old Nether-Saxon family who produced several well-known scholars, and in particular the important 19th century economist Wilhelm Roscher.[4] One Johann Roescher (1589-1668) was court preacher for a duke of Brunswick-Luneburg just prior to the time when Leibniz entered the service of this house.[5] Reschers have been substantial landholders in Hesse at least since the 17th century.[6] There were R-schers pretty well scattered throughout the German-speaking realm. However, my own ultimate ancestors were Swiss. The clan of von Rascher was an old family prominent since medieval times in the town of Chur (Coire) in the canton of Graubünden (Grisons), the most remote and perhaps the most backward region of Switzerland. Ennobled in 1550, the family divided in the troubled times of the Reformation. In 1580 its Catholics emigrated to Vienna, leaving the Protestants in possession of the home ground in Switzerland.[7] By the early 1700's this emigré branch of the family had prospered and was again raised to the minor nobility—this time in Austria.[8] It was to this group that my own forefathers belonged.[9]

The first paternal ancestor whom family tradition identifies by name is my grandfather's great-grandfather Albrecht Heinrich von Rascher, who was born in Austria around 1750. The younger son of proud and prosperous parents, only recently ennobled, he outraged his family by making an "unfortunate" marriage which severed him altogether from his relations. The young lady he chose to make his own was Jewish, and to obtain her hand in marriage he agreed to have their children brought up in his wife's beliefs.[1] Their son, Johann Jakob, was accordingly raised in this faith, and in loyalty to his mother's memory, he eventually named his own son—my father's grandfather—Nehemias, after the Old Testament hero. But this son's adherence to his grandmother's religion faded away in time, and he resumed the Christianity of his forefathers—not, however as a Catholic, but in the standard German Protestantism of the Lutheran-Evangelical stripe.

His marriage having alienated him from his family, Albrecht Heinrich von Rascher left Austria in the early 1780's and resettled in southern Germany, near Mannheim in Baden. Dropping the nobiliary prefix *von* as unsuitable to his changed circumstances in life, he also altered the name to Röscher, attuning its orthography to the local Swabian dialect.[11] I do not know just how he earned his livelihood; apparently he was never prosperous. He died around 1810. As a result of his move to southern Germany, the destiny of my ancestors unfolded in Baden and Württemberg, and the theater of their activity came to lie in the valley of the river Neckar—in Mannheim, Stuttgart, Tübingen, and their environs.

Albrecht Heinrich's fateful marriage produced one son, Johann Jakob Röscher (named, so family tradition has it, after Jean Jacques Rosseau), who was born around 1780. Eventually he came to enjoy a modest prosperity as a proprietor of a business in the small town of Hochberg, in Baden. Around 1815 he married a local girl who was about a decade younger than himself. They had several children, but all died in infancy except one boy, Nehemias, born in 1828. The father died (in his middle fifties) in June of 1835, when the son was only seven, and the mother followed her husband to the grave a year and a half later, still in her early forties.

My father's grandfather was thus orphaned as a little boy of eight. I do not know who took charge of his upbringing or just where he was raised. However, there was no financial difficulty. His father's business had prospered and adequate funds were available for the boy's immediate needs. He received a good schooling, which he concluded in 1848. During 1848–49 he discharged his military service obligation in the army of Württemberg, and then proceeded to study the medical basics at the University of Tübingen. After further medical study at the University of Würzburg—at that time perhaps the best medical school in Germany—he took his M.D. examination in the summer of 1852. Later that year he settled in the rural hamlet of Schrozberg (not far from Stuttgart) with his new bride, Emilie Isar, the twenty-year-old daughter of one Leopold Isar of Sonthaim-on-the-Neckar. By then he had already simplified the spelling of his name from Röscher (= Roescher) to Rescher.

Throughout his working life Dr. med. N. Rescher practiced medicine as a *Landartzt* in Schrozberg. He was very popular in the village, and on the 30th anniversary of his service there his fellow citizens held a special celebration in his honor. Family tradition depicts him as the typical old-time country doctor, struggling to make ends meet to support his growing family. As the son of his son Alfred wrote me, "I well remember my father saying how, on cold winter nights, he often hitched the horse and buggy and would drive his father into the country to attend a patient, and of how, very often he was not paid for his services, which he gladly performed on the basis of need, or was paid small amounts, often only in kind with a few eggs or vegetables." Dr. Rescher was quite handsome—as evidenced by a fine, old lithograph of him as a young man which remains in the family. (It was made in 1849, when he was a young medical student of 21 years, and shows him in the characteristic tighwaisted jacket of the day.) He died of a chronic ailment in 1885, at the relatively young age of 57.

My father's grandfather had married twice. His first wife, Emilie, bore him seven children, of whom only four survived to adulthood: Otto b. 1853 (my own grandfather), Adolf b. 1856, Emma b. 1860, and Julie b. 1865. The marriage had lasted some seventeen years when Emilie died in March of 1869, leaving the bereaved physician with sons aged 16 and 13 and daughters aged 8 and 4. The family evidently needed a mother, and so, after a minimally seemly period had elapsed, my father's grandfather remarried in December of 1869, then aged 41. His second wife, Nanette, was the 28-year-old daughter of Alexander Gunzenhausen, a businessman from Mannheim. In the course of the next ten years she gave birth to eight children, four of whom survived to adulthood.[12] Notwithstanding the rigors of almost annual maternity throughout the decade of her 30's, she lived to a ripe old age in America, where she eventually emigrated with all her children.[13] They settled in Denver, where she died in 1925 at the age of 84. The subsequent history of this part of the family forms an independent unit, and a somewhat sad one, since the Rescher name now stands at the brink of extinction in this "American Branch" of Reschers, launched by the children of my great-grandfather and Nanette Gunzenhausen Rescher.[14]

The Schrozberg doctor's first marriage had produced two sons. The second, Adolf, was born in 1856, and in due course became a successful businessman in Stuttgart, where he resided throughout his life as a prosperous pillar-of-the-community type. (Around 1878 he married a local girl, and this union resulted in the birth in 1883 of a single child, Oskar Rescher, who was to become an eminent but eccentric Arabist.[15]) The other son—the elder—was my own grandfather Otto, born in 1853.[16]

On reaching adulthood, my grandfather, Otto Rescher, left his parental roof in Schrozberg together with his brother Adolf to make their way in the business world of Stuttgart. Their father had hard work of it to support the growing family of his second marriage on a modest medical practice in a rural village, and could not afford to send his sons to the university. However, the lads were apparently endowed with business acumen, and both ultimately prospered. Otto Rescher became an importer and wholesaler of textiles (largely woolens imported from England). By his late forties he had made a substantial fortune. He then sold his business, and went into retirement, living in an apartment in the Bad Cannstadt section of Stuttgart. He devoted himself to the maintenance of his (as he thought) delicate health, pursuing the then-common hypochondriac routines of vegetarianism, bottled waters, and extensive spa visits, and so continued pretty much hale and hearty until his death at almost eighty years in 1932.

Around 1888 Otto Rescher married Emilie Haarburger, the daughter of a prosperous Stuttgart manufacturer.[17] Born in 1861, this young lady bore the name of his own mother, Emilie, but was nicknamed Emmy. They had five children in all, of whom only two survived infancy—my father Erwin Hans, born in 1890, and his sister Gertrude, born in 1903, whom I remember well from my childhood. She was a charming, rather flighty woman—married numerous times, with all of her marriages ending in divorce.[18]

As this brief family history indicates, the Reschers of recent generations have all been solid, middle-class professional people: physicians, businessmen, lawyers, scholars. Moreover, they have usually been well-to-do, with a more than ordinary ability in matters of business. They have generally shown considerable drive and tenacity in making their way in the world. Finally, they have also often exhibited a streak of decided eccentricity, manifested in grandfather Otto's hypochondria, the eccentricities of great-uncle

Oskar, and even in Aunt Gertrude's succession of marital mishaps. They have been people outside the common run, with more ability and more "character" than one ordinarily meets with.

B. Father

My father was born in Stuttgart on April 21, 1890. He grew up in the midst of a prosperous, bourgeois, Forsyte-like family circle. All I know about his early youth is that his uncle Adolf was a great favorite of father's, who as a child loved to go on long rambles with him in the woods around Stuttgart. My grandfather was apparently not much given to small-talk, and so it was from Uncle Adolf that my father learned about the struggles of the Rescher brothers for business success in the Stuttgart of the 1870's and 80's.

After completing his schooling at a humanistic *Gymnasium* in Stuttgart, my father attended the local university in nearby Tübingen. During the period from 1909 to roughly 1912 he there lived the life of the typical university student of Kaiser Wilhelm's Germany: hard work, good companions, beer, and, of course, a duelling society (called the "Allemania," I think). Throughout his life, father wore across his left cheek the duelling scar that was the characteristic badge of such a fraternity. His Tübingen studies completed, father transferred to the University of Berlin, where he enrolled in the Faculty of Law. He completed his legal studies in 1914, just in time to join the ill-fated throng of young men being herded over the precipice of World War I.

In the fall of 1914 my father received a commission as a lieutenant in the army corps which the King of Wurttemberg contributed to the military cause of the German Reich.[19] He trained initially for the cavalry, and after mastering such splendidly obsolete skills as the use of a lance on horseback, spent four years in the trenches of the Western Front. Amazingly, he survived the war, emerging from four years of Army service as a senior grade lieutenant, the holder of the Iron Cross (second class) and some lesser decorations. I remember well the tale of father's Iron Cross. One day the commanding general of his division inspected his unit. He commented on father's lack of decorations and father replied that he had no deeds of special valor to his credit. The GOC asked how long the young lieutenant had been in service at the front and father said he had been there for some two years. "That's valiant enough," said the GOC, and ordered the award of an Iron Cross.

The majority of my father's friends and classmates were devoured in the senseless slaughters of the Western Front. When I was a boy of five or six years, we visited Stuttgart and walked in the cemetery where my father's own father had recently been buried. There father showed me the great cenotaph for local victims of the war, many of them the companions of his youth. (Fewer than one in ten in father's Gymnasium class survived the war.)

After the demobilization, father returned to the law, taking up an internship as "assessor" with a law firm in Frankfurt an der Oder. With this training completed, he settled down in 1922 to practice law in Hagen, in Westphalia. Initially he was in partnership with another attorney (one August Fischer), and they maintained an office in the "Hagener Zeitung" Building. However, after a couple of years he set up on his own. No doubt he had a strugglesome time of it at first, but by the later 1920's he had built up a flourishing practice.

My mother entered this picture in 1924 when she came to work in my father's office as his secretary. She was a young woman of great beauty and charm, and it is little wonder that they soon fell in love. They were married in September of 1925; when father was 35 and mother just under 20.

At first they lived in a small flat in the Hohenzollernstrasse (at the corner of the Körnerstrasse), but shortly before I was born in 1928 they removed to a larger apartment in the Ruhrstrasse, which then became my birthplace. Not long afterwards they purchased a family-sized house in the more suburban Leibnizstrasse.

The early 1930's must have been "the years of wine and roses" for my parents. Father was building up a thriving law practice. Mother busied herself not only with child and home, but also an active social life, and, above all, with athletics. At this stage mother was an enthusiastic gymnast and sportswoman, who, weather permitting, spent part of each day at the local sporting ground.

My parents' good fortune came crashing down in flames with the onset of the Nazi regime in 1933. Father never troubled to conceal his dislike of the Nazis and what they stood for—imprudently, for a practicing attorney. As the Nazification of the judicial system proceeded, lawyers known to be unsympathetic towards the Nazi cause simply stopped winning cases.[20] In consequence, clients, of course, went elsewhere. By the middle 30's my father's law practice was *kaput*. Economic hardship, dismay at political developments, and the approach of the day when, on reaching the age of ten, I would soon have had to join in the compulsory activities of the "Hitler Youth," combined to set my parents to think of emigration. In 1936 they sold the house on the Leibnizstrasse. That summer father went to the U.S.A. for an exploratory visit, and he returned permanently the next year to arrange for a place to live and a means of livelihood. After a circuit of farewell visits, Mother and I crossed the Atlantic to join him in 1938.

The transatlantic migration was financially ruinous for my parents. One could bring only a modicum of personal possessions, and the Nazi regulations prohibited emigrants from taking more than 100 marks apiece in cash (then some $25). Fortunately, father was able to transfer a modest sum of around $1,500 surreptitiously through Switzerland.

The most immediate problem facing my father was clearly that of earning a living for himself and his family. He was unable to resume his career as a lawyer, the differences between the German and the Anglo-American systems being so substantial that this would have required several years of preparation in a law-school, which was obviously out of the question. In an America still caught up in the slump of an unconquered depression, the obstacles to the useful employment of an immigrant aged almost fifty were formidable. So father turned for a career to his hobby, photography. With the money salvaged via Switzerland, he started a small photographic business.

After 1939, he shared a small storefront at 161-11 Northern Boulevard in north Flushing with a friend who operated a sporting-goods shop—a somewhat curious arrangement! This business went on in a modestly adequate way. (By 1940 we were even able to afford our first car, a 1936 vintage Studebaker, whose acquisition for some $300 impressed me greatly, since in Germany we had never owned—nor indeed needed—an automobile.) Mother would sometimes help out in the studio, and father brought home to her all pictures for coloring, which in those days was done by hand-painting. In this way, my parents managed to eke out a modest livelihood.

Things went along reasonably smoothly until catastrophe struck in the wake of America's entry into the war upon Japan's attack on Pearl Harbor in December of 1941. As part of the military security precautions launched after America's entry into World War II—measures which most notably included the internment of Japanese-Americans—a regulation was instituted prohibiting all "enemy aliens" who lived within 300 miles of the seacoast from owning cameras. The point, it seems, was to prevent their taking pictures of military installations, war plants, shipping, troop movements, and the like. At this time, however, father was still a German national—he did not acquire U.S. citizenship until late in 1942. Overnight, his photographic business was finished, and he had to sell his stock at a substantial loss. For the second time in a decade father's vocation had been pulled out from under his feet and his livelihood destroyed by the rude intrusion of political developments. Over fifty years old, he once again stared economic disaster in the face—this time in a still unfamiliar and unaccustomed environment.

What to do? Father met with courage and good humor the difficulties of a man no longer young confronting the task of making his living in a strange place. He turned to being a self-taught bookkeeper and accountant—first at Bloomingdale's large department store in Manhattan, and then as the war-economy expanded in a small shipyard in Whitestone. After 1946—when it became clear that the shipyard, a wartime product now transformed into the "Whitestone Woodworking Co." could not survive during peacetime conditions—father's place of employment shifted to the head office of

Drake's Bakery in Long Island City. The work was doubtless tedious, but it provided a modest and secure income.

Father's spare time was always devoted to reading and writing. Amidst the routine and largely uninteresting occupation which had replaced his shattered career, he turned to the development of inner resources. Gradually my father made himself over into something he had never had the time to be in Germany—an intellectual. He spent his leisure hours (and very little money) building up a small but solid library of German and English literature—especially his favorite Goethe. And he even turned out a couple of rather amusing short stories. His reading covered a wide range of English literature, with 18th century authors among his favorites—Sterne, Goldsmith, and, above all, Boswell's *Johnson*.

The late 1940's were a time of much financial stringency for our family, but they were also a time of security and stability—a comparatively happy period after a decade of turmoil. Around 1950 circumstances were eased slightly by the onset of a modest monthly compensation payment to those who had lost their professions in Germany during the Nazi era. Now finally—when he was some sixty years old—the family's finances were once more relatively comfortable.

But it was too late. In 1951 father began to show the signs of a distressing and dangerous heart condition (*angina pectoris*). Though occasionally painful, it did not stop him from getting about—on a visit to Washington in the summer of 1952 (where I was then stationed on military service) or on a final visit to Germany that August—the first and last time father revisited his native land after emigrating in 1937. Suddenly one evening in late October of 1952 he died of a heart attack just after turning in for the night. His body was cremated a few days afterwards, as he had instructed. Not until a decade later did his ashes find their final resting place—in the peaceful little cemetery by the newer Quaker meeting house at Middletown, Pa. near Philadelphia (where my mother's ashes were eventually to join his, more than a quarter century after his death).

Father lives in my memory as a man who, though strict, was warmhearted, kind, and endowed with a sense of humor. When my interests turned to mathematics and technical philosophy, they diverged increasingly from his, but we nevertheless were always close—especially during the latter 1940's. Father was unquestionably an officer and a gentleman, and in various ways a rather admirable person. I still find it surprising and impressive that he was able to keep up his good spirits and even temper throughout all those upheavals, at any rate as far as all external appearances went: his resilience of spirit must indeed have been substantial! He was rather "unflappable," as the English put it. The experiences of World War I had impressed his personality with a degree of Stoicism. *"Kommt Zeit, kommt Rat"* (roughly, "We'll cross that bridge when we get there") was one of his favorite sayings, and another was the Roman legal maxim *Ultra posse nemo obligatur* ("No one is obligated to do more than is possible"). The strength not to lose heart in the face of adversity is among the most difficult of human accomplishments. It is to my father's great credit that he managed to achieve this.

C. My Mother's Family

My mother's father, Wilhelm Heinrich Ludwig Landau, was born in 1869 in Kreis Waldeck in Hesse. In my recollection he stands out as a characteristic German type—a fine, bluff, somewhat irascible old gentleman who forms one of the vivid memories of my childhood. He was one of the younger sons of Karl Landau (1825-1898), a flourishing farmer in the rural hamlet of Goddelsheim. The Landaus had been settled in Waldeck since time immemorial, taking their name from the village of Landau (near Arolsen). However, by the 17th century the family no longer lived there, but had removed first to Neukirchen and later to Goddelsheim. The Lutheran parish register at Sachsenberg traces our line continuously from Johannes Landau(1665-1735), a miller of Neukirchen; in fact, the Landaus owned and operated the mill at Neukirchen throughout the 17th and 18th centuries.

Subsequently the Landau family owned a large farmstead in Goddelsheim through succeeding generations, maintaining the property intact by the old expedient of letting it pass always to the oldest son.[21] Thus young Wilhelm—as a younger son—went off around 1890 to seek his fortune in a nearby city, and somehow found a niche in the sales office of the Andreas Brewery in Hagen, Westfalen. He worked in this office for some fifty years until his retirement at the age of seventy—rising gradually to become manager of the sales department. I remember the tale that in his earlier days he carried a large rubber syringe on his public relations rounds of the *Bierstuben* that featured Andreas beer ("Edelpils"), so that he could secretly empty the *kleines Helles* pressed on him by a convivial innkeeper, accepting hospitality without impairment to his working efficiency. He died in 1943 on the ancestral lands in Goddelsheim, where he and grandmother had moved "for the duration" to escape the bombings of industrial Hagen, so that I never saw him again after we left Germany in 1938.

My maternal grandmother, Adele Landau née Kämper, was born in 1878. The Kämpers lived in Gevelsberg, near Hagen, but also had some family connection in Goddelsheim. (Family tradition has it that these Kämpers came originally from the Netherlands— and that one of their ancestors was a pirate named Klaus Störtebekker (?).) On the morning when Adele was born, her father returned home in such a condition from revels celebrating the anniversary of the German victory at Sedan in the Franco-Prussian War that he did not learn of his new daughter's arrival until several days after the event.

Wilhelm and Adele Landau had two daughters, my maternal aunt Luise (b. 1903)[22] and Meta Anna, my mother, born on December 14, 1903. Grandfather Landau very much wanted a son and was so furious that mother was a girl that for a time he would not speak with my grandmother! Grandfather had a choleric strain, and did not lead his wife an easy life. During my childhood in Hagen they lived in a small apartment house (of perhaps five units) at 69 Bergstrasse. The building was owned by grandfather himself, and it was an open secret in the family that if any tenant was financially embarrassed when the rent fell due on the first of the month, grandmother would dip into her carefully nursed savings to make the rent-payment possible on time. For whenever someone's rent was overdue, grandfather Landau became increasingly irritable with each passsing day, so that grandmother's apparent altruism was very much a matter of self-interest.

I remember the Bergstrasse house well from childhood, for mother and I lived there with my grandparents during 1936-38, after my father's departure for the U.S.A. The building was burned out in the incendiary bombing raids of World War II, and grandmother sold the land to the city after the war for reconstruction. Another small apartment-house was erected on the site and grandmother continued to live there for the rest of her life.[23] On visiting her there in September of 1963, I recognized in the immediate neighborhood only one old building across the street which housed a shop whose two old-maid shopkeepers remembered me from a quarter-century before. Among local houses, it alone survived the incendiary raids, thanks to the efforts of the two brave old ladies who manned their roofs during air-raids with buckets of sand to extinguish the firebombs.

Grandmother Landau was my only grandparent to survive into my adulthood. (She died in 1966, so that I got to see her again during visits to Germany after the war.) It was, I suppose, the fact that I was her first grandchild that created a special bond between us. At any rate, during my German boyhood I felt that of all nonparental adults it was she to whom I was especially close, and we spent a good deal of time together.

D. Mother

My mother was born in Gevelsberg near Hage, Westfalen on 14 December, 1905, her parents' second daughter (and last child). Mother and her sister Luise ("Ise") had a typical German childhood of the period, including the deprivations of World War I and the very difficult immediate post-war period. Upon completing her schooling in the early 1920's, she first spent a year in a finishing school for girls that principally trained them in "home economics," inculcating the mysteries of Hausfraudom. Then she spent another year or so in secretarial school. At the age of 18, in early 1924, she finished her training and was ready for her first employment, which she found in my father's law-office. She must have made a deep impression, for she was a strikingly beautiful young woman, as the photographs of this period attest.[24] A little more than a year later my parents were married (in September of 1925). Some three years after that came the birth of their only child, myself.

The decade from 1923 to 1933 must have been a time of ease and happiness for my mother. But the next 25 years were a period of constant difficulty and anxiety. She had to support her husband through a steady stream of catastrophes: the collapse of his career in 1934-35, the transatlantic migration in 1937-38, the struggles to gain a foothold in a strange country during 1938-40, the collapse of father's business in 1942, the economic stringency of the early war years (when mother held down one makeshift job after another to help keep us afloat), the war's severance of all contact with her parents and relations, a time of ill health around 1944-46, my father's period of (ultimately fatal) illness during 1951-52, and then the difficult readjustment to living on her own. One after another the hammer blows of ill fortune came down on mother. Yet, nothing daunted, she carried on throughout it all cheerfully and constructively. Her own inner spirit somehow equipped her with resources to cope with difficulties for which her early years of secure girlhood and affluent matronhood must have left her utterly unprepared.

After 1941, until her "retirement" in 1970 at the age of sixty-five, mother held a varied succession of jobs. During World War II she worked for a time as a saleslady at Macy's Department Store in Manhattan. From 1944 until my father's death she worked in the same capacity at Henri Bendel, a fashionable ladies-wear shop on West 57th Street. After moving to California in 1955, she continued in this line of work for some months in a similar establishment in the 400 block of Wilshire Boulevard in Santa Monica.[25] But then she changed gears. In 1955 she became assistant to the director of the Friends (Quaker) International Center at UCLA. Then from 1955 to 1957 she directed a Quaker work-camp for young people at Tlaxcala in Mexico, and then spent another year there helping to run the Quaker hostelry Casa de los Amigos in Mexico City. Thereafter, from 1961 until her retirement in 1971, she served as the "Official

Hostess" of Westtown School, the Quaker boarding school near Philadelphia. After retiring she stayed at Westtown until the Fall of 1972, living at "The Farmhouse" on the school campus. Mother then moved to Illetas near Palma in Mallorca, where she lived for almost two years. At the present writing (August, 1974) she lives in our house at No. 6 Cunliffe Close, Oxford. She enjoys Oxford where she keeps busy with activities in the North Oxford community center (The Ferry Center) with volunteer work—especially for the little Oxfam Shop on Oakthorpe Road in Summertown—and with participation in the Quaker Meeting.

As this brief account shows, my mother is a versatile and resourceful woman, with great powers of adjustment to varied settings, and equally at home in a German, English, or Spanish environment. She is a warm, enthusiastic, outgoing person who makes friends easily—gregarious on the surface, though not without some reserve and attachment to privacy underneath. She is a lady of enormous charm and great practical good sense. I have always loved her dearly and with the passage of years I have come to admire her as well.

TWO

A German Childhood
Hagen: 1928-1939

(Age 0-9)

AFTER THEIR marriage in the spring of 1925, my parents lived in an apartment on the first floor of a large house on the Ruhrstrasse, in a pleasant residential district of Hagen in Westphalia. It was there that I was born on Sunday, July 15, 1928. I am the only person I know of among my contemporary acquaintances who was born at home rather than in a hospital. My mother's obstetrician believed in this if the parents could arrange to hire the necessary help—an idea nowadays sporadically returning to favor in Europe. I was christened Klaus Helmut Erwin Rescher, becoming Nicholas only in 1938, after our emigration to the U.S.A. (The Germans shorten NICKOLAUS = NICHOLAS to KLAUS from the second half of the word, the English to NICK from the first.)

When I was about a year old, our family moved to a two-story, family-sized house with a many-gabled roof of brown tiles, "standing in its own grounds," as the English say, at the top of the Leibnizstrasse (No. 3). I remember the pleasant, grey-green stucco house well, for we resided there until I was seven years old. The entire neighborhood was then an attractively suburban area, and I enjoyed roaming over it on exploratory rambles.

This period of my early childhood was the era of my parents' greatest prosperity. My mother was at this stage very energetic and greatly devoted to sports and gymnastics. She spent much time at such activities, and until I was four years old or so I was mostly committed to the care of a nanny. Thereafter, mother did many more things with me, and for a time I became her steady companion. Father was generally away at his law office, and so remained somewhat on the periphery of my life. Until 1934, his legal practice thrived, and he joined an active social life to his busy professional one.

As a small child I spent much time with my Grandmother Landau who lived in a spacious apartment in the Bergstrasse at the other end of town. Grandmother and I would often make long excursions across the fields and meadows of the nearby countryside. I adored "found objects" and invariably brought home various treasures— bits of rusty old iron and the like. I was, of course, less close to my paternal grandparents, who lived in far-off Stuttgart. I recall only very dimly a visit to them 1931, the last time I saw my grandfather Rescher who died the next year. (I remember somewhat better yet another visit to Stuttgart in 1934, when we left flowers at his grave.)

My memories of early childhood are for the most part happy ones. Much of my time was spent playing in the large, sloping garden of the Leibnizstrasse house, digging in some unused corner, building rock constructions, playing games with my little friends, and the like. I was basically a good child but also mischievous. On one occasion in 1933 or 1934 a friend and I came upon some catechism books left by some pupils from the neighborhood Catholic girls' school who, their classes over, were playing in a local park. We promptly threw the books into the lake while the girls were busy at their games. On another occasion around this time, while mother and I were on holiday at Bad Honnef on the Rhine, I released the numerous occupants of a rather large rabbit-hutch, and appeared in our hotel room with my apron full of little bunnies.

In the fall of 1933, at the age of five, I was enrolled in a kindergarten—a small, privately run affair under the care of Fraulein Irmgart Ritter, a pleasant young lady who struggled three or four mornings a week to channel our youthful energies in such constructive directions as drawing and paper cutting.

At this time I also began to read—apparently quite spontaneously. I had learned the alphabet when $4\frac{1}{2}$ years old from an alphabet picture-book that my parents had given me. (It still remains in my possession!) After this I would amuse myself by spotting letters on store-signs, placards, and the like, having taught myself how to put letters together into words. One day, aged just over five, I surprised my mother by reading her all the signs along the trolley-route into town.

In the fall of 1934 I began the first grade of school at the public (state) elementary school in the neighborhood. Little about my initial school year now remains in my memory apart from two things: that I rather liked school itself, but that during playtime in the schoolyard I was regularly oppressed by the class bully—an obnoxious little boy a year or so older than I, who had somehow managed to lose the first joint of one of his thumbs. I was not displeased when we moved away at the end of the school year and I was transferred to another school.

Increasingly after 1933, the shadow of National Socialism lengthened across Germany—and across my father's career. The Nazi movement made itself felt on every side. No opportunity was lost for holding a parade or rally or comparable demonstration of physical presence. Uniforms sprouted forth everywhere—the makers of brown shirts and leather straps and jackboots must have made a fortune. It was known in legal circles that father was decidedly not a Nazi. One small but symbolic episode sticks in my mind. In 1933-34 many boys—even the little ones of my own age—started to sport swastika armbands in imitation of the members of the Brown-Shirt brigades who were always strutting about. I launched an agitation with my parents to be allowed to have an arm-band like the other boys. Finally they gave in and let me have one—but with a difference. Instead of the Swastika, the arm-band mother made me a small-scale version of the old three-striped black-white-red German flag. I was disappointed and felt that this was "just not the same thing." And I'm sure that that's exactly what other people thought.

Though my parents kept their worries about political developments to themselves, I could not help learning that something was amiss. I still recall various signs of this. The summer of 1934 we were to take a holiday in Switzerland. We started out with a visit *en route* to my grandmother in Stuttgart, where we were also to pick up some travel documents. These were denied to us, and so we went for a (very pleasant) visit to Baden-Baden instead. Again, later that year my father was called in for the extra-thorough tax audit—a device used to annoy persons deemed unfriendly towards the Nazi regime. I recall his spending several days at home worriedly compiling his records and documents. On another occasion, my father received a summons to attend a meeting in the Town Hall, and he and mother were greatly concerned about this. It transpired—to my parents' great relief—that the occasion was merely one of distributing some medal being awarded routinely to those who had served as officers during World War I.

Behind all this loomed one crucial and crushing fact. After 1933, my father's law practice was increasingly moribund as members of the bar who were known to be cool to the regime found fewer and fewer clients. And so the spring of 1935 saw a development that was truly momentous for my parents and for me—the decision to emigrate to the U.S.A.

As the first preparatory step, my parents sold the house in the Leibnizstrasse during that summer. Thereupon we went to live in two rooms of my grandparents' large flat in their house in the Bergstrasse. I attended the local elementary school *(Volksschule)* in the fall of 1935, and continued there until early 1938, with various interruptions for travel on farewell visits to relations. As best I recall the system, the class kept its same teacher from year to year. I remember my teacher well—a kind, intelligent, and sensible Herr Feist, who was eventually killed as a soldier on the Russian Front. Only a handful of school incidents of this period remain in my mind, most prominently my first caning in the office of the school principal for some trivial offence. At the time, I regarded this punishment as unmerited by the minor transgression that occasioned it. Only later did I learn that it had actually been instigated by my own mother, who suggested to Herr Feist that the experience "might be good for me." We spent many hours playing games in the schoolyard, and I recall that at the time I was very enthusiastic about soccer.

My various playmates of this period are now dim in my memory. They included Dieter Nölle whose father was, like mine, an attorney; Günther Alles whose parents owned a leather-goods shop, and Günther Grote whose father owned a photography shop. One boy in particular remains vividly in my mind because of an amusing incident often retold in my family. Wolfgang Maier, a friend of my own age (then 8) whose father was an agent for a pharmaceutical company, in my presence once asked mother in a very serious, grown-up sort of way, just making polite conversation, "Haben Sie viel Last mit dem Lümmel?" (Does the good-for-nothing give you much trouble?). I cannot say whether I was more shocked by his nerve or impressed by his maturity.

The things I principally enjoyed doing as a small child were the usual ones—play with my friends, outings with my parents, games with adults at my grandparents' place. Perhaps only two of my interests were developed beyond the level of the ordinary at this stage: woodworking, which I soon gave up altogether, and reading, which has remained my prime avocation to the present day. The stories of Wilhelm Hauff were among my favorites. And I still have in my possession the copies of *Robinson Crusoe, Dr. Doolittle,* and *Little Lord Fauntleroy* in the German versions in which I first read them at age 7-8.

In early 1936 my father made a short exploratory visit to New York. The next year he crossed the Atlantic for good, mother and I traveling to Hamburg to see him off. Hamburg impressed me greatly as a beautiful, prosperous city, liberally sprinkled with greened copper roofs. The year 1937-1938 was largely given to preparations for emigration. I attended school rather intermittently at this stage, though various attempts were made to assure that I did not stop doing school work altogether. My mother arranged with a young nun from a local convent, who had lived in England for a time, to tutor me in English. She used *Mother Goose* as a text and for some reason thought it well to begin with "Humpty Dumpty." I found it most strange that the English would use the word for *egg* (German *Ei* pronounced just like the letter I) as a term meaning *myself* (I).

One vivid recollection of that last year in Germany relates to the plebiscite of 1938. In April of that year, a month after the *Anschluss* of Austria, Hitler appealed to the citizenry of the new Gross-Deutschland for a renewed 4-year mandate of power. (He won it by over 99%.) Among the last memories of my childhood in Germany is my going with mother to the voting place on this occasion. Since the two different styles of ballots (yea or nea) were preprinted, with only the affirmative ballots made available at the polling stations, the whole thing struck me as silly. What, I thought, could be the point of holding an election when there were no alternatives for a choice? Young innocent that I was, the deeper ramifications of the political process were quite beyond me!

The two years between father's first exploratory trip to the U.S.A. in the spring of 1936 and the summer of 1938 when mother and I joined him there were spent in a sort of limbo as far as our own family life was concerned. Mother and I became planets orbiting the family of my grandfather and grandmother. I am now surprised that this did not seem strange to me, but as I think back to my early years, I am struck again and again by a child's ability to take things in stride and adapt to drastic changes without thinking anything amiss.

After our emigration to the U.S.A. became a settled issue, it transpired that a development of significance for our lives had taken place more than a decade before. In the 1920's my father's father had made plans to emigrate to ancestral Switzerland. Among the preparatory steps, he had transferred the bulk of his fortune to the care of the Schweizerischer Bankverein in Basel. However my grandmother dug in her heels. She had lived in Stuttgart all her life, and most of her friends and relations lived there. Understandably enough, she was reluctant to move away to a new and strange city.

Though natural, this was also unfortunate. For the Nazis eventually forced the repatriation of these assets and ultimately confiscated them. (But for grandmother's stubbornness, I might today be a wealthy man—and perhaps a Swiss one as well.) Yet even a black cloud can have a silver lining, for grandfather's Swiss fund made it possible for father to get a modest sum past the fiscal controls imposed by the Nazis.

One day in early July in 1938 mother and I made the trip by train to Bremen, accompanied by grandmother Landau. There we boarded the U.S.S. President Roosevelt for the transatlantic voyage. I left my native land without much sorrow or regret. My thoughts dwelt wholly on the adventures that lay ahead—the reunion with father and life in a new country about which I knew little more than I had seen in the Keystone Kops movies, which were popular in the Germany of my childhood.

What sort of boy, now nearing ten years of age was crossing the Atlantic? I was (I do believe) good natured, and of a friendly, outgoing disposition, reasonably alert and intelligent, rather fond of reading, and fond also of sports and physical activities. (I made the error of taking my never-to-be-used soccer equipment along.) But there was nothing whatever to indicate special ability in any particular direction, such as art or music, which children so often manifest at a tender age. My work at school had been mediocre—not egregiously bad, but by no means outstandingly good. I was an altogether ordinary boy—good of heart, but quite average in abilities. And I certainly lacked any crystalized ambitions or aspirations.

Was our leaving Germany for a fresh start in a new and foreign land a wise step or a foolish one? I have never hesitated for a moment to regard it as eminently wise. Conceivably, our lives might in some ways have run smoother course in "the old country," for there is no doubt that a time of very real hardship lay ahead for my parents. Yet things would probably have been far worse in Germany. The Nazi pestilence was a present and worsening reality, and a major war lay in the foreseeable future—a war in which, young though I was, I might well have been caught up.

Over the years my thoughts have often dwelt on that force in human affairs to which the Romans gave the name of *fortuna* and that we call fortune, luck, chance, or the like. Its role becomes paramount in extraordinary conditions (war, disaster, revolution) when the "normal" circumstances of quiet life are ruthlessly abolished. The whole experience of emigrating from Germany and placing an ocean between ourselves and the Nazi catastrophe and its concomitant war left me with the strong conviction that it is safer and wiser to sidestep rather than grapple with world-historical disasters. The sensible course in such circumstances is not, alas, that of valor and heroic confrontation, but that of prudence and discretion. When the cattle stampede or the avalanche thunders down, there is no point in standing pat. It seems wiser to follow the course of prudence and get out of the way than to undertake a hopeless struggle against potent and malign forces wholly beyond one's control.

Dr. Nehemias Rescher
(Great-grandfather as a medical
student in 1849, age 21)

Otto Rescher
(Grandfather ca. 1885, age 32)

Erwin Hans Rescher
(Father as a student in his
duelling fraternity outfit,
Tübingen 1912, age 22)

Meta Landau Rescher
(Mother at the time of her
marriage in 1925, age 19)

Oskar Rescher (Osman Reşer)
("Uncle Oskar" in 1965, age 82)

Nicholas Rescher
(1971, age 43)

Nr. 3 Leibnizstrasse, Hagen,
Westphalia (Boyhood home ca. 1934)

Klaus Helmut Erwin Rescher
(The author in 1936, age 8)

A Family Portrait (1976)
(Mark, Dorothy, Catherine, Nicholas, Owen)

THREE

An Immigrant Boy
Beechhurst: 1938-1942

(Age 10-13)

M<small>Y MOTHER</small> and I sailed on the U.S.S. President Roosevelt from Bremerhaven on the 8th of July, 1938. After brief stops at Le Havre in France and Cobh in Ireland, the ship crossed the Atlantic on a smooth voyage of which I still have various pleasant recollections. As any boy would, I loved roaming about the large vessel, breathing the sea air, sensing the unaccustomed motion of the ship, and being awed by loud blasts of its great horn.

At the synthetic "horse races" in the ship's lounge one evening, a kind elderly gentleman placed a 25¢ bet for me, and I won a dollar or two, which I saw as a good omen. I recall the thrill of first sighting the Statue of Liberty and the impressive view of the New York skyline. We landed in the early morning of July 16th, the day after my tenth birthday. This new year of my life was to see a new start in an altogether strange place.

It was exciting—and somewhat odd—to be in a foreign country with a different language. But I was very pleased to be reunited with my father, whom I had not seen for over a year. We soon cleared through customs and made our way by taxi out to Long Island. I was glad to leave Manhattan behind. It seemed over-powering to me: intimidatingly massive, overcrowded, and—after the tidiness of German towns—rather dirty. Still, an aura of excitement hung over the hustle and bustle of the place, and a mixture of wonder, apprehension, and hopefulness filled my mind.

Our first residence in the U.S.A.—where we lived for some six months after our arrival—was an apartment in a recently built duplex which father had rented in a newish, red-brick, residential suburb somewhere on the outskirts of Flushing. My recollections of that summer form a kaleidoscopic series. I particularly remember working in the garage to make things out of orange crates (a boat, hauled to a distant beach by public transport on a very hot August day, only to sink instantly upon launching). Then too I recall the excitement occasioned by a succession of hold-ups at a local bar.

1938 saw the opening of the New York World's Fair, which took place virtually in our own back yard, so that we often went there. By and large, the national exhibitions made relatively little impression upon me. The industrial ones were a different matter, however. Several of them had a futuristic orientation, and I was fascinated by the robots, the fanciful automobiles, the ultra-modern houses, and other accoutrements of twenty-first century cities as seen from the vantage point of 1938. This reinforced the sense of new horizons and challenging possiblities opened up by our transatlantic move.

That fall I took my place as a student at the local public elementary school. The first day of the new school year came on a hot day in early September and I reported with an open shirt—without a tie. The school rules required boys to wear ties, and I still remember vividly how the teacher's vain attempts at explanation were followed by the vista of a surrounding sea of boys and girls, pointing at their necks or mine, tugging their ties, some enthusiasts even taking theirs off to wave in the air. I got the idea, and henceforth appeared duly tie-equipped.

The school made a special effort to help me adapt to the grade into which I had been placed according to age. I was excused from some of the usual classes to have special lessons with one of the reading teachers. She helped me to work my way through the whole curriculum of readers, beginning with the "baby-books" used in the first grade. After a time she left me pretty well to my own devices, just giving me books and struggling to resolve any questions I might have (she knew no German). I made good progress—heaven knows how—and at the end of ten or twelve weeks was getting pretty well caught up in reading. Gradually I began to settle into the routine of the place.

But another change was in the offing. Early in 1939 we made a further move—this time to the village of Beechhurst on Long Island Sound. Here father had found a larger and more pleasant apartment, not greatly removed from the house of a refugee physician and his family who had been friends of my parents in Hagen.

Beechhurst in those days was a small, virtually rural hamlet of some six thousand souls, with only a few shops—a grocery, a dry cleaners, a drug store, and perhaps one or two others. Located a bit further out than Whitestone on Long Island Sound, the only civic amenity of the place was a small public beach. And the only residential structure of larger than domestic size was our new home—a large apartment complex known as "The Beechhurst Towers," located at 160-65 Seventh Avenue. The building itself was a somewhat pretentious brick pile, with stone facing here and there, which had been erected in the economic euphoria of the 1920's. The establishment had offered a good deal in its prime, but had fallen on hard times with the Depression. Even so, it still afforded an amazing range of amenities, albeit in a state of ongoing decline. There was a pair of tennis courts, a beach with a pier extending into Long Island Sound (as well as a dilapidated and already virtually useless beach-pavilion), a recreation room equipped with ping-pong tables, and a private bus service which linked the Towers to the subway railhead in Flushing and also took the children back and forth to the local school. All this erstwhile grandeur of the place was slowly decaying from lack of upkeep in the new era of financial stringency. But my playmates and I did not require the splendors of well-manicured facilities—the old tennis-courts, the ping-pong tables, and the beach provided us with endless hours of pleasure, not withstanding their declining state of repair.

The Towers was important to me not just as a dwelling, but as a *social* unit on which I drew for most of my friends and which provided the stage-setting of our communal activities (tennis, ping-pong, swimming. etc.). Being an inhabitant of the Beechhurst Towers provided the first bit of community identification that I achieved since our American migration.

When we arrived in Beechhurst, my knowledge of English, though progressing, was still imperfect. I distinctly recall being somewhat hampered by language difficulties that spring during a birthday party for Jack Beddell, one of my Towers playmates—my very first social occasion in the U.S.A. But my English now improved with leaps and bounds, and I soon managed "to pass for native."

After we settled in the Beechhurst Towers I began to attend P.S. 30, the local elementary school. Housed in a little red brick schoolhouse that accommodated only the first six grades, it afforded a rather modest physical plant, and an unkempt, minimally equipped schoolyard. The human element was, happily, more auspicious, for the staff was both dedicated and competent.

Miss Jones, the principal, was a petite, red-haired lady who looked kindly on the red-haired immigrant boy being committed to her charge. She placed me in Miss Sabbathé's class, the fifth grade, which suited my age, though not my language-skills quite yet. This class was just one year from the top of the school, since only one further class, Miss Ferber's sixth grade, followed within this school itself. Our home-room teacher taught us all subjects except for penmanship. This was Miss Ferber's specialty, and I fear I must have taxed her patience sorely in trying—never with full success—to convert my Germanic hen-scratches into the smooth loops and whirls of Palmer penmanship.

The thing that impressed me very much about P.S. 30 can be summarized in the words *good will*, for a great deal of it prevailed throughout this small and modest school. It seemed to govern the relationship of all concerned, of teachers to students, students to teachers, and teachers to one another. Miss Sabbathé was a most kindly and helpful person. She began each morning with a reading from the psalms (the 23rd was her favorite), and the majestic verses of the King James Bible were the first pieces of English prose I learned by heart. One of my favorite times each day was the brief period alotted to free creative activity. (I was particularly fond of modeling with clay.) The fastidious Miss Ferber—who taught the sixth grade—seemed to me rather severe at first, but I came to like her immensely once she became my regular teacher in the sixth grade. It was her custom to spend that last 15-20 minutes of each day reading us a story on the installment plan, and listening to her do this was always one of the highlights of my day. The entire period I spent in this school from early 1939 to June of 1940 was a thoroughly happy time for me.

One of my Beechhurst friends who made a deep impression on me was Thomas Floyd Buckley, whose family lived in a large detached house around the corner from the Towers. Our friendship deepened only gradually, for Tom was some two years older than I, and in boyhood even two years makes a big difference. With his two somewhat younger sisters, his charming mother, and his bluff and imposing father (a professional actor whose gruff voice served for the radio-characterization of Popeye the Sailor), the Buckleys formed an attractive group which I have always regarded as the archetypically American family. Tom was a very bright and gifted lad, with a remarkable gift as public speaker and as a writer. (He eventually would end up on the staff of the *New York Times*.) Tom was something of a hero to me because there was about him an aura of easy assurance, of secure place in the fabric of the society, which I myself certainly lacked. (The experiences of my family had instilled in me a trace of uneasiness that no matter how well things seem to stand, circumstances beyond one's control can always intervene with disaster.)

My other close companions of this period were three occupants of the Towers, the two Merwin brothers, Donald and Philip, and John Beddell. Jack was the only one of my boyhood friends with strong scientific inclinations. He was a dabbler in chemistry and biology, tinkerer with electric gear, and devotee of science fiction, and eventually went on to study engineering in college. A blond, lanky, and somewhat moody lad, he tended to be more of a "loner" than my other friends. Of the Merwin brothers, Donald, a year or so older than I, was the intellectual, while Philip, a year or so younger than I, was a friendly, carefree, happy go lucky youngster. They were my constant companions and true friends. To my regret, I have long ago lost track of them. (Both, I believe, eventually entered careers in social service of some sort.) But throughout my years in Beechhurst these lads loomed large in my life and we whiled endless hours away in one another's company. Boys of ten through twelve are naturally gregarious creatures. They flock together, and the center of their world is populated by their fellows—adults live very much on the outskirts.

What did we do? We walked and talked. We took long aimless rambles along the East River shoreline. In bad weather we played Monopoly or even roulette (on a home-made wheel). On Saturday afternoons we would sometimes go to the 25¢ matinee at a movie house in nearby Whitestone. Ping-pong in the Towers' erstwhile clubroom was another indoor favorite. In good weather we swam and played on Beechhurst Towers' pier on the East River or played "boxball" on the sidewalk or in Tom Buckley's driveway. Tennis was also popular with us, and much of our time was spent on the Towers' gradually decaying tennis courts.

I am keenly alive to the great debt I owe to these lads-companions of my boyhood—for their companionship, their friendliness, and not least, their *teaching*. For the time we spent together was a precious learning experience for me: the testing of ideas and opinions in discussion, the perception of other views, the rubbing of one personality against another. One owes to one's childhood friends a debt which, unless repaid in kind at the time, can never be repaid at all.

I was amazed in retrospect at the speed with which my acculturation was accomplished. I had arrived at P. S. 30 in early 1939 as a "different" boy who stuck out in the setting of American school like a sore thumb. But by mid-1940 I had become transformed into an indistinguishably American boy. That this was possible is a tribute to the atmosphere of the school and to that of the wider Beechhurst environment of which it was an integral part. I cannot explain the process of Americanization, it was something that just happened—like growing up itself. Imperceptibly I felt less distanced from my fellows, and came to view the American past as part of my tradition. (Now, almost four decades later, I always feel that I am among "my people" when I return to the U.S.A. from abroad. When I visit my native land, I feel among strangers.)

Upon completing the sixth grade at P.S. 30, we were transferred to the rather large P.S. 79 in Whitestone, where I began the seventh grade in the fall of 1940, having just turned 12. At first we still went there by the Towers' private bus, but this stopped operating in the spring of 1941, and thereafter we travelled the two miles or so on the standard yellow school bus. This new school involved an innovation: the weekly "Assembly" of all the children in the school. A white shirt was mandatory for boys on assembly day. Early on, I came to assembly several times "out of uniform"—I cannot recall whether I did not own a white shirt or just forgot to put it on. One of my classmates thereupon gave me a new white shirt as a present. I felt grateful for this gift, but distinctly sheepish at being the recipient of such a charity. Still, this act of kindness produced the desired effect. Never again did I appear on Assembly day without the appropriate garb.

Games and outdoor activities were more organized at P.S. 79 than I had been accustomed to. Mostly we played softball, which bored me because one is inactive so much of the time. But I did enjoy the "clubs" held at school for one appointed hour each week. I particularly liked the stamp club. I had started collecting stamps in Germany and continued as an enthusiastic philatelist until my latter teens. I also liked the science club and acquired from it an enthusiasm for science that was to be dampened by poor instruction in high school later on.

At this time I began to acquire some taste for "literature," including poetry. Already in P. S. 30 we had had to memorize various poems. (Of these I now only remember the inevitable "Trees," which I thought rather silly—though it did lead me to take a closer and more appreciative look at this form of vegetation.) I now acquired a taste for poetry that endured until college days (but faded away swiftly thereafter). Our literature teacher in the seventh grade at P.S. 79 was a kindly spinster who had no capacity for disciplining her class, with the result that the students had no respect for her and disorder sometimes prevailed. Her very incapacity in this regard seemed to provide my fellow-students with a challenge to produce this result. This was my first memorable encounter with the need in human affairs for that trait of character called "capacity for leadership," the ability to elicit cooperation amidst centrifugal tendencies.

At school I was not one of the cleverest children, but I always did my work competently—and always received an *A* in "conduct." Had I grown up in the securer ambience of my native land, there would almost certainly have been more mischief about me. But now, being—or *feeling*—somewhat different from my fellows, I wanted to remain inconspicuous and not attract unfavorable notice. That difference itself, however, namely that I was *German*, was something that the ethos of the war era led me to deemphasize—certainly to others, and perhaps even to myself. This feeling did eventually lessen, but it nevertheless left its effect on me. It unquestioningly provided an added stimulus to thought: it drove me more into myself, and made me more introspective and cerebral that I otherwise would have been. We borderers who dwell at the interface of different cultures tend to be more reflective about things.

Brief and limited though it was, I am glad to have had a glimpse of American life before World War II. Now more than a third of a century past, it seems like the image of another world—one that belongs to an earlier generation, though (thanks to the movies!) it will never become quite as dead as the ethos of earlier eras. Still caught up in the aftershock of the Depression, it was the day of a people tried by great hardships and not found wanting. The America of the 1930's is scarcely an era to evoke nostalgia, but there is much about it that deserves admiration, for it was a time of people who cared for standards of achievement and ideals of heroism, despising the merely tawdry, and eager to look upwards towards those people and actions that have an element of the larger than life.

The Japanese attack on Pearl Harbor on 7 December 1941 for a time—a regrettably brief time—produced little change in our peaceful microcosm. The next day the school was a buzzing hive of chatter and speculation, but then all settled back into the normal routine—except, of course, for an occasional air-raid drill. (Who, in heavens' name, was going to bomb Whitestone?) The whole war saw periodic outbreaks of air-raid hysteria in New York: blackouts, sky-watchers, air-raid wardens, the whole silly charade (mainly calculated, one suspects, to "keep up morale" by creating a harmless outlet for people who "just *had* to do *something*" to help the war effort).

However, as the weeks passed, the effects of the war soon began to make themselves felt. My father's business was an early casualty. It had to be sold—at a substantial loss. For the second time in less than a decade economic catastrophe struck the family.

I was too young at the time to be in a position to remember much of the collapse of my parents' social and economic world in 1933-36—too young, or perhaps too preoccupied with the travails of a boy just beginning school. But the second disaster in 1942 had a quite different effect upon me. Not that I was ever for a moment anxious or apprehensive on my own personal account. Youthful innocence, combined with a total trustfulness in parents, always led me to feel that we would be provided for somehow—that I would not have to look into the face of disaster absolute. But I did feel rather acutely that we were not as others; that for other people circumstances were by and large smooth, but for us difficult.

Still, my own feelings—whatever they were—mattered little in the face of the massive problem that now arose. For what was to be done now that my father's business had collapsed and our livelihood with it? Somehow father turned up a makeshift job at Armonk in Westchester County, New York, and we moved there in the spring of 1942.

At Beechhurst my feet had come to be placed on increasingly familiar ground. Now, for the second time in a few years, came another major upheaval. Fortunately, it was confined to the now-familiar American context. In this regard, at any rate, a great transformation had come over our lives since the time—less than four years back—when Mother and I set sail for "the New World."

Four

High School Days 1942-1946
(Age 13-17)

My primary schooling came to its end at the Armonk village school in Westchester county. I attended this establishment only for a few months in the spring of 1942 and still recall pleasantly the diminutive but impressive graduation exercise of that June, for which I had to acquire my first-ever white summer suit. There were perhaps twenty children in my class, but the only Armonk schoolmate of whom I now have any recollection is a pleasant, lanky boy named Richard Landers. He came of an old local family, and used to take all the history prizes as a matter of course until I arrived to give him some competition. As best I recall, he was my only schoolfriend at this stage. I was thrown on my own resources a good deal during this time, for we lived in a rather isolated spot several miles from Armonk itself. So I now became an even more avid reader than heretofore.

In September of 1942, I entered Pleasantville High School located in the Westchester town of that name. We were shuttled back and forth from Armonk by bus, but this ride was often made unpleasant for us younger boys by some older bullies. I came to feel that the child who can walk to school is fortunate.

I well remember little of Pleasantville High apart from the roomy, much bewindowed classroom in which we now began the study of Latin, a language of which I came to be very fond. As (supposedly) mature high school students, we were left to our own devices during the lunch hour, and I soon discovered the delightful small public library, located near the school, which I visited with great regularity. Libraries have ever since remained among my favorite haunts—I can walk into one in any corner of the globe and feel immediately at home.

Throughout my high-school years I was an enthusiastic stamp collector. I had already been an active participant in the stamp club at P. S. 79 in Whitestone, and used to extend my collection by trading there. Eventually, however, I decided to specialize in 19th century European stamps, largely because I did not want to get involved in a pursuit of unending proportions and welcomed the idea of working in a limited domain. Thereafter I could only proceed by making purchases, so I came to devote most of my (always small) "allowance" to buying stamps. Fortunately, other interests—in schoolwork, in social contacts, and in tennis—eventually pushed stamp collecting aside.

Late in 1942 we removed to Summit, New Jersey to follow up some brighter job prospect that beckoned to my parents there. It must not have answered fully to expectation, because our stay lasted only for some six months. During that time I attended Summit High School and mildly enjoyed it. The compulsory class in mechanical drawing gave me a chance to discover my lack of artistic ability, but in general my performance in school was adequate, though I recall getting bogged down with long division of polynomials in algebra. I liked the school library, however, and used it a good deal for miscellaneous reading. Adventure stories (especially Robert Louis Stevenson) and swashbuckling historical novels (especially those of Alexander Dumas) were my favorites in those days.

While I was on casually good terms with several of my schoolmates, I did not form any close friendships in Summit and cannot now recall the name of a single one of my classmates or associates there. At home I was left to myself a good deal and tended to live the somewhat interiorized mode of life, doing a good deal of miscellaneous reading. It was, I think, at this stage of adolescence, when I was much left to my own devices, that I first began to think of who I was and what I wanted to be. In a vague sort of a way I now sensed within me the first stirrings of an aspiration to make something of myself. At this stage I was rather given to day-dreaming and the building of "castles in the air," indulging myself in this during leisurely walks to and from school through a pleasantly residential section of the town. It is just as well that an early move shifted me to a more active and sociable setting.

In the spring of 1943 we returned to the North Shore of Long Island—to Flushing. There we moved into a large, dark-brick apartment block at 36-20 Parsons Boulevard, just off its intersection with Northern Boulevard. The site was only about three bolcks north of Flushing High School—just around the corner from the attractive setting of the old Bowne House and the great Weeping Beach Tree. Our apartment here consisted of an entrance hall, a kitchen with attached dinette, a living room, a bathroom, and a single bedroom. It was cramped quarters for a family of three. I often slept on a convertible studio-bed in the living room, but when my parents stayed up late, mother did so instead.

I still think of this small apartment as the home of my youth. When we moved to Flushing in early 1943, I was only a fourteen-year-old high-school freshman, and my mother continued to live there after my father's death until early 1954. Accordingly, this apartment house was my family's home for over a decade, a period that included most of my high school years, all of my time in college and graduate school, the beginnings of my academic career at Princeton, and the whole of my military service. (I myself lived there until leaving for graduate studies in Princeton in 1949, a period of six years; to this very day in 1974 I have never resided so long at a single address.) The apartment complex lacked physical charm, but sheer familiarity bred a certain attachment. It was unquestionably convenient: only a short distance from my school, within an easy walk of the Public Library, the subway, and the center of town—and the movie houses, which I often frequented during my high-school years.

With its large and motley group of students, Flushing High was not one of the elite schools in the New York system. But there were many excellent teachers and a small core of able students who regularly met together in the more challenging courses and created a stimulating environment for one another. Here my academic inclinations first manifested themselves in a serious way. I liked Latin—though it was sometimes strugglesome going for me (in part, I now realize, because we were not really taught all that well). I always enjoyed history and social studies and still fondly remember a Mr. Harry Esterowitz who taught the latter subject in an uncommonly lively way.

I took to French from the very first. Our teacher—a middle-aged Mademosielle whose name, alas, eludes me—was a very able teacher and a great Francophile. French was the only language I ever learned really easily, and I loved every minute of it. I began to study the language in the spring of Operation Overlord, the allied cross-channel invasion of the Continent, and it was exciting to mark the progress of the allied forces across Normandy on the large map of France that hung in our classroom. As my study of French made headway, I became increasingly enthusiastic about this beautiful language and did much reading above and beyond the call of duty. On occasion I travelled to town to see French films, and I often read the French newspaper then published in New York. From time to time I attended a French-language lecture on some aspect of French thought sponsored by the *Alliance Française*, an organization of wartime expatriates concerned to promote the appreciation of Gallic culture. Gradually I acquired a reasonably good command of French—now alas much eroded.

Mathematics was unquestionably the subject that I made mine above all others. I have never been fond of arithmetic, nor had first-year algebra been a great success with me, but from my first exposure to geometry in the fall of 1943 I loved this subject and, through it, all of mathematics. (Just imagine—being able to dispense with the whole business of arithmetical computation!) Charlotte Knag, our unusually gifted teacher in algebra, at whose blackboard I first learned about mathematical induction, still remains fondly and vividly in my memory. The discovery of a penchant for mathematics was undoubtedly the high-point of my high school career.

Not that everything was peaches and cream. Some of the teachers seemed to me very bad inded. Strangely enough, their names stick in my mind while those of their more competent colleagues have often vanished. A Miss (and Dr.) Mann taught me biology in my first term at Flushing High School and did so in a way that killed forever any wish on my part for further formal instruction in the subject. Dr. Lilian Lieber was the head of the Mathematics Department and author of some strange books—works not exactly of mathematics but of a propaganda of sorts for mathematics. (The chief of these productions was entitled *The Education of T. C. Mits*—that is, "The Celebrated Man In The Street.") She made a poor impression on me because the classtime we should have devoted to learning mathematical techniques was given over to boring discussions of one or another of her books. I resented our being made a captive audience. Had my interest in mathematics not been firmly established by the time I arrived in her classroom, it too might have gone the way of biology. My contacts with chemistry were somewhat less traumatic, but also negative. It is a chastening thought that for most students a subject is made or unmade not by the intrinsic interest of its subject matter but by the personality of its teacher.

German, to be sure, was something I never studied formally at all. I did, however, read a good deal of miscellaneous classical literature on my own at this period, including Goethe's *Faust*, Schiller's *Wallenstein*, and the stories of Johann Peter Hebel, which I enjoyed immensely. It seemed to me that there was no point in wasting good courses on what came naturally. My ceasing to feel any sort of personal allegiance to Germany as a nation never diminished my appreciation of and admiration for the cultural products of German civilization.

In early 1944 I went to some Manhattan courthouse with my parents to arrange for my citizenship papers. I cannot say by what mysterious alchemy I had become transmuted into an American. Nowadays it might appear that I am something of a citizen of the world. My roots lie in Germany, the land of my youth. I am attached to England and spend a considerable period of each year there. I do much travelling and lecturing elsewhere—in Canada and in European countries. My scholarly attention has been devoted extensively to the products of Mediterranean civilization—the intellectual products of classical antiquity and of the Arabian peoples. Yet there is no doubt whatever in my mind that America is my homeland and Americans are my people. Though I never set foot in the U.S.A. until after my tenth birthday, Franklin, Washington, Jefferson, and Lincoln are an integral part of "my" historical heritage.

Throughout my high school years in Flushing, I often took the bus to Beechhurst for Saturday visits with my friends of Beechhurst Towers days. Jack Beddell had moved away, but Donald and Philip Merwin and Tom Buckley were still there. We would go on rambles or, more frequently, just sit around and talk—of our reading, our activities, or our various interests.

During the spring of 1944 Philip Merwin had become involved in a study-group run by a middle-aged dentist on Henry George's *Progress and Poverty*. By some mysterious process, a few cells of the "single tax" movement launched by Henry George in the 1880's had somehow survived into the New York of the 1940's, laboring to indoctrinate youngsters with the economic merits of a policy of restriction of taxation to land alone. Though the sessions had alrady been under way for some weeks, Philip persuaded me to accompany him and join in, and I attended this group for some 6-8 weeks. I came away from it with an utter scepticism about this (or any other) socio-economic panacea and with an enhanced opinion of my mental powers. It seems to me that I was able to detect many flaws in Henry George's reasonings, which, on the other hand, seemed totally convincing to our dentist-leader.

My father must be numbered among the close friends of my high school years, for around this time we became closer than before, drawn together by a shared interest in secondhand books. We often spent Saturdays combing the second-hand bookshops on Fourth Avenue in downtown Manhattan. These Saturday excursions had the effect of confirming me in my scholarly inclinations. I gradually built up a library of several hundred miscellaneous philosophical and literary volumes. This could be done at very little cost, since many second-hand treasures were available in the 25-75¢ range. The combination of a human fondness for bargain-hunting with a high school boy's penchant for collecting meant endless pleasurable hours among the dusty shelves of the obscure little bookshops which in those days littered that part of downtown New York. These Saturday outings—downtown by subway combing the bookshops, lunch in some self-service cafeteria—provided an inexpensive, constructive, and pleasant activity. I learned a good deal from my father, not so much by way of specific facts, as by the transmission of attitudes and predilections in bookish and academic directions.

During my high-school years I spent much time reading. I regularly walked over to the Flushing Public Library (as usual, a Carnegie foundation), and did a good deal of general miscellaneous reading. At first, Alexander Dumas appealed to me. Then P.G. Wodehouse became a great favorite. (He was already in those days a long-established author—a virtual classic—and it is startling to think of him as still alive and productive at this writing (1974), thirty years after the days of which I speak.) I also went through a Sherlock Holmes phase. But detective stories in general never had an appeal for me, nor did science fiction. I was interested in real life, and novels, biographies, and histories have always been the staple of my diet.

In summer I regularly spent much of my time on the tennis courts of the Whitestone Tennis Club. When the Beechhurst Towers stopped maintaining its tennis courts for reasons of economy in the spring of 1940, a group of three or four Towers couples had joined to purchase this very modest four-court establishment, which soon passed into the exclusive possession of John and Beatrice Hackenberg, a childless couple who had lived in the Towers until recently. The club's days of prosperity came when the Whitestone Yacht Club was closed in mid-1942 for the duration of the war, and many of its tennis enthusiasts came over to "our" club. Until 1947—throughout high school and on into my early college days—I was a "regular" of this establishment throughout the tennis season.

I was on friendly terms with many of the adult members of the club. But it also yielded much contact with boys my own age. One lad whom I now got to know at this time was John Frankenheimer, who later came to fame as a film director and producer. His family was one of the wartime exiles from the Whitestone Yacht Club, and Johnny had had the benefit of professional coaching. He played far better tennis than the rest of us, and when I met him in the finals of one of the club's junior tournaments, he massacred me by something like 6-1, 6-2. He was a decidedly self-impressed young man, and though I respected his prowess on the courts, I was put off by this.

Jack Clarke was a very different sort of youth. He was a typical "good time Charlie," an outgoing Irish American with a consummate gift for blarney, a fellow of infinite jest and good humor, ever fast with a quip and handy with a story—one of the most glib raconteurs I have ever encountered. He was a latecomer to the tennis club, a lad somewhat older than I (he had seen service in the Navy and had been discharged on some trivial medical ground). He had an impressive mastery of the American tongue, and an immense quota of native wit. We became fast friends during the summer of 1944 while both enrolled for summer studies at the Garden County Day School. Our friendship reflected the attraction of opposites—he had no academic inclinations whatever, and could think of little but larks and girls (subjects at that point but seldom on my mind). Considering the difference between our personalities, I honestly cannot say exactly what brought us together, but we were fast friends at this stage. After I entered college we drifted apart, and lost sight of one another. Many years later I heard that he was married, settled someplace on Long Island, and had a successful law practice. This last did not surprise me at all. If anyone ever had a natural gift of plausible gab Jack Clarke did—I feel certain of his ability to convince a jury of anything.

While I was shooting pool with Jack at the Flushing YMCA one rainy evening in the fall of 1945, a call was put out for an extra person for a duplicate bridge game. I was interested and, since Clarkie had other things to do, agreed to fill in. My partner, it turned out was a Mr. Charles Diels, a fine white-haired old gentleman of seventy-some years. I must have impressed him as promising raw material—eager and teachable, even if somewhat unskilled—for he expressed an interest in playing with me again the following week. This was the beginning of a collaboration that lasted for almost two years. I don't know that we won very often, but we regularly came in among the first few, save for a handful of occasional catastrophes (no doubt of my doing) which saw us finish at the bottom of the ranking.

We must have seemed a strange pair, separated by some fifty-five years, and I don't quite know what kept us together week after week. I suspect that on his side it was the appeal of dealing with someone not a septuagenarian. As to me, I felt that Mr. Diels was counting on me and that it would be wrong to let him down. Then too, I welcomed this unorthodox opportunity to interact with someone of an older generation, a surrogate for the grandparents I had left behind in Germany.

During my high school days I had little interest in girls until the last year (1945-1946). Even then I never had any one particular "sweetheart," but there were several girls in school who were my good friends, and of whom I was fond in that ill-defined, semi-romantic way that is seldom far removed in the friendship of young persons of the opposite sex. The recollection of most of these friendships has now grown so dim that for the most part I cannot even now recall the names of the young ladies.

In the course of the 1944-45 academic year I was elected to Flushing High School chapter of ARISTA, the scholastic honorary society. This was important for me in two ways. For one thing, it had a marked effect on the development of my self-image: I began to think of myself for the first time not simply in atomistic terms, as one student distinguished from others by the pattern of his personal interests and activities, but as a member of a certain group, an *intellectual*, a member of an elite distinguished by academic interests—in books, ideas, and issues.[26] Moreover, by throwing me into closer contact with those of my schoolmates whose orientation was in essentials congenial to my own, membership in ARISTA had an expansive effect on my contacts and friendships. For the first time at Flushing High School I entered into an active social life. This broke the pattern of isolation and self-sufficiency into which I had been thrown since Beechhurst days by the shift succession of moves to Armonk to Plainfield to Flushing. Eventually, the shift to college in 1946 broke up these high school friendships, but these classmates still stick in my mind, and I remember them well and fondly.

The greater part of my high school career unfolded against the background of the Second World War, which ended only some six months before my graduation. As best I recall, we students never talked about the war with each other, though no doubt, some attention was devoted to it in the current affairs part of social studies courses. To be sure, we read the newspapers and heard the radio and were acutely aware of what was going on. But we were determined to live our lives in a "normal" way.

As the panorama of the war passed before my fascinated gaze during these impressionable teen-age years, it all seemed very far from home. And for me it never came close. I read avidly of the generals and their campaigns, eagerly studying the maps to follow the vast struggles of far-off armies. I was ever anxious to see how "our side" was doing. There was never a moment of doubt that the U.S.A. was "my country" and that it held my absolute allegiance. Although I had at this stage spent the lesser part of my life within its borders, I could not have been a more convinced and unquestioning patriot had I descended from ten generations of native Americans. This is not to say, however, that I was personally anxious to enter the fray. I signed up for the draft at age 17 as was required, but was thoroughly pleased when the war ended before I was of age to be called up. I was acutely conscious that only the lucky accident of a well-timed birthdate enabled me to view this world-catastrophe as a spectator rather than a participant.

The war undoubtedly made its greatest impact on me through films. Intended for propaganda and morale-building purposes, they manged to endow the whole process with an aura of unreality that a casual reading of newspapers could never offset. Only in later years, after reading books and, above all, myself seeing military service during wartime, did I begin to form a realistic picture of what was involved, a picture that gave me deep sympathies towards that sincere pacifism that is not a mere cover for personal convenience.

During high school days, I had two brief periods of Saturday employment: one as packer at the Loft candy factory in Long Island City, and one as counter boy at a Bickford's diner in Elmhurst. The latter involved getting up at around 5 AM and travelling on the subway for over a half hour. It made for a miserable, drawn-out day, for little pay and next-to-nothing in tips. It was generally unpleasant and unproductive and I gave it up after two or three Saturdays. The candy packing job was deadly-dull assembly-line labor of the most routine sort. But one's companions were other high school kids with whom one could joke and talk. I kept this up on Saturdays for a period of some months, before concluding that I would really rather have the time than the money (probably around 40¢ an hour). However I derived lessons of great value from these two brief spells of common, unskilled labor. I learned how enervating and thought-erasing work of a totally routinized nature could be and so became reinforced in my determination to "make something of myself"— and to avoid at all costs having to toil at meaningless work in a deeply uncongenial occupation. I was determined to get a good education and put myself into the position of earning a livelihood with my head rather than my hands. Above all, the need to go to college became a settled idea with me.

Towards the middle of my high school period my thoughts regarding a career began to take some more definite shape. I now began to toy with the idea of the Diplomatic Service. (I was fluent in German and making headway in French, with some talent for learning languages, and a strong interest in histsory and international affairs.) But this idea was demolished sometime in 1944 when I wrote to the State Department to get information regarding the qualifications and training for the appropriate civil service examinations. I learned to my dismay that a naturalized citizen could only enter the service after holding his U.S. citizenship for 15 years. Since I obtained my citizenship only that year, I could not see my way clear to contemplating a career that I could not enter upon until years after completing all the necessary training. Though disappointed, I realized that it is pointless to fret over what cannot be mended.

In the spring of 1944 I had my first experience as a teacher, tutoring mathematics to a French immigrant boy a little younger than I who lived in our Flushing neighborhood. I succeeded rather well in this teaching effort and found it enjoyable and satisfying. The cumulative impression of this experience and some others of a similar nature later on implanted in my mind the idea of teaching as a vocation—an idea which took increasingly firm hold with the passage of time.

When I now look back, it strikes me as curious—and even in some degree unnatural—that my parents left me entirely to my own devices in this regard. As best I can now recall, they offered no suggestions and gave me little if any advice and counsel. It is perfectly conceivable that I could have had a successful and satisfying career along lines very different from the actual ones—as a physician, say, or an architect. And I suspect I could easily have been impelled in such directions. But for better (as I now think) or for worse, no such impetus was provided by my parents.

Indirectly their influence was crucial, however. For one day in early 1945 my father brought home a copy of Will Durant's *Story of Philosophy*. (Father had some amateur interest in philosophy and was particularly interested in Arthur Schopenhauer—to say nothing of that semi-philosopher Goethe, to whom he was greatly devoted.) I had soon devoured Durant's book and found it fascinating. This was my initial discovery of philosophy. I went on to other miscellaneous reading—some Schopenhauer, some Descartes, and quite a lot of Hume. I was altogether captivated, and came to the view that philosophy was something really worthwhile, something in the doing of which one could rewardingly spend the rest of one's days. Neither then nor for some years afterwards did philosophy displace mathematics completely from the forefront of my interest. But it was clear from the first that these two fields were the really live options for me. And happily, it soon appeared that these disciplines were more complimentary than divergent—at least from one perspective. For I discovered symbolic logic.

At some point during my high school career I was enrolled in a mathematics course with Mrs. Charlotte Knag, then a recent graduate of Queens College (who had just married the treasurer of that institution). On one of my book buying excursions I had acquired a copy of Andrew Paul Ushenko's *The Theory of Logic* from a secondhand bookshop. I read it with interest and I found symbolic logic utterly fascinating. Mrs. Knag—with whom I talked about this—made some other reading suggestions, and she told me about a Professor Hempel at Queens who was an authority in this field and an excellent teacher. I looked forward to going to Queens and working under him. Since logic lay at the border-area between philosophy and mathematics, it afforded a perfect way of combining my two paramount interests.

In January of 1946, at seventeen and a half years, I graduated from Flushing High School with a place well up on the honors list. I now made ready to begin collegiate studies—in the middle of the academic year—at Queens College. At this stage, there was still much about me that was indeterminate and formless, but nevertheless I had begun to make some headway in the process of maturation and self-definition. To be sure, I never thought of myself as a person of outstanding talents in comparison with the ablest of my contemporaries (quite the reverse!). But it now became a settled thing, at least in my own mind, that I was to make my way in the world by means of brainwork. The idea of an academic career began to loom in my thoughts. I recognized clearly that in realizing this aspiration I would be quite on my own, since my family lacked useful contacts and connections. But while I may not have had many splendid opportunities to look forward to, I was set on making the most of those that would come my way.

Five

Queens College: 1946-1949

(Age 17-21)

My undergraduate studies began at Queens College in New York in January of 1946, at the midpoint of the 1945-46 academic year. Located in what was then a largely undeveloped no-man's land be tween Flushing and Jamaica, this institution was still in its infancy. It had commenced operations only a few years before in the converted buildings of a former boys reformatory, soon supplemented by a few wartime prefabs. In 1946 its only new building was the student union—even the library was still housed on an upper floor of the old administration building. However, the austerity of the physical plant was more than offset by the excellence of the faculty at that time.

The Queens College philosophy department contained a group of men of capability and good repute: Herbert G. Bohnert (a disciple of Rudolf Carnap), William Callaghan (a charming Irish-American Catholic who was a neo-Thomist of sorts), Donald Davidson (a disciple of W. V. O. Quine, then just beginning his academic career after wartime service in the Navy), John Goheen (the chairman, who maintained interests in ancient and medieval philosophy, but devoted his main efforts to administration), Carl G. Hempel (a German emigré logician and philosopher of science), and Arnold Isenberg (an aesthetician). They were a likeable group of people and always helpful to me. Moreover, there were, on the whole, dedicated teachers. To be sure with the hubris of callow youth, I regarded them as ordinary mortals of ordinary abilities, the one outstanding exception being Hempel, a man of obvious ability and massive power. Primarily, however, what held me to philosophy was not so much the example of its teachers, as the fascination of the subject itself. Once I had discovered the field in Will Durant's *Story of Philosophy* as a high school sophomore, my interest was firmly locked in place. The more I came to grapple with the issues that filled the pages of the great philosophers of the past, the more my enthusiasm for the subject grew.

To be sure, mathematics for a time proved to be a temptation, exercising a potent lure. The Queens College mathematics department then afforded an impressive array of talent. T. Freeman Cope, the chairman, taught classical analysis with a clarity and precision that amounted to elegance. And his staff consisted of very able people indeed: Leon Cohen (who specialized in the theory of functions), Banesh Hoffman (applied mathematics), and Leo Zippin (topology), among others. Professor Cope in particular had one impressive and amazing trait. In working problem upon problem at the blackboard and presenting a wide variety of proofs, he never made the slightest slip-up, not even a minor error in calculation. This gave a certain virtuosity to his teaching performance which was not in other ways particularly colorful, keeping us in suspenseful waiting for that slip-up which never arrived. The other mathematics professor who most impressed me was Leon Cohen who joined the faculty at Queens in my Junior year. His course in Analysis of Real Variable was a sheer joy to me. Cohen really loved mathematics and managed to endow its presentation with excitement and warmth. He in particular among my teachers ultimately became a friend, and I continued to see him from time to time later on in Washington, when he had left Queens College to head the Mathematics Section of the

National Science Foundation in the early 1950's. I am grateful to these men for making the study of mathematics an intensely exciting and rewarding experience throughout my college years. And my efforts in this field were not unsuccessful; I was sometimes the ablest student in the class, and always among the two or three best.

Not long after graduating from high school, I learned quite accidentally from a friend that the competitive examinations for the New York State Scholarships were to be given shortly. (To their discredit, my teachers and advisors at Flushing High School had left me quite uninformed about this whole venture.) I put my name in to take the examinations only a few days before they were actually offered, and had no chance to prepare—I could not even obtain information as to the *sort* of thing at issue. I thus took the examination in a rather casual spirit, simply gambling on the off-chance that something might come of it. To my surprise and pleasure, I did succeed in winning one of these scholarships. They then paid $750 per annum, with no strings attached, to any New Yorker attending an in-state college or university. The purchasing power of the dollar was in those days such that this modest amount was far from contemptible. Since Queens College was a tuition-free, publicly supported institution, it more than sufficed for all my expenses for books, fees, transportation, lunches, etc. What particularly pleased me was the fact that this windfall freed me of any pressure to earn money by irrelevant summer jobs, so that I could now devote my summers to recreation and study. Whenever I am minded to grumble about taxes—a not infrequent experience nowadays—I remind myself of this debt to the taxpayers of New York.

In my college work I was relatively hardworking and serious-minded. I carried a joint major in mathematics and philosophy. Philosophy never made great demands on me—it was like coasting downhill. But mathematics was a different story, and while I enjoyed it greatly, I also worked at it quite hard.

What drew me to philosophy and mathematics? As with all too many students, I was activated by the sheer impetus of interest. It never occurred to me to look at the matter in practical terms. Then too, no countervailing forces were at work—no successful uncle to beckon me into his banking house or flourishing architectural practice. Had such opportunities been at hand, I do not doubt that I could have been diverted—whether for ultimate good or bad it is impossible to say.

Classics was another area I pursued seriously, continuing with Latin and commencing Greek. I much liked and respected Konrad Gries, the professor of classics, who was a person of substantial capabilities. But, while I expended considerable effort at classical languages, I feel that I never attained that real facility at Latin (or at Greek) which the time devoted to these subjects might lead one to expect. Though the instruction we received was certainly competent, I now think my training was seriously defective in point of pedagogical strategy. It lacked that constant review of grammatical fundamentals, that well-structured plan at building vocabulary, and that systematic program aimed at developing a capacity for rapid reading, which ought to be a prime aim of the teaching of dead languages.

I much enjoyed the study of literature—in French and classical languages as well as English. (I recall being particularly appreciative of Edwin Knowles in whose class I studied Chaucer's *Canterbury Tales*, and Paolo Milano with whom we read some of the *philosophes* of 18th century France.) I was very much interested in drama and read masses of plays from Shakespeare to Shaw. I also began at this time to be interested in the history of art and architecture. But I viewed all these interests in diverse cultural matters as ancillary to my philosophical concerns. Under Oswald Spengler's influence—whose *Decline of the West* made a deep impression on me—I inclined to view all cultural phenomena, philosophy included, as belonging to one over-arching and unifying (albeit evolving) intellectual tradition.

Throughout my Queens College career I lived at home in our Parsons Boulevard apartment, traveling to school by the public transport system's Jamaica bus—a trip of perhaps 20 minutes or so. But while I continued to reside at home, the old patterns changed and with them the nature of my familial and personal relationships. My ties to old Beechhurst friends grew more tenuous—they were now away at college and we only had some sporadic contact in the summers. And my relationship with my parents gradually changed too—as my horizons broadened they, as is natural enough, no longer cast quite so large a shadow over my life.

My first term at Queens College saw the burgeoning of my first relatively serious feminine interest. That spring of 1946—aged seventeen—I became attracted to my first real "girl-friend," a girl called Lorna from Jackson Heights. (Lorna what?—I cannot even recall the name, though I do know that it wasn't Lorna Doone.) I took her to various entertainments and sporadically visited her at her house. My interest could not have been too serious. While she was away on vacation for that summer, I never wrote her, being too busy playing tennis. When college resumed in September, I found that she had taken this much amiss, and our friendship came to an end.

More important was my attachment to Jean H. which commenced late in 1946 and lasted throughout my college years. She too was a mathematics major, a year ahead of me in the program, who was much interested in logic, and was also an enthusiastic ping-pong player and devotee of bridge. (It was, I think, the floating bridge games in the Student Union that first brought us together.) We became good friends and relatively constant companions, sharing various common activities and interests. She was an attractive, dark-haired girl, of middling height and build, neither svelte nor plump. Her personality was pleasant and cheerful, and she was highly intelligent though perhaps a bit impassive. For years on end we spent much time together, and in due course of time an understanding evolved that we might eventually marry.

Although I had many casual friends of my own sex at college, I was not a close companion to any of them. My work certainly absorbed much of my time and energy, and my social life centered around the friends I shared with Jean, with whom we would generally do things together (especially play bridge). Only a handful of my college contemporaries made a lasting impression on me. These include Richard Myers, an intense young man who was an authentic mathematical genius, and Joan Drakert, an exceptionally bright and sharp-tongued girl who went on to a Ph.D. in physics. Another person I was in regular contact with was Cornelius Ryan Fay, a philosophy major who was some two years my senior. His parents were Catholic and had a large family of boys, so that Neil had some five or six brothers. They all lived at home, and those who were still in school held down part-time jobs. When there were any financial needs or difficulties, father Fay would go to church to pray for guidance, the result of which was generally an increase in the "rent" all of his sons were charged. They were a charming and attractive typical Irish-American Catholic family.

During the summers of my college years, the pace of my life ran a more leisurely course. One summer I worked as a factotum in the Foreign Language Department of the Jamaica Public Library. Whereas earlier my free time went to tennis, I now became more sedentary and intellectual.

It was at this stage that I was first introduced to the writings of Freud which made (dare I say it?) a very poor impression on me. Accustomed to the rigors of academic philosophy—to say nothing of those of mathematics and natural science—I viewed him a sloppy thinker, inclined to fanciful leaps from scanty data to remote conclusions. Nor did I think it plausible to view sexuality as the controlling factor in life's dealings—it has always struck me as just another of man's biological drives which, important though they are, scarcely constitute an all-encompassing pivot of human affairs. I deemed Freud, as I had deemed Henry George before and was to deem Karl Marx later on, as just another 19th century one-track thinker who had an oversimple, monolithic solution to a complex manifold of issues. This was my view as a brash undergraduate, and I still hold it to this very day.

During my final college years I audited several mathematics classes at Columbia University. Professors never bothered to take attendance in the large classes there, so that bootlegged knowledge could be had for the taking. I enjoyed these classes and profited by them. One of these courses made a particularly vivid impression on me—Samuel Eilenberg's lively lectures on Algebraic Topology. Eilenberg was a very clear and well-organized lecturer and projected a striking, if somewhat abrasive, personality. Once, for example, he repeatedly declined to recognize a questioner, and then at a later stage interrupted his presentation to address him personally: "Now *this* point has answered your question hasn't it? I knew you were bright enough to spot the difficulty, but felt it best to let it be resolved in the natural course of things."

The Mathematics Department at Queens College required all its majors to take a comprehensive examination towards the end of their career. This served a dual purpose, both as a general proficiency examination in the major field and as a prize examination. I took this exam prematurely at the end of my Junior year (in the Spring of 1948). Nonetheless, I tied for first place. As a prize I could pick a mathematics book of my own choice, and I selected Alexandroff's *Topologie* which I still have, but to my shame have never finished reading.

For a brief time this success impressed me with the (probably mistaken) idea that I might succeed as a professional mathematician. Going on with mathematics in graduate school became an increasingly live prospect. But several things prevented it. One was the feeling that a real mathematician needs not just an adequate talent for his subject, but a positive genius—a truly extraordinary gift for it, and that this was something which I lacked. Though certainly competent at mathematics, I never sensed the inner power of real creativity in this field, and never felt that intense commitment to it, analogous to near demonic dedication of the real chess player.

In philosophy, on the other hand, I thought I could do well. I believed (heaven knows for what reason!) that none of my classmates at Queens were more capable in this field than I. To be sure, I did not credit myself any extraordinary gifts of intellect. But I combined dedication and willingness to work with an intense interest in the field. More than most, I had an ability to cut through to the core without irrelevancies: a capacity to get a job done. The subject appealed immensely to me, and I "felt in my bones" that I could do well at it.

Moreover, I saw my interests in philosophy as altogether compatible and congenial with those in mathematics, the sciences, and the humanities. Philosophy cannot do its work on a pedestal set apart, but must labor in the very midst of other concerns. The philosopher is entitled to be a jack of many trades—perhaps even required to be so. Philosophy cannot operate *de haut en bas:* it must address the materials secured by other branches of learning rather than lord it over them.

What attracted me to philosophy was the chance to deal in a serious and hard-headed way with issues that are both challenging in themselves and of substantial human importance: the nature of the world, the business of acquiring knowledge, the source of value, and the like. I succumbed also—and especially—to the siren call of logic, and was keenly alive to the beauties of formal reasoning and the almost aesthetic appeal of a clear analysis of complex issues.

As my college years progressed, it somehow jelled in my mind that I was going to go on to graduate school. My professors represented a type—the professional academic—that was new to me and that I found appealing. The prospect of being able to dwell within the realm of ideas exerted an ever-increasing appeal for me. Grappling with the things of the mind struck me as a venture vastly preferable to dealing with the hurly-burly of the world's practicalities. Gradually I was captivated by the idea that "this is the life for me"—that there is nothing else I would rather be doing. At that point my professors ceased being just my teachers and became my role-models as well.

When I sent out applications for graduate school scholarships in the fall of 1948, I also applied to several schools in mathematics. But my thoughts and aspirations by now turned mainly in the direction of philosophy, and my main hopes were placed in those applications I made for graduate study in this field.

When the returns were in, I had two offers from mathematics departments—from Syracuse and some other, now forgotten university—but I was also offered scholarships in philosophy at Harvard, Yale, and Princeton. (Hempel had advised me in my applications, and the whole department had supported them—obviously to good effect.) The Princeton offer had the greatest attractions for me. The field was philosophy, the institution was of good repute, and its location was within easy visiting distance of home. Last, and not least, the financial terms were attractive since the grant covered all the tuition expenses and most of my living costs as well. Without much hesitation I decided that Princeton was to be the place for me.

On a warm and pleasant day in June of 1949 I attended the graduation exercise and listened to the usual commencement platitudes from the mouth of Judge Charles S. Colden. (I still remember him, not because of his message, but because he was a remote descendent of Cadwallader Colden, one of America's earliest philosophers.) I received my B.S. with honors in mathematics and was graduated *magna cum laude*.[27] I looked forward to the rest and relaxation of the summer—even more to the challenges of Princeton that lay beyond.

The years of adolescence and young adulthood generally see some struggle at learning about oneself, largely by toilsome trial and error, to determine just where one's potential lies and what one can and cannot do. This self-definition is certainly not a matter of simply making up one's mind—willpower of itself has little to do with it—it is largely a matter of natural selection by way of trial and elimination by actual failure, a painful process because it is never easy for human beings to face up to their inadequacies. The issues often take years to resolve and may well exact a heavy psychological toll. I was fortunate that in my own case my natural bent came to the fore readily, so that the period of uncertainty was reasonably painless and mercifully short. Realizing fairly clearly where I wanted to go, I could settle down and address myself to the task of getting on with it. By the time of my graduation from Queens College, still at the age of 20, I knew pretty well what I would ideally want to do with myself in life: to be a teacher and student of philosophy.

Considering the formative years at issue, I naturally left Queens College in June of 1949 a very different person from the raw youth who came there in January, 1946. I had acquired a good deal of knowledge and skill, but—more importantly—an enhanced confidence in myself and my intellectual abilities. And, above all, I had formed a determination to put these abilities to work. My college experience had provided an incentive to broaden and enlarge my interests and a stimulus to develop them. To credit this result to an educational institution is to give it high praise, and I have felt—then and ever since—greatly indebted to Queens College.

Six

Princeton University: 1949-1952

(Age 21-23)

I RECALL clearly the balmy day in early September of 1949 when my mother saw me off at the Flushing depot of the Long Island Railroad to start the train journey to Princeton. I had never lived away from home before. Mother, of course, cried bitterly, despite my embarrassed urging that this was really quite uncalled-for—considering that I was a full-grown young man of 21 and would, in any case, be only two hours' journey away from home. But in my heart of hearts I too was struck with occasion, which was clearly an augury of coming changes.

After the Pennsylvania Railroad had deposited me in Princeton late that morning, I settled into my assigned room in the grey-granite, neo-Gothic pile known as the Graduate College. I had brought along the Everyman's Library edition of Fielding's *Tom Jones* and spent an hour or so reading it in an armchair by the open dormer window of my small third-floor room trying to get into the "feel" of the place. That afternoon I set off for campus. I began with a visit to the Philosophy Department offices in 1879 Hall for an orientation interview with W.T. Stace, who was then in charge of graduate studies in philosophy. I let no grass grow under my feet. After completing registration for my courses, I went off straightaway and passed my French and German language-proficiency examinations that very day.

One thing still stands out in my mind regarding that interview with Stace. He gave me a list of courses and asked me which four I would like to take. I indicated several, including one by Jacques Maritain, the celebrated French neo-Thomist. Stace pulled a face and indicated I would do well to select something else. The situation was strange to me, and in any case I was not brash enough to demur from the views of the Director of Graduate Studies. Only later did I learn that Stace and Maritain had quarreled in print about religion and were ideologically at loggerheads. Opposed to all Christian orthodoxy, Stace was reluctant to see a student come under the influence of this eminent Catholic thinker. Though I came to like and respect Stace, this incident left a blot on his image, and whenever in after years I heard talk of the anti-Catholic animus of American academics, this episode leapt to recollection.

My first impressions of Princeton on that September day of twenty-five years ago are still vivid in my mind: the little train station, tidy and clean beyond any of my acquaintance in the big city; the handsome campus, incomparably greener and more picturesque than those I knew in New York; the people—students and faculty alike—who, in comparison with those of Queens or of Columbia, seemed to me so much more leisurely, self-assured, and at ease with the world. The town itself, then a mere village, seemed a compact and congenial little place whose sole reason for being was catering to the needs of students. I was by now a New Yorker who had scarce left the crowded and untidy confines of the metropolis for the past six years. By comparison, Princeton struck me as a veritable heaven on earth. I thanked a kindly fate for having set this phase of my life's drama on such a splendid stage, revelling in the prettiness of the place, somewhat daunted and overawed by it all, but proud to be a little fish swimming in so noble a lake.

I registered for four courses that first term: Alonzo Church on logic (which was taught in the Department of Mathematics), Walter

Terence Stace on recent philosophy (Bradley, Whitehead, Russell), Andrew Paul Ushenko on epistemology, and Arthur Szathmary on Descartes. I also sat in on two courses in mathematics, one of them the very excellent lectures on algebra by Emil Artin.

Stace's course that first term was particularly interesting to me, partly on account of the material, but largely on the account of Stace himself, who had a vivid personality and an engaging style of presentation. Stace—then aged sixty-three—was certainly not a professional philosopher of the usual sort. After academic training at Trinity College, Dublin, the bulk of his professional career has been spent in the Ceylonese civil service, where he had risen to be mayor of Columbo, the capital city. A tall, impressive man with a somewhat bluff manner, it was clear that his concern for philosophy was deep and real. In a pleasantly disarming way he was not always sure he fully understood the thinkers whose ideas he was presenting, but it was clear that he thought them of importance and value. He was thus able to get us to take seriously philosophers like Bradley and Whitehead whose way of thinking and writing was altogether antithetical to the temper of the time. Stace's many years in the East had awakened an interest in religious mysticism on his part, an inclination towards which I then felt no sympathy, but which did somehow augment his interest in my eyes.

Andrew Paul Ushenko was rather an enigma. Although he was a soft-spoken little Caspar Milquetoast of a man, the epitome of the shrinking violet, the concept of *power* played a central role in his philosophizing. He had a genuine dedication to philosophical ideas and inquiry. I thought his seminar on aesthetics managed to identify some points of interest in a pretty bleak terrain. He had a good sense of where the important problems lay in philosophy and was eager to come to grips with them. This, to my way of thinking, did much to offset his lack of charisma. Moreover, I felt a debt to him because of the impact that his logic-book had made on me in high-school days.

Alonzo Church, of the department of mathematics, was a unique figure. A more dull and pedestrian lecturer can hardly be imagined. But this hardly mattered, since the man was scholarship personified—accurate, painstaking, and amazingly widely informed, in fact, a walking encyclopedia of the subject. He made a deep impression and did so by intellect alone, unaugmented by any trace of impressiveness of personality. He was bulky in mind and body alike, and moved slowly and ponderously—a juggernaut weighted down by the burden of prodigious learning. A scholar of the highest standards and capabilities, he stood in a class by himself, though, to be sure, the comparison class to which he belonged, or at any rate to which I assigned him, was that of logicians and not philosophers as such.

The graduate program in philosophy at Princeton was in those days a relatively small affair—there were perhaps eight students in the entering class and altogether a total of some twenty in residence taking courses. The individual seminars had around eight members. They met in sessions of two or three hours and usually consisted of an hour's lecture followed by a somewhat longer period of discussion. Occasionally (but rarely) the participants would be asked to present seminar papers about which the group then deliberated as a whole with eager and generally constructive criticism.

I had no reason to be discontented with my formal academic fare. Still, I profited as much—or more—from contacts with my fellow students, some of who were truly outstandings: Rogers Albritton, who possessed a keen albeit labyrinthine philosophical mind, and was a very good discussant with an unusual capacity for insightful criticism. Fadlou Shehadi, an enthusiastic young Lebanese, who was at this stage very much of a beginner at Western philosophy, but had an impressively deep dedication to philosophical ideas. James L. Cole, an Oberlin "faculty kid" and graduate, who had a good head and rather out-of-the-way philosophical interests—having been a psychology major as an undergraduate, he tended to look at things from a viewpoint rather different from mine. And in a more casual way I was in touch with many nonphilosophers—chemists, romance linguists, classicists—who contributed both to my intellectual and social nurture in the monastic fellowship of the Graduate College.

My routine during these days ran somewhat as follows: Arising around 7:00 A.M., I dressed and went downstairs to breakfast. Then I would work in my room until class-time at 9. Returning for lunch at noon, I would thereafter work—or go to class—until the middle of the afternoon. Around 5 P.M. I would go round to a friend's room for talk and a glass of sherry until dinner at 6:30. After dinner I would work until 10 o'clock—or sometimes go to a film or for a social visit off campus with a married friend. I was always back in my room by 10:30, and would then spend a final half hour or so with light reading to clear my head of philosophical cobwebs before going to bed. (I now first read the *Autobiography* of Herbert Spencer, which I liked immensely, and which began a lifelong interest in philosophical autobiography. However, my usual reading fare tended towards English novels—Fielding, Smollet, Jane Austen, Disraeli—and towards books on American history.) Generally, I must have spent some ten hours of the day at work in or out of class—8-12 noon, 1-5 P.M., and (frequently) 8-10 P.M. I never drove myself and never burned the midnight oil, maintaining a slow, steady, even pace of reasonably efficient application to the tasks at hand, with little wasted motion. I was perhaps not so much of an all-work-and-no-play sober-sides as such a schematic account may suggest. While I tended to approach the work in hand with zest, I generally did so with a bit of humor as well. It never seemed to me that philosophical concerns precluded a certain detached amusement towards the issues and a willingness to treat them with an admixture of fun.

Class-work aside, I pursued a major project of my own devising during this first year of graduate studies. Over the preceding summer, I had begun a study of the philosophy of Leibniz with a view to developing a suitable project that I could carry with me to graduate school that fall. (I already possessed my life-long tendency to "steal a march" on the future by getting a head start on the discharge of its commitments.) My Queens College friend, Cornelius Ryan Fay—who had already begun graduate work at Columbia—had drawn Bertrand Russell's *The Philosophy of Leibniz* to my attention, and Russell engaged my attention for this fascinating thinker. His many-sidedness and especially his genius for the utilization of logic and mathematics towards philosophical ends exercised a powerful appeal for me. I spent a good bit of that fall of 1949 reading whatever Leibnizian material I could lay my hands on. In particular I discovered Louis Couturat's *La Logique de Leibniz*, and this splendid book gave me much stimulation. But while it was two figures of a past generation (Russell and Couturant) that led me to Leibniz, it was Leibniz himself who held me there. And so throughout the 1949-1950 academic year I enthusiastically pursued a study of Leibniz' cosmology, producing a substantial essay as a vehicle for my ideas.

In early May I told Prof. Ledger Wood about this writing project. I asked him if he could suggest some faculty member to read it with a view to judging its potential for development into a dissertation. He replied that he had best read it himself, seeing that Leibniz was as much in his area of interest as anybody's in the department. I gave him a copy of my script. A fortnight later he called me into his office to discuss this project. He said he felt this to be a very good piece of work and eminently suitable as the first draft of a dissertation. He proposed that, as I was so far along, I would do well to try my hand at the General Examination for the Ph.D. which was due to be given in 10 days time. He assured me that failure would not be held against me in these circumstances. I accepted this proposal eagerly though not without trepidation.

Perhaps to everyone's surprise—certainly to mine—I not only sustained this battery of examinations, but (so I was told) performed well enough to have passed "with distinction" had not my ethics paper been relatively weak—which certainly did not surprise me, since I had never taken even so much as an undergraduate course in the subject.

Clearing the hurdle of the General Examination had important implications for me. After a single, relatively unpressured year, I l had now completed all the official obligations of the doctoral program apart from the dissertation. And even here I already had in hand a first-draft version that only needed some polishing which I could attend to, in the main, over the summer months.

Thus when I returned to Flushing in June of 1950 the work for the Ph.D. lay almost completely behind me. In other ways too I had made progress, having at last been required to live on my own and be responsible for myself. By some glacial and inconspicuous process I had become a relatively self-sufficient young man.

At this stage my attitude towards my parents also underwent a significant change. Living away from home led me to view them with greater detachment—to see them as people rather than as simply a part of my family unit. I came to respect them more, to appreciate their good qualities, to take them less for granted. In sum, I became fonder of them. But I became distanced from them as well. I certainly wished them well in every way, but was now fully committed to proceeding on my own.

Then too, I now at last became fully independent in point of finances. The graduate scholarship I had held during my first year sufficed for the tuition fees and also went part-way towards defraying my room and board. But there was still a deficit to be made up—partly from a small nest-egg I had saved from my New York State Scholarship, but principally by the contribution of my parents. Now, however, I was promoted to the somewhat more elevated status of University Fellow, a post whose ampler emoluments just about covered the whole of my expenses. From this point on I was able to stand on my own financial feet. (And none too soon—considering that I was now turning 22.)

This seems a proper place to record my deep sense of debt to the various strangers who helped decisively to make my participation in higher education finanacially possible: the officials of New York City who set Queens College up as a public institution, the legislators of New York State who established the system of state scholarships, the benefactors of Princeton who gave funds for scholarships. To all of these I feel an immeasurable gratitude. I realize what a tragedy it would have been for me had higher education not been attainable—as it would otherwise almost surely not have been, considering the tight financial straits into which my parents had been plunged.

One important development occurred at this juncture. I had dated Jean H. ever since my second year at Queens College. But as the years passed the relationship gradually wore stale. Moreover, being away at Princeton had changed my perspective. I came to see my life in a different light and Jean no longer seemed a necessary part of it. Perhaps our friendship had just dragged on for too long. Perhaps the shift to graduate school and the opening of new horizons made me eager for new contacts and new experiences. At any rate, I now broke off our relationship—doing this so abruptly that it was actually cruel. Jean deserved better of me. But I felt that there had to be an ending, and did not trust myself to make it at all if this were not done in a swift and decisive way. I felt—and still feel—that the unkind *manner* of this inevitable breach casts no credit on me. In his *Autobiography* Benjamin Franklin speaks of certain *errata* in the typography of his life that he wishes it were possible to correct. For me, this lack of consideration towards someone who deserved far better of me was such an erratum.

That summer of 1950 I was relatively lazy. I revised the thesis and did some desultory philosophical reading. In the main I saw friends and occupied myself with tennis and other recreational activities.

After a relaxed summer, I returned to Princeton that fall refreshed and eager. Having sustained the General Examination, I was now free of any obligation to take courses formally, but I audited a variety of offerings in various departments. Apart from some philosophy courses, I recall another session with Alonzo Church on logic and William Feller's lectures on probability in the Mathematics Department, and in Classics I attended Whitney Oates' seminar on Aristotle's *Metaphysics*. Otherwise, I polished my thesis, socialized with friends, and lived in the relative comfort that an increased fellowship stipend afforded me in the easy circumstances of the Graduate College. I particularly enjoyed interaction with some of the lively and interesting members of the newly incoming group of graduate students: Vaclav Benes, Jerome Schneewind, and Jerome Shaffer.

Unfortunately, I began to have a succession of headaches at this stage. I thought at first that they might be occasioned by eye troubles, but this possibility was soon eliminated. What, then, might be the cause? The suggestion came that they might perhaps be of psychological origin. I found this difficult to believe—for had I not just recently put various prime sources of psychological pressure behind me? Still, I thought it best to consult "the experts." Accordingly, I visited the Health clinic's psychologist, as well as another such practitioner who was recommended to me. I was surprised and impressed at the ease with which these men proposed diagnostic etiologies that placed my problems squarely within their favored framework—be it Freudian or whatever. But I was no less surprised when the problem cleared up overnight a week or so later when a tooth with an infected root canal was extracted. This experience did nothing to alter my already low estimate of the psychiatric craft.

Now at last I began to practice the career for which I felt myself destined. My new fellowship called for instructional duties, so that for the first time I became a practicing teacher. I served as "preceptor" for various courses, meeting with groups of 8-10 students in Princeton's version of the Oxbridge tutorial system. Next to authentic individual tutorials, this process of small group colloquies has always seemed to me a near-to-ideal method of philosophical instruction. At any rate, teaching in this context was a new and highly pleasurable experience for me.

I now began work on what was to be my first published paper, appearing under the title of "Contingence in the Philosophy of Leibniz" in *The Philosophical Review* (vol. 61 [1952], pp. 26-39). In fact, my dissertation on Leibniz had inaugurated an ongoing concern on my part with the work of this outstanding thinker, and as the years went on, I was to be frequently preoccupied with this great man. I periodically taught seminars devoted to his work, wrote a succession of articles about him, and in 1967 published an exposition of his philosophy, parts of which drew on my dissertation of some 15 years before.

In November of 1967 Leibniz scholars from all the world gathered in Hanover, Germany to commemorate the 250th anniversary of his death. Dr. Wilhelm Totok, the able and enterprising head of the Nether-Saxon State Library, was the leading spirit behind this celebration, and on its occasion he took the decisive steps towards launching an International Leibniz Society. It was founded at a meeting at which I was present, and I was chosen a member of its Council (*Beirat*), an office I continue to hold to the present day (1974). I also became a member of the editorial board of its official journal, *Studia Leibnitiana*. (Indeed, it was my plea for a Latin rather than German title—made for reasons of internationalism and in homage to Leibniz' boundary-transcending spirit—that led to the selection of this title in the place of *Leibniz-Studien*.) When the idea of an American Leibniz Society first came to be mooted some years later, I was also involved, helping to organize the society and becoming a member of its Executive Committee.

The inspiration of Leibniz is clearly present in some of my books (e.g., *The Coherence Theory of Truth*), and is discernible in my general approach to the conduct of philosophical work. I do not view myself as an adherent of his teaching or doctrine, but rather of his mode of philosophizing. Leibniz is to my mind the master of us all in the use of the formal resources of symbolic thought in the interest of the clarification and resolution of philosophical issues—a role-model for the way in which one wants to introduce exactness and rigor into one's philosophical work. Many of my books accordingly exhibit the Leibnizian tendency to use some formal notational or symbolic mathematical or logical or diagrammatic, device for the elucidation of philosophical issues. Moreover, I have always felt a certain spiritual affinity with Leibniz, in that we have both faced a broadly common situation in a broadly common way. We both came to philosophy after a generation of iconoclasm—represented by Cartesiansim in his case, and logical positivism in mine. In each instance, there had been a prior phase of annihilation of traditions and search for a fresh start, for building up everything anew on a novel foundation erected on the ruins of the older structures. This created a common mission of our philosophical generations: to build a bridge across the rubble left by our demolitionist predecessors—a bridge able to reach the far bank of the rich philosophical heritage that lay beyond. In any case, my Princeton dissertation proved to be the first step in an ongoing preoccupation with Leibnizian themes and variations.

Throughout my Princeton career I kept in touch with Alonzo Church. Though an uninspired teacher, he was a scholar of such substantial ability and vast erudition that it was a stimulating experience simply to see him at work. He now enlisted me as a reviewer for *The Journal of Symbolic Logic* and made extensive use of my services in this regard. During 1951-1953 I contributed to the journal some 40 reviews of papers on a wide variety of logical topics. This experience provided a most useful training in critical analysis and compact exposition.

During the second term of the 1950-51 academic year, a visitor from Oxford, James O. Urmson of Corpus Christi College, made a deep impression on all of us fledgling philosophers at Princeton. A disciple of J.L. Austin, his seminar on epistemology introduced us to the mysteries of "ordinary language" analysis as cultivated by this master of the new vogue of Oxford philosophy. We endlessly dissected how talk about knowledge proceeds in the "ordinary language" of "the plain man," contrasting this with the supposed distortions at work in the knowledge-talk of philosophers like Descartes—to the not insubstantial disadvantage of the latter.

In the early spring of 1951 I attended for the first time an annual meeting of the American Philosophical Association (or rather the Eastern Division thereof), held on the Swarthmore College campus. The Princeton philosophers contributed two car-loads or so, and I was included. I had never seen so many philosophers in one place before—the 300 or so who came struck me as an enormous throng. Nowadays we meet in big convention hotels in the major cities, with nearly ten times as many in attendance. The past quarter century has seen American academic philosophy change—be it for better or for worse—from a small fraternity of mutually familiar colleagues to a large, amorphorus, and rather more impersonal profession.

Only towards the end of that academic year, in the spring of 1951, did I begin to give serious thought to the future. But whatever anxieties I may have had were soon dissipated by the offer of an Instructorship at Princeton for the academic year 1951-1952—at a salary of $3,500. This was less than many a graduate fellowship at this time of writing (1974), but was an amount which then seemed quite ample to me, and I took the naive view that my foreseeable future was now securely arranged.

With the conclusion of that academic year, my graduate studies came to an end as well. I now received my official commission as a Doctor of Philosophy—my membership in that truly international branch of scholars licensed to teach in institutions of higher learning throughout the world. And I now had a "handle" to my name as *Dr*. Rescher, an addendum which took a long time to sound natural to my ears. My doctoral work had progressed at a surprising speed—yielding the Ph.D. in two years, when I was still only twenty-two years old.

The summer stood before me. It was necessary to put aside some money against the coming year's expenses. But it is one thing to have a degree, and something quite different to have a job—even a temporary one of the sort I had in view. I approached the office of Student Employment for ideas. A prospect developed there which I took up if not with glee at least with contentment. The Elizabethtown Consolidated Gas Company in Elizabeth, N.J. (conveniently sited on the Pennsylvania Railroad's Princeton-New York run) had just converted from selling its own manufactured gas to natural gas imported on the Texas pipeline. In the confusion created by the change-over, its domestic customers had been systematically overcharged. The New Jersey Public Utilities Commission had ordered a repayment for all duly entitled customers. The company was consequently hiring a handful of young men (mainly college students home for the summer) to carry out the work of calculating these refunds. To this essential but infinitely dull task I dedicated my labors that summer at a recompense which, small though it was, enabled me to put aside several hundred dollars. For a happy conjunction of events made it possible for me to live very inexpensively.

The Assistant to the President—one Colonel Fox—was devoting himself to the hunt country of Virginia over the vacation and wanted some reliable person to take care of his house and female cat—the apple of his eye—in exchange for quarters in the place. I took on this assignment together with my friend and fellow student Jennings Mangum (who was soon to forsake philosophy for the greener pastures of banking), and it provided us with comfortable yet cost-free lodging for the summer period. One weekend when Jennings was away, and I in charge, the colonel's cat escaped from her huge complex of interconnected cages—a vast multilevel structure that was veritably a cat-palace. Fortunately she reappeared after a day or two. When I met the colonel once more a week or so after his return, he complimented me on the care of the cat, stressing her plump and well-fed appearance. I worried about the implications of this circumstance, but happily the litter I saw with my mind's eye never materialized.

My closest Princetonian friends at this stage were James L. Cole—a fellow graduate student in philosophy—and his wife Barbara. The son of a psychology professor at Oberlin, Jim had strong interests in this field as well and ultimately transferred to it. Barbara was the daughter of a prosperous insurance broker from Pen Yan, N.Y. Jim had met her at Oberlin. She combined a fine sense of humor with an inveterate addiction to gossip. (She was also the greatest horse-enthusiast I ever encountered.) They were a couple blessed with infinite good will and good humor, and I became very fond of the Coles and grew close to them.

On two or three occasions I joined the Coles on vacation visits to the cottage of Barbara's parents on Lake Keuka near Pen Yan. Like many another happy young couple, they felt that all their bachelor friends should marry, and Barbara was in any case a natural matchmaker. She began bringing me together with various girls in the Pen Yan area. None of them made much of an impression on me, save one, Barbara's old childhood friend, Frances Short, to whom she introduced me in the spring of 1950.

Born in 1925, and thus a few years older than I, Frances was a slender, smallish girl, two inches or so over five feet in height, with a light complexion and blonde-brown hair. She had majored in Political Science at Lake Erie College, but she now lived with her mother and brothers out in the country near Rochester, N.Y., and worked in this city as a social service caseworker for the New York State Department of Public Welfare. Her father was the scion of an old WASP family whose mother, the first woman to earn an engineering degree at Ohio State University, had married Henry Howe Short, a pioneer in the electric-traction industry in the U.S. However the family had fallen on hard times during the Depression, and the father, its main provider, had died years before I came on the scene.

Much impressed by Frances, I began to correspond with her in the fall of 1950. After a courtship carried on by correspondence, and three brief visits in one another's vicinity, we were married in early September of 1951, at the outset of my Princeton instructorship.

Frances possessed many good qualities, being intelligent, thoroughly honest in head and heart, and straightforward in human dealings. But she also had some less positive traits of personality—traits which were ultimately to outweigh the good in the context of our relationship. She was tenacious about getting her own way with the things of everyday existence and intensely possessive of the people in her life. Character is fate, the Greeks said sagely. The personality of Frances already contained—as yet writ small—the makings of difficulty in fitting in with my own.

At first we occupied a small apartment consisting of the upper floor of a private house on Harrison Street (No. 185), rented out by the widowed and very talkative landlady who lived downstairs. But after two months or so we were fortunately able to move into unit No. 412B of the Graduate Student Housing Project on Butler Avenue—a cluster of prefab structures that had once accommodated Naval trainees in a World War II crash program. I embarked upon my teaching duties, and Frances secured a job in Princeton's Firestone Library. Since most of my compatriots in the graduate program were still on the scene, we led an active social life.

The teaching duties of my Princeton instructorship were not onerous. As best I recall, they consisted of one class (in the *Philosophy of Science*) and several preceptorials (in the *History of Modern Philosophy: Descartes to Kant*). The latter were an unadulterated pleasure, but the former posed problems.

At this stage, I generally geared my teaching closely to the assigned textbook. I did this partly from beginner's caution, but also because I have always believed that students should find reading and lecture materials mutually supportive rather than wandering off in different or discordant ways. (I think it unfair to ask the students to buy a book for a course and then not to teach them what's in it—however much one might also go *beyond* it.) Unhappily this basically reasonable policy proved counterproductive in my Philosophy of Science class because the predetermined text was rather a poor book. Perhaps, if I had been a more experienced teacher, the shortcomings of the text could have been overcome, but as it was, I found the going something of an uphill struggle.

The historical preceptorials went very well indeed, however, and I always came away from them with the feeling that I had really helped the students to gain a solid understanding of what these philosophers were about. (This impression was happily confirmed when some fifteen years later I met a young philosophy professor—his name now eludes me—who had been a student of mine on this occasion.) I became confirmed in the view that I had now found my profession: I felt that I could function effectively as a philosopher and teach successfully when dealing with material that was congenial to me.

Early in the Fall of 1951 I bought my first car—a venerable 1936 Willis. Among my friends were Judson Lamour Ihrig and his wife Gwendolyn. Jud was a very able young chemist then at work on the experimental research for his doctoral thesis. He was studying the effects of strong magnetic fields on certain chemical reactions, and revelled in the intricacy of his equipment—he was the most naturally gifted person at things mechanical I had ever encountered. Deeming it a disgrace that here was I, a young man over 21, quite unable to drive, Jud insisted that this should be put to rights. He would teach me himself and in my *own* car to boot. And so he took me to a junkyard where we bought an ancient blue Willis sedan for $30. We spent a couple of afternoons (and perhaps another $15.00 for materials) working on the car, with me sanding and repainting the exterior, while Jud put the nonfunctional electrical system to rights. Soon the car was running as nicely as can be, and for a month or so we would go out on driving lessons, with Jud indoctrinating me into the mysteries of a manual gearshift. By Thanksgiving I was an accomplished driver, and greatly enjoyed my new-found mobility.

Late in 1951 I met Paul Oppenheim through the mediation of Carl Hempel, my old undergraduate mentor. Oppenheim had originally been a German financier, and had occupied a seat on the board of directors of I.G. Farben. A clever man, he had the sense to realize early on that the rise to power of Hitler and the Nazis spelled a real danger to Jews. He liquidated all his holdings and took them—and himself—out of Germany in 1933, going first to Belgium, and subsequently to the U.S.A. This prescience saved his considerable fortune. He invested this intelligently, and managed to live very comfortably on the proceeds in an elegant but compact modern house in Princeton.

Withdrawal from business enabled Paul to devote himself to his hobbyhorse, the promulgation of a particular philosophical viewpoint regarding scientific knowledge. He recognized that he could not, as an amateur, do this in a way that would exert any influence without securing the collaboration of able professionally qualified collaborators. Already in Belgium he had enlisted the help of Hempel, and they had collaborated in the early 1930's on a book on the conception of *type* in the light of modern logic (*Der Typusbegriff im Lichte der neuen Logik*). In after years, Hempel became Paul's academic talent-scout and during the early 1950's he recruited John Kemeny, Hilary Putnam, and myself (among others) to work on various projects with Paul. In the 1951-52 period I collaborated with him on an essay on the conception of a *Gestalt*, carrying out a line of investigation he had begun in Europe with Kurt Grelling some fifteen years before. This collaboration issued in a paper, "Logical Analysis of Gestalt Concepts," which eventually appeared in the *British Journal for the Philosophy of Science* (in vol. 6 for 1955). My own efforts had otherwise been absorbed largely by Leibniz and symbolic logic, and this work provided a useful occasion for concern with issues in the philosophy of science.

Through the Oppenheims I came to meet some academic notables. The most eminent was Albert Einstein who was an intimate of Paul's—every Sunday morning they tok a long walk together. Einstein lived up to expectation: kindly and unassuming in person, and utterly eccentric in dress. (He went shirtless under an old sweater, and wore no socks, so that, when seated, his trousers rode up to expose his uncovered ankles.) He gave the impression of one who viewed life as made for thinking and best left undistracted by the trivia of the conventional proprieties. Bertrand Russell too was a friend of the Oppenheims and stayed at their house whenever he came to Princeton. (He was in town for a lecture at the time of his being awarded the Nobel Prize in Literature in 1951 and received notice of the award at the Oppenheims.) Russell seemed to exude an aristocratic condescension, regarding the ordinary mortals of this world in much the same way as operatic *prima donna* might look on the members of the audience—a necessary nuisance without whom one would be playing to an empty house. But Russell's evident self-esteem did not yield much to that of the almost equally eminent Hans Riechenbach, whom I also met several times at the Oppenheims.

No sooner was my new career launched on its way than a development occurred which at the time struck me as utterly catastrophic. As long as I had been a student I had had no draft problems at all, and as the end of my studies was approaching, my draft board had assured me in April of 1951 that these deferments would continue and that I could take up my post at Princeton without difficulty. But in November of that year the picture had changed. The draft levies for the Korean War had put increasing pressure on them, and they felt compelled to call me up. Notice now came that I would be inducted some twelve weeks hence.

When this bombshell burst upon me, I took immediate action. At the suggestion of a helpful mathematician, I arranged to call on John von Neumann at the Institute for Advanced Studies. At the appointed hour I was ushered into his office. It seemed vast to me and rather imposing. But the impressive little man came out from behind his large desk at the far end of the room, shook hands in a very cordial way, and was most friendly and helpful. I explained my problem to him, telling him about my training in logic and mathematics and expressing the hope that this could be utilized in some way in the course of my military service. (I passed in discreet silence over the fact that I had no stomach for routine infantry duty.) Von Neumann understood the issue at once, sympathized, and promised his aid. He had some ideas; would make some inquiries; and would be in touch with me again shortly. And he was as good as his word. Within a fortnight I had heard from him. His friend, an Army colonel whose name I have long forgotten, was in charge of some sort of scientific activity at the Aberdeen Proving Ground in Maryland. His unit could use the services of bright young men with training in mathematics. Once the date for my reporting for induction was fixed, I should let the colonel know. Further arrangements would then be made and instructions given. I breathed much easier.

Nevertheless a serious blow had been dealt, and the period from mid-November 1951 to mid-February 1952 was very much of an interregnum in my life. The sharp break with normal plans for the future put my affairs into a condition of suspended animation. I carried on my regular activities in a routine, sleepwalking sort of way, always conscious of the great change that lay just ahead. But the time passed quickly, and early on the morning of February 17, 1952 I entrained to New York to report for induction into military service. A turning point was clearly at hand and I looked with a mixture of apprehension and interest towards my projected new role as a junior scientist in Army service.

I had come a long way during this Princetonian period. I had matured as a person and was now settling down in life as a married man. I had completed my higher education, written for publication, and placed my feet firmly on the initial rungs of the ladder of a professional career. That brisk midwinter day, the Pennsylvania Railroad was carrying from Princeton a young man substantially more educated and seasoned than the eager young scholar it had brought there only two and one half years before.

Seven

U.S.M.C.: 1952-1954
(Age 23-25)

A RUDE surprise awaited me when I reported to the draft induction station at Church Street in lower Manhattan that chilly February morning in 1952. My papers—indeed every fifth set of papers—had a big black U.S.M.C. stamped on them. The explanation was simple: I was destined for the Marines. This proud volunteer organization was unable to secure enough enlistments to meet the demands of the military build-up for the Korean War, and had to resort to the draft. A random one-fifth of the inductees were being sent in this direction, and I was to be one of them. By one swift pinprick, fate burst the balloon of my carefully arranged Aberdeen plans. My military career was to evolve in a wholly different direction, that of the United States Marine Corps, a sphere unhappily beyond the reach of John von Neumann's influence.

That night we were put up in an unprepossessing Manhattan hotel, and the next morning we were gathered together, bussed to a local airfield, and embarked on a World War II military biplane. This rude and unluxurious vehicle propellered sedately southwards towards the Carolinas. There was a refueling stop at Quantico,

Virginia, and I recall my naive surprise at the substantially warmer temperatures encountered as we travelled south on this February day. The flight—my very first—was somewhat primitive, but not uncomfortable, and the time passed by rapidly, between conversing with my young Latin-American neighbor and reading in the first volume of Winston Churchill's *History of the Second World War*. (I wonder what strange inspiration led me to begin my new career with this rather martial bit of reading matter.)

Upon arrival at the airstrip in Beaufort, South Carolina, we were again herded into busses and transported through the subtropical coastal lowlands to our new home away from home, the sprawling Marine Corps Recruit Training Depot at Parris Island.

I shall be brief about the course of basic training itself. Its purpose was clear: to harden our bodies and to adjust our minds to the conditions of military service. The objective was to instill obedience and discipline in slack, soft, and wholly unmilitary young American lads. The measures taken towards these ends were certainly unenjoyable, but they were seldom cruel, and were unquestionably effective. The drill instructors' bark was worse than their bite, but sufficiently compelling to break us in to the harness of military life. We entered Parris Island as ordinary civilian lads and nine weeks later emerged as fledgling marines able to operate rifles and pistols, convinced of the benefits of gas-masks, and exposed (at a safe distance) to the workings of flame throwers and hand grenades. I did not like the transforming process, but cannot gainsay its effectiveness—nor question its necessity given the aims of the enterprise. One episode still sticks in my mind. As we were being issued various items of clothing and other gear, someone told me to pick up "that jacket" and move along. I looked blank, for I had my jacket on. "That jacket," he said, pointing. "Oh," said I, "that's not a jacket, that's my coat." At that point a bystanding corporal gave me a blow in the chest that knocked me down. "Don't you tell a Master Sergeant what's what!" he growled. I got the point—it's *their* system and, like it or not, you're going to have to do things their way.

As the end of basic training drew near, we were given classification questionnaires and interviews to determine how our efforts were going to be utilized by the service. The NCO in charge of this screening process was impressed with my competence at language—not so much the defunct (Latin and Greek) as the living (German and French). So he proposed assigning me a "military occupational specialty" category number of 0300, designating the Military Intelligence service, which employed linguistically equipped people for document translation, prisoner interrogation, and the like. I leapt at this idea with alacrity, being eager to serve where I could use my head instead of dedicating more rudimentary skills to being a rifle-carrier in the infantry. But once again, I learned how easily the best-laid plans can go wrong—especially in the military. For when it came to the actual assignment process, the only unit then actively seeking classification 0300 people was the Second Amphibious Reconnaisance Battalion at Camp Lejeune, North Carolina, and it was there that I was sent in due course to take up my first military assignment.

So many Parris Island trainees went on to Camp Lejeune that we were bussed there *en masse*. And so one fine Sunday afternoon in April of 1952 I arrived at this huge Marine base, whose bleak appearance and regimented arrangement I found overawing in a depressing sort of way. It was well after working hours by the time I found my way to the inauspicious prefabs that housed the unit for which I was destined. I was received by the current officer of the day, a friendly and enthusiastic young lieutenant who gave me a guided tour of the area and explained to me the nature of the unit's activities.

The military is always refighting the last war. In World War II as the Marines went island-hopping across the Pacific, frog-men were sent out at night from submarines to reconnoiter the approaches, examining the beach area for obstacles, defensive installations, etc. It was to *this* sort of "intelligence" work to which I (a virtual nonswimmer—but with linguistic capabilities!) was now being assigned. I applied straightaway for the short leave to which new-trained recruits were entitled, determined to try to seek out some more appropriate line of activity.

I had heard that the Marines operated a correspondence school in Washington, D.C., and it occurred to me that this might well prove my best hope. I made a bee-line for Washington to see what might be arranged. On arriving there I proceeded to search out the site of the Marine Corps Institute (MCI). This was not all that easy, because, while I knew its site was at a certain address (as best I recall at 5th and G Streets), I failed to realize that there are *four* such addresses in the Washington grid system. But after a couple of false tries, I found the place in the Southwest quadrant. There I entered a large, old, redbrick schoolhouse and proceeded to make inquiries of the Lieutenant Colonel in charge. Could they use someone with my training? To my pleasure and surprise, it turned out they could. The sergeant in charge of higher mathematics was shortly to be discharged. Would I be able to grade calculus papers? I was willing, nay eager, for the assignment. Within the hour, a happy meeting of minds was reached by all concerned, and I left with the euphoric feeling that I had managed—quite on my own initiative—to redirect the lines of my military career in a happier direction.

But all did not go so smoothly. On my return to Camp Lejeune I immediately applied for a transfer, only to have my papers "get lost" after being routinely disapproved by the commanding general, who was unwilling to see men pass from his command after less than a year's service. Not until two months later, and with intervention from Washington, did this finally get straightened out. (In the meantime I was, however, shifted from amphibious reconnaisance to less obnoxious activities in "Special Services," an operation which provided the troops with various forms of leisure-time support, from entertainments to correspondence courses.)

The transfer issue finally resolved, I waited eagerly for the day of transition. When it finally came, I hitched a lift on a Military Air Transport Service plane going up to Naval Air Station at Anacostia. (I also managed to collect the train fare for the trip—in the military one soon learns to have no scruples about cheating one's employer.) Thence I proceeded to my new home away from home, the Marine Barracks at 8th and I Streets, Southeast, the small but historic military station where the personnel assigned to the Marine Corps Institute were based.

"Eighth and Eye" was an unusual Marine installation. Then exactly one city block in size, it was shared by four very strange bedfellows: the town-house living quarters of the senior Marine generals stationed in Washington—including the Commandant of the Corps—the U.S. Marine Band, the Drum and Bugle Corps, and the personnel of the Marine Corps Institute.

The Institute—a correspondence school pure and simple—was a rather strange sort of military operation, and was staffed by an odd mixture of Marines. Many were young draftees—college men with a background in various academic subjects. Others were professional Marines, World War II veterans who had decided to make a career of it, and who generally taught the more military subjects (map reading weapon maintenance, etc.). Everyone got on pretty well. We were an informal, easy-going bunch and it required the constant vigilance of our officers to maintain the principle that we were Marines first and office workers afterwards. And day-to-day life around the barracks was not unpleasant. The people were generally congenial, and the food was good (the baker—who produced goodies for us along with those for the bigwigs in the generals' quarters—was a true virtuoso).

For the first few weeks in Washington I lived on base, going home to Princeton every second weekend on the rotation scheme virtually universal for Marine installations. But immediately upon settling in at Marine Barracks, I had applied for accommodations in a naval housing project. Informed that it would be half a year or so before this would become available, I turned to the rental market and set myself the (by no means easy) task of finding a reasonably pleasant but yet affordable apartment in the Washington area. After some weeks I finally located one, and made arrangements for the move from Princeton. But on the very morning that the movers started loading the van, I also learned that something had gone amiss and that the apartment would not be available after all. I set out immediately and had the luck to find a suitable apartment at 3900 Fourth Street, deep in the Southeast suburbs. I concluded these arrangements just in time to notify the movers as they were ready to start from Princeton with our few worldly possessions.

An episode occurred during my service at M.C.I. that deeply affected my political orientation, and in fact turned me into a lifelong Republican. This happened during the 1952 presidential election campaign. We were all called together and given a lecture by our commanding officer, Capt. Charles Stevenson, to the following effect: He did not want to tell us how to vote, but just wanted to put some information at our disposal. It had been his observation over years that Democratic presidents generally favored the military services and Republican administrations generally meant more stringent times. In particular, Eisenhower was no friend of the U.S.M.C. and had supported its absorption into the Army. While some of us might be indifferent to such considerations, those of us who were dedicated Marines should be careful in drawing our lessons from them.

These remarks proved profoundly counterproductive in my case. With attitudes shaped in reaction to my recent experiences I took the view that any opponent of the Marines was a friend of mine, and that any party that expected the military services to render value for money had entirely the right idea. And in due course, I was never to lose sight of the fact—which struck me as deeply symbolic in this light—that a Democratic administration took the country into the conflict which led to my rude extraction from civilian life, and that a Republican president had wound down the Korean war, thereby creating conditions under which my projected release from military service could be realized. In later years, the regime of Lyndon Johnson, with its intensification of the Vietnam War after running on a peace-platform campaign against the supposedly hawkish Barry Goldwater, was also to confirm my long-standing suspicion that, when it comes to war and war-like activity, Democratic presidents are given to talking in one direction and acting in another. Even at the height of the anti-Nixon hysteria in the wake of the Watergate scandals of the early 1970's, I was always mindful that this was the man who had successfully extricated us from the morass of Vietnam, and had done so under conditions more favorable than anyone had previously thought attainable. (As I saw it, the subsequent debacle in Indo-China was not Nixon's fault, but that of those who were intent on pulling him down, regardless of the cost.) In any case, it is curious how trivial developments of one's impressionable youth can often exert a totally disproportionate effect in determining the direction of future developments.

In the context of matters political, this period of life in the nation's capital proved one of the real advantages of my military service. Washington is—or then was—not only a very pleasant and liveable city, but one made particularly interesting by the presence of the apparatus of government. Its newspapers, its people, and in fact its entire atmosphere of life is saturated with the ebb and flow of political affairs. And it affords a variety of politics-related experiences that were in the highest degree broadening and interesting. (For example, I was able to attend one of the sessions of the Army-McCarthy Hearings in the spring of 1954.) Life in Washington was in many ways an educational experience, and while I was by no means happy about the circumstances which led me there, I nevertheless recognized that a silver lining came with the cloud.

A most grievous development for me during this time of military service was the death of my father in October of 1952, at the relatively young age of 62 years. His heart had been giving him trouble for somewhat over a year, but his condition seemed to have been stabilized by regimen and medication, so that his sudden death was quite unexpected. I took leave to help mother with the necessary arrangements and then returned to M.C.I. in very low spirits. I loved my father dearly and he meant a great deal to me in ways that are made no less real by the fact that they do not admit of precise articulation. When things go as they ought, the father plays a guiding role in the life of a son that differs not only in magnitude but in quality from that played by any other individual. With his departure something irreplacable is lost for good.

Then and since I have frequently ruminated on the unhappy vicissitudes of my father's fate: the 1914-18 war, the economically difficult times of the 1920's, the destruction of his livelihood in the Hitler era, the transatlantic uprooting of the late 1930's, the collapse of his new-made livelihood in 1941, and the very straightened circumstances of the subsequent decade. Every phase of his adult life brought its own sort of hardship. Yet throughout, he maintained a cheerfulness, a good humor, and a dedication to intellectual interests that I do not for a moment believe I myself could have manifested in comparable circumstances. I greatly admire the even temper he preserved in adversity and the Stoicism with which he generally made the best of extremely difficult conditions.

Early in 1953 my name on the application-list for Naval housing was finally reached, and we were able to move into a small unit at the edge of the Anacostia Naval Housing project (right next to the Naval Research Lab—at No. 9, Compass Green). For the remainder of my military service this modest but comfortable wooden bungalow-style structure was to provide the home-base from which I set off in the mornings to do my stint at the Marine Corps Insititute. Here we lived for the next 12 months or so, struggling to inject an element of domestic normality into a life traumatized by the continual and diversified demands of Marine Corps service.

In the spring of 1953 the Marine Corps Institute moved from the old schoolhouse in S.W. Washington to an upper floor in a large warehouse at the Naval Gun Factory not far from our base at Marine Barracks. After these changes, life settled once more into a relatively predictable routine. Reporting to the barracks for the morning check-in, we rode in busses to the Gun Factory and ascended by service elevator to our far-flung office loft. We mathematicians had a row of facing desks (partners-desk style) and sat there, manning bottles of green ink and grading our papers. At lunch time the lads who lived on base were bussed back for their meal, while we "brown-baggers" who lived off base broke out our lunch-pails in the office and gathered around each other's desks in small congenial clusters. Weather permitting, one could go for walks about the interesting Gun Factory compound, or one might simply find a convenient packing crate to sit on and watch the Potomac flow by. In the late afternoon we bussed back to the barracks, gathering in the locker room for a quick change into civilian garb, and then departed for our respective domiciles. This, at any rate, was the usual routine, though there was ample variation, not always of a welcome sort—guard duty, drills, and inspections.

The position of the Marine Corps was—and I daresay still is—that one is a Marine first and a cook or recruiter or correspondence school instructor secondarily. We were thus called upon for all those "duties" expected of a Marine: guard-duty, clean-up duty, mess duty, etc. Once a week we got out our rifles to play soldier in Anacostia Park—until the city fathers complained of our tearing up their grass. We were then shifted to the National Guard Armory, a vastly preferable site because, being indoors, we were sheltered against the vicissitudes of the weather, and also because it was too far afield to march to, thus yielding the comforts of bus travel.

Moreover as Marines stationed in the Washington area we were called on to participate in the staging of various ceremonials. In January, 1953 we marched in President Eisenhower's Inauguration Parade, and we later escorted the Declaration of Independence in its move from the Library of Congress to the National Archives Building. We participated regularly in the Friday Sunset Parade, a display of military ceremonial then—and for all I know still—put on during summertime for the edification of the public. Happily, I managed to escape virtually all the ceremonial details—because I wore glasses in those days, and the Corps disliked admitting in public that there were Marines who lacked 20-20 vision.

There was, however, one very special service we were called upon to provide whenever Ike went (as he loved to do) to the presidential retreat in the Catoctin Mountains in Maryland—which for some mysterious reason was a Navy installation. We furnished the perimeter security-guard while the Secret Service guarded the house with the President himself. I served on this special Presidential guard detail some three or four times. It worked roughly as follows. We would set out by bus on Friday afternoon for the drive of some two hours to the presidential compound which F.D.R. had named "Shangri La," but Ike had renamed Camp David after his grandson. By the time the President arrived in the late afternoon—by car from some nearby helicopter landing—our security operation was in place, consisting of a perimeter patrol by armed riflemen walking along the inside of the wirefence enclosure. (Since our M-1 rifles held live ammunition, the inspecting Officer of the Day made sure one heard him coming on his rounds, in consequence of which some of the lads—I not among them!—made free to "sit down on the job.") We lived in basic but (in summer) perfectly adequate smallish cabins of the sort one might expect in a National Park. We ate in the mess-hall operated for us and for the Secret Service men by the Navy cooks from the Presidential yacht. (The food, as I recall, was of a very good standard.)

Had it not been for the nuisance of having one's weekend plans broken up, the Camp David detail could have been viewed as a not unpleasant diversion. One's guard-circuit involved a rather enjoyable if monotonous ramble through the scenic woodland paths. I shall always remember one particular morning in the spring of 1953 when I walked the 4-8 A.M. patrol through this very attractive tract of woodland, with dawn gradually coming on and dozens of different species of birds waking up one by one, until the whole forest was vibrant with song. I recall too one pleasantly balmy Saturday that summer when I had nothing to do all afternoon but lie on my bunk reading Benjamin Franklin's *Autobiography* with great enjoyment, and with keen appreciation of the shrewdness of the man. I had not read it before, but it has been one of my favorites ever since.

The presidential week-end concluded, we would return to Washington by bus on Monday mornings. On one occasion we were given a guided tour of the main house after the President's departure and got to see some of Ike's paintings which I found surprisingly attractive. Though I saw Ike from afar on several of these occasions, I never got to speak to him, and don't think that any of us did, possibly excepting the commander of the detail who may—I would hope—have been accorded a personal word of thanks. One amusing facet of the enterprise was the marked contrast between us "tough Marines," the cerebral M.C.I. types, and the mere civilians of the Secret Service guard, a very rough lot answering to one's picture of Miami Mafia enforcers, all ablaze in loud sportshirts left over from the days of Harry Truman's Florida vacations.

Of the many young men who figured among my acquaintances at M.C.I. three stand out as particular friends:

Herbert Curl was a young Ph.D. in biology—a limnologist to be precise. Perhaps a year or two older than I, he also was married and had a child. Possessed of a sedate disposition and commonsensical outlook, he had a wry sense of humor and was companionable in a rather self-contained way. We were good friends at work, but had no contact off base.

C. Maury Jones had recently graduated from Princeton, which gave us some points of contact. Maury was also married, and his pleasant, outgoing wife gave birth to their first child around this time. A graduate of one of the better prep schools, he came from a wealthy background. (His father was an affluent New York oddlot stockbroker who served in the Esquadrille Lafayette in WWI and his mother a power in the American Red Cross, and a *grande dame* of the best American type—maternal, yet clearly the bearer of considerable social and political weight.) Maury was bent on becoming a mogul in the advertising industry after completing his service. I have no idea how he subsequently fared in the pursuit of this ambition, but in any case he was bound to inherit a substantial fortune.

Walter Harman was a late comer who arrived in early 1953. Perhaps a year younger than I, he was well enroute to a Ph.D. in zoology, and already held an appointment in the Zoology Department at Louisiana State University in Baton Rouge. His specialty was earthworms, and on his days off he scuried about the countryside collecting specimens. He was a pleasant, good natured, and rather easygoing young man. He frequently visited in our house, where his kindness and good humor made him always welcome. He was attracted to Gwen, an attractive and thoroughly pleasant girl who also came from Louisiana. He was then locked in a chronic struggle to make up his mind to marry her—which he ultimately exuded the manner of a "gentleman of the old school."

Though at the time seemingly endless, my two year period of military service moved along day by day, and I daresay that on balance it went well enough. In June of 1953 I was promoted to corporal, thereby becoming a "non-commissioned officer," a status which entailed various small but useful privileges, NCO's being exempt from most types of dog-work. Later that year I even passed the various hurdles for promotion to sergeant and would have achieved this exalted rank—so I was informed—had my period of service been prolonged two months longer. My files contained several letters of commendation (relating to proposals of mine for improving the work of the office), and I think my superiors always found reason for satisfaction with my contributions. Though I disliked the service I did not let this deflect me from my general tendency to try to do well at whatever task was put into my hands.

Perhaps this account has given a misleading "fun and games" tenor to my period of military service. The thing I found most objectionable about military service was the combination of uncertainty and helplessness. One never knew what tomorrow might bring—a special guard detail, a stay with the President at Camp David, perhaps even transfer to "the front" in Korea. There was no way of telling what would come next, and whatever did come, there was no way of averting the decree from on high. This feeling that one's life lay wholly outside the grasp of one's own control was for me the most distasteful aspect of the whole business. My direst apprehension was a prolongation of the period of service by our being drawn into replacing France's collapsing efforts in Indo-China, and I shall be eternally grateful to Dwight Eisenhower that—despite considerable pressures—he did not permit this to happen during his administration.

What did military service mean to me? I would be less than honest to deny that I disliked every day of it and looked forward keenly to its termination. For I felt acutely the wastefulness of it all. I was an impatient young man eager to get on with the business of building my academic career, and I regarded the two years of my service as a massive loss of opportunity. I believe that the reason I became "indefatigable" in my professional work—as somebody once remarked in reviewing one of my books—was at least in part due to a sense of the need to make up for lost time.

And yet in the retrospect of over twenty years I really cannot bring myself to regard this period of service as a total loss. There are many useful lessons that one can only learn under conditions of personal adversity, and I have had the not wholly welcome opportunity to learn some of them. I also learned some facts about human nature and about my own reactions to various problems and situations that were to prove of use in other situations. I experienced life with men under conditions of shared proximity, rubbing shoulders at close range with Americans of a type that would otherwise have been as remote from me as the natives of Patagonia. And I learned the fundamental aspects of military discipline—the basic pattern of life in cantonment that has not altered significantly since Roman times. These lessons were worthwhile not only for the human being but for the philosopher. From this aspect, my father's pet saying *"Das wird man Dir im Militär schon zeigen"* ("They'll teach you about that in the service!") was to prove markedly true.

When one considers the relatively secure and comfortable channels in which my own life has generally run, one might incline to think that here is a person who has no understanding of the lot of ordinary working people. Yet on various occasions, extending over an entire decade, I have been exposed to the totally routine and utterly mind-annihilating sort of work to which the daily efforts of all too many are perforce dedicated. During a formative period of my life I repeatedly saw the workings of "unskilled labor" from the inside: As an assembly-line candy-packer in the Lofts factory in 1943, as a counter-clerk in Bickford's diner in 1944, as a library-underling in the Jamaica Public Library in 1947, as a clerk in the Elizabethtown Consolidated Gas Company in 1951, and as a basic trainee in the U.S. Marine Corps in 1952. Such activities took me outside the academic orbit of studies and students within which my life has otherwise been lived, and gave me a profitable different slant on things.

Edward Gibbon spoke of his teachers at Oxford as people "whose eyes are dazzled by the light of philosophy." He deemed them abstracted academics—otherwordly narcissists, given to contemplating their own intellectual navels. If nothing else, my period of military service prevented me from becoming a person of this sort. Most of my younger colleagues have never done anything since the age of four or five except to get up in the morning and go to school—first as a student, then as a teacher. This is a situation from which fate has preserved me. My years in the Marines and even the period at RAND threw me together with people (and military people in particular) of a sort not to be encountered in academic settings. They gave me exposure to "the real world'—an experience by no means useless to a philosopher. Insofar as my reflections have dealt with issues of life rather than issues of thought alone, this is done in good measure to these years spent outside the precincts of the academy.

Still, throughout my Marine Corps service, I kept in touch with philosophy, finding some Sunday hours to devote to it even during the Parris Island months. During the spring of 1953 I taught Introduction to Philosophy in the evening program at American University—a strictly illegal proceeding for someone on active service, but one which brought me considerable enjoyment and a little money. At Alonzo Church's behest, I continued to write some reviews for *The Journal of Symbolic Logic*. And I managed to do a bit (a very little bit) of work at the Library of Congress to keep abreast of current work on Leibniz. The maintenance of my self-image as a philosopher was important to me.

As my discharge from the service began to draw ever closer with the passage of 1953, I had to give serious thought to the job problem. A letter from Professor Robert Scoon, then Chairman of the Philosophy Department at Princeton, offered a resumption of my instructorship there. But it was clear that this would be an interim measure, with little prospect for the long term. After the upheavals of the past two years, I felt a strong disinclination to enter upon yet another temporary arrangement. And so I decided to look in other directions.

I wrote some fifty letters (unwisely on yellowish stationery) to the philosophy chairmen of various colleges and universities. The replies, though sometimes hopeful, were uniformly unproductive. The postwar student boom was just ending, and academic institutions throughout America were in a desperate state of retrenchment and decline. The academic job market was a shambles. Given my disinclination to accept the Princeton offer, the prospect of finding an appointment in philosophy looked very gloomy.

I thus began to think about other possibilities. For one thing, I was offered (at his instigation) the opportunity to succeed David Baumgardt as resident philosopher in the Library of Congress, but this somehow did not appeal to me. For another, it was now suggested that I explore the prospects of working for one of the various military think-tanks which were thriving in this era of the "Cold War" and the Korean conflict. The idea sounded potentially interesting, and I made the rounds of the Washington offices of various operations-research agencies ORO (Army), NRO (Navy), RAND

(Air Force), and WSEG (Joint Chiefs). Both the latter two indicated interest in me; the others wanted only physicists at the time. But RAND's proposal was far and away the most tempting. They offered me a post in the Mathematics Division of their main office in Santa Monica, California, at the princely-seeming salary of $7,200 per annum. The job sounded interesting, and California had the appeal of novelty. The whole prospect seemed challenging—and anyway, no more attractive alternatives lay to hand. I decided to accept.

By the end of May all preparations for the move to California were completed (down to the purchase of a new Chevrolet sedan—cheaper on the East Coast than the West and shipped cross-country at RAND's expense). One rainy day at the start of June, a Baltimore and Ohio train heading westwards to Chicago left from Union Station in Washington, leaving behind a city that had, for some two years provided the stage for my military service—such as it was. I left Washington happy to have this detour behind me, with a new and interesting-sounding job in a new part of the country lying ahead. The tune of "California, Here I Come" ran in my head, and I faced the prospect of new scenes and activities with a mixture of curiosity, hopefulness, and excitement.

Still only 25 years of age, I had now carried my education through to the doctorate and discharged my obligation of military duty. At last I could enter upon a regular job. And yet, though filled with the enthusiasm of youth, a certain apprehensiveness lurked at the back of my mind. Political developments had driven me from the land of my birth in 1938, international conflict had deflected me from a philosophical career into military service in 1952, and economic conditions had now blocked my prospects for a suitable academic post. Running beneath a surface layer of natural optimism was an undercurrent of awareness of the everpresent potential for the unexpected and unwanted in human affairs. I have always lacked, more than most people seem to do, an assured confidence that all will go according to plan and that we can count our lives secure against the untoward interference of "circumstances beyond our control."

Eight

The Rand Corporation: 1954-1956

(Age 25-28)

CHICAGO WAS the point of transfer to the Santa Fe Railroad, whose Superchief service then provided perhaps the most comfortable means of train travel to California. This railway journey in June of 1954 was a memorable one for me—my first transcontinental trip. I can still recall vividly some snatches of the route: the "dark, satanic mills" of the steelworks at Gary, Indiana; the active bustle of the Chicago railway stations; the seeming endlessness of the Great Plains; the barren panoramas of the California desert. The trip lasted two days and three nights—a limited time that yet seemed interminable. But one sunny morning we finally pulled into the handsome Union Station in Los Angeles. After the luggage had been gathered up, a taxi provided transport to 1700 Main Street, then as now home office of the RAND Corporation in Santa Monica.

Housing accommodation was initially furnished in a nearby beachside hotel. But serious house-hunting began right away, for years of wandering from one residential make-shift to another had fostered an eagerness to settle and let down some roots. Upon seeking advice at RAND and inspecting various possibilities, it appeared that Pacific Palisades offered the most promising locality as a pretty residential area with affordable house-prices. While several days were spent looking, with some ten houses actually visited, the final choice settled on the very first one inspected. This was an attractive single-level, California-style, three-bedroomed house at 14907 Bestor Boulevard. With its handsome lawn in front and large garden in back, the house was prettily sited on a pleasant residential street, redolent with the perfume of Southern California flora. It cost a nowadays incredibly low sum of $22,000, but the realization of this then enormous-seeming amount called for every musterable penny of credit: not only a mortgage, but even a small loan from Florence Simpson, the helpful real estate saleslady who had assumed charge of these househunting efforts. (Ever since I have always lived under my own roof save during periods of transition, and this has proved a sound financial practice throughout a generally inflationary era.) Occupancy of the house had to be postponed until the furniture van finally arrived, some days after Frances and I watched from the window of the empty living-room the traditional 4th of July fireworks set off from a Navy ship anchored in Santa Monica bay. In due course we settled in and began to explore our new habitat, gradually growing accustomed to the shaplessness of Los Angeles and the strange semi-tropical beauties of Southern California.

The initial weeks of my employment at RAND were spent "in quarantine" in an outer section of the building populated by people who also had not yet received their governmental security clearance for access to a "classified facility." Most of my time here I spent in reading material in the mathematical theory of games, which was then central to the interests of RAND mathematicians—though as it turned out I never made the slightest use of it in connection with any of my own work there.

As my pre-clearance period was nearing its end, a young man named Fred Thompson, of whom I knew nothing at all, dropped by to ask if I might be interested in working with him and some other Mathematics division colleagues on some economic issues they were researching. This was the first time anyone at RAND had shown the slightest awareness of my presence. So I agreed with alacrity, feeling that this would be a great improvement on the rather boring inactivity that was currently my lot.

My recruitment to project work at RAND was typical of its then-current mode of operation, at any rate in the Mathematics Division. By and large, work was done on a free-consent basis. The Air Force tried—often unsuccessfully—to persuade RAND to undertake a project. If the organization's directorship was interested, it tried to persuade one of its senior staff members that this might suit him. He in turn made the round of his otherwise uncommitted colleagues to try to recruit their collaboration. The voluntary contribution of effort was the rule, not just in theory but in actual practice as well.

The project we now launched had at its aim the design of a large scale computerized input-output model of the workings of a national economy. The inquiry was bound up in some vague way with the issue of how much damage the American economy could sustain in a war of bombardment and yet continue to maintain a military effort. The leading spirit of the venture was Frederick B. Thompson, then in his mid-30's, who had earned his Ph.D. in mathematical logic under Alfred Tarski at Berkeley a few years before. Fred was a person of intense drive and energy, a super-salesman type. Intelligent and hardworking, he seemed to live for his work alone, driven by a strong yearning for recognition. I admired him for his good qualities and learned lessons from his bad ones, which included, above all, a tendency to set image above accomplishment. For Fred, to see his way roughly clear to solving a problem and then to convince others of his *capacity* to do so was quite enough; the need for completing a finished product available for general use was not recognized. The futility of a powerful machine that ceased operations just short of producing an actually available result made a lasting impression on me, and made me determined that the fruits of my own work would always be full-ripened and duly packaged for public consumption.

Something I found very impressive about Fred Thompson, however, was the depth of his commitment to hammering away at the tasks in hand. When he arrived at work in the morning (never late and generally early) it was obvious that a good deal of thought had been given since the end of the preceding day to the nature of its residual problems, to the steps that lay ahead, and to the general organization of the work. And there was a kind of driving eagerness to "get on with it," an infectious and enthusiastic concern to push the effort forward to its next stage that exerted a near-inspirational impetus. Then and since I have regarded Fred as the very model of dedication to work and workmanship. Only as the end drew near did Fred's interest in the venture wilt. And so our computerized economic model—which I still consider as in some degree a pioneering achievement—was allowed to die by neglect on the very verge of completion.

My second RAND activity was a joint effort with Fred and the economist Frederick B. Moore to make an assessment of the extent of the human and economic carnage that would be brought about by an all-out Russian nuclear air assault against the U.S., given the best available estimates of their then-current capabilities according to USAF intelligence. The project was named VAMP for "Vulnerability of American Military Potential"—I myself dreamed up this acronym and was quite pleased with it.

As best I recall, the project came to the conclusion that while the economy could readily restore the physical damage within a couple of years, we would have lost some 20% of the population in the attack—largely as victims to radioactive fallout—so that the destruction of life and its concomitant social disruption could be expected to put all considerations of an impact on economic productivity into the shade.

After parting ways with Fred sometime in early 1955, I worked on a project on my own making; a speculative assessment of how, given then-extant Russian military capabilities, a preemptive nuclear "counterforce" attack against U.S. retaliatory potential might be designed. Interestingly enough, considering the reputation for war-mongering hawkishness that RAND came to have in the academic community during the 1960's, all of my own work there was primarily of defensive orientation, as indeed were most projects of which I had knowledge. (RAND was responsive to the moods of the military, and, with Pearl Harbor fresh in mind, the Air Force of the 1950's was more worried about being sinned against than sinning.)

The head of Mathematics Division in those days was John D. Williams, author of a clever introduction to game theory entitled *The Compleat Strategist*. He was a man of rare quality. I did not get to know him well enough to gauge fully the creative power of his mind, but I could readily tell that it ranged far and deep. What struck me as the most original aspect of the man was his approach to research-administration. His rule was to secure the services of people he deemed competent, and then to give them virtually unrestricted freedom, leaving them at liberty to work as interest and opportunity might list. Some simply rambled off in pursuit of their own academic goals. Others dedicated themselves to the serious problems of the corporation, and their self-motivation produced a respectable average level of activity. It seemed to be Williams' idea that a high structure requires a base of seemingly wasteful proportions. Though I had my doubts at the time, I have since become increasingly alive to the possible merits of such a theory of administration.

One of the most interesting people at RAND was Olaf Helmer, to whom I felt personally closer than to any other RAND colleague, thanks to the philosophical bent of his interests. Olaf was a German emigré who had originally trained as a philosopher, earning a Ph.D. under Susan Stebbing at the University of London in the late 1930's, before coming to the U.S.A. He was a person of great charm, clever inventiveness, and a certain unrealism with respect to practical affairs. Futurology was his pet—a then unheard of sphere of inquiry. Olaf was one of the inventors of the "Delphi method," involving the use of questionnaires to elicit from "experts" opinions to be used as a basis for prediction.[28] He was very interested in the epistemology of prediction outside the natural sciences, and we would talk about these issues from time to time. Sometime in 1955 we decided to write a paper on the subject, and so once a week we held an evening work session either at his house or mine. His (third?) wife Maggie was a charming and vivacious person, and I spent many pleasant evenings in their home in Mandeville Canyon Road talking epistemology with Olaf. I count him as a kindred spirit who helped to make my years at RAND more pleasant.

Lester Ford came to work in the Mathematics Division about a year after I did, and became peripherally involved in the VAMP group for a time. A gifted mathematician, he soon became interested in theoretical questions in queing theory and network theory and drifted off into pure mathematics. But I got to know him and his large family very well (he had some seven daughters at this stage). Lester was a very easygoing chap with a good sense of humor and a relaxed, uncomplicated approach to the problems of life which struck me as admirable and sometimes amusing. I liked him greatly and we came to be good friends.

Norman Dalkey was another RANDite I grew to know and like. Norm too had started out as a philosopher. A person of great charm, he combined a penchant for rather outlandish but interesting ideas with a certain disdain for the down-to earth labor needed to give them shape and substance. He came to do his best work later, when RAND's interests ultimately shifted from military to civilian concerns, and the atmosphere of the place became more congenial to socially oriented issues.

Working at RAND afforded me an opportunity to meet many outstanding people—and to see some of them in action (for wargaming was then a vogue). Curtis LeMay, Charles Lindbergh, and John von Neumann were among the luminaries who came to visit. One extraneous chance encounter from those days also sticks in my mind. On one of my Washington flights on some RAND business it happened that Gen. Omar Bradley was a fellow passenger. Though a prime leader of our World War II efforts in Europe, a former Chief of Staff of the U.S. Army, and the Chairman of the Board of a major corporation, he did not travel in the First Class, but shared humbler accommodations with ordinary mortals in the Tourist Class. He made himself available to his fellow passengers, strolling along the aisle talking with anyone who wished to chat, a step which—considering that he was not a candidate for public office—I found even more suprising. This episode was, for me, a useful lesson about leadership in a democracy, and I was impressed. Only in eventual retrospect did it strike me that Bradley's folksiness might be every bit as much of an image-projecting pose as Douglas MacArthur's proverbial aloofness.

One lesson I had driven home to me during my years at RAND was the difference in cast of mind, intellectual approach, and—above all—operative effectiveness between the theoretician and the practical man of affairs. RAND had its quota of impractical, "mad scientist" types in those days—my friend Olaf Helmer being a good example of this species, and Herman Kahn a rather more opportunistic one. But it seemed to me that the views of such people never stood a chance of making any difference to the way in which things happened at RAND—the things that mattered. Between them and real influence in the corporation, either internal or external, there invariably stood a handful of practical men of "common sense," themselves not scientists either by training or intellectual inclination. The president of RAND, Frank Collbaum and his nearer advisors, a palace guard of influential consigliores—all solid and able men of limited vision and capability—were those in whose hands the fate of the corporation and its efforts actually rested. To say all this is not to say that theoreticians and speculators labor in vain. (The ideas of Marx, after all, have made a vast difference!) But the work of the theorist begins to make an impact on the real world only when the men of action pick it up and turn it to their own ends.

In this regard, one episode in particular opened my eyes. Late in 1955 or early in 1956 I became involved in a collaborative inquiry—carried out at the behest of the Air Intelligence directorate—whose aim was to examine the prospects of a possible U.S.S.R. surprise attack against the U.S. in the oncoming missile age. One of the prime participants in this study, Jack Raymond, had a theory about a rapid build-up of Soviet missile forces which differed from the more conservative position currently favored at RAND. He was in process of building this view into his contribution to the project. But when his more orthodox colleagues noted this, the result took the form not of reasoned counterargumentation, but of a simple power-play that effectively ousted Raymond from the project. (Shortly after he left RAND for a much better job elsewhere—one of the several instances in my experience of a person ejected from one post putting forth under duress the initiatives that in fact lead to a major advance in his career, a curious phenomenon that often makes "failure" a highroad to "success.")

I kept at philosophy in a desultory way during the RAND years. I read some of the journals and wrote a couple of (rather trivial) papers. On two or three occasions I attended philosophy meetings at UCLA. My main effort along these lines revolved about the philosophy of social science and especially history, and culminated in the essay on "The Epistemology of the Social Sciences" which I co-authored with Olaf Helmer 1955-56. Looking back on it, I am sensitive to the difficulties of working "outside the context" without the stimulus of students and colleagues and formal commitments to teaching and lecturing. In this light, I came to feel a boundless admiration for C. S. Peirce, who produced first-rate work in philosophy for over 30 years in the splendid isolation of the wilds of the Pennsylvania countryside.

One interesting philosophical acquaintance I made at this stage was Rudolf Carnap, the eminent positivistic philosopher of Vienna Circle fame. Periodically Olaf Helmer, the statistician James Savage, and I met with Carnap at his house to discuss issues of induction and probability. Young whippersnapper that I was, I felt too much in awe of Carnap to enter freely into these discussions, although Carnap himself was an unassuming little man who made up for a lack of sparkle with painstaking care and elaborate laboriousness. He was unpretentious, and at times almost diffident, but his evident dedication to the work in hand set an example from which a fledgling scholar could profit.

Shortly after settling in Los Angeles I became interested in Quakerism. Frances and I now began to attend the local Friends Meeting in Santa Monica. Three aspects of the sect strongly attracted me: its utterly simple yet deeply meaningful mode of worship, its lack of any creedal commitments that might jar on a critical philosophic mind, and its dedication to pacifism. (My experience of war, however distant, and of military service, however unwarlike, had convinced me that the way of peace is best, and that pacifism albeit difficult in practice, is an ideal that merits all the support it can obtain.) In due course we joined the Santa Monica Meeting, and the fellowship that this provided was one of the pleasant highlights of these California years.

Only after getting settled in Pacific Palisades and adjusting to working at RAND and living in the Los Angeles area, a process pretty well accomplished by early 1955, did life become settled for Frances and me. Our marriage had heretofore witnessed a series of rapid changes, marked by repeated shifts in locale and career: its four years had seen us living in six different domiciles, with me following three very different careers—as a philosophy instructor, a Marine, and now as a RAND researcher. But at last stabilization seemed to be at hand.

This circumstance was to prove shattering. The shifts and jolts of the recent years had served to mask the tensions and incompatabilities between us. The fact is that we were ill suited to one another in personality and, above all, in what we wanted from life. I loved travel and changes of scene, while Frances was glued to her home and hearth. I was a social creature, enjoying to be entertained and to entertain others, while Frances had no relish for the presence of others in her house. I viewed marriage as providing a domestic base for venturing forth into the activities of the environing world, while she regarded it as a safe harbor from whose security one only reluctantly departs. To be sure, I never had been one to "go out with the boys," I did not hunt or golf or play poker or the like. But I have always relished work and its involvements—colleagueship, professional meetings, research-connected travel, etc. For Frances any foray outside the domestic orbit on my part was virtual treason. She made marriage not a haven but a prison. The long and short of it is that we were incompatible—immersed in that uncommon situation where a glib cliché like "the wrong chemistry" can do good service.

I long refused to look this fact in the face. I regarded myself as a "logical" person, and logical people hate to confess error. And various social and moral pressures were at work as well. But I now began to face up to the idea of a break with Frances and talked to her about it. However, she was dead set against divorce, which was apparently viewed as a heinous crime in her family because of some traumatic episode of the past. And I shrank from taking so decisive a step unilaterally. Things dragged along for some months in a thoroughly unsatisfactory condition, when external circumstances intervened. The inner strains of our relationship were once again dampened by outer challenges, and we agreed to hold our marriage together as we embarked on plans for a second cross-country move in a little over two years.

In March of 1956 I had gone to Washington for a few days to transact some RAND business with the Air Force intelligence people. Shortly after arriving, a telegram was forwarded to me telephonically to the Hay-Adams Hotel, where I invariably stayed in the nation's capital because I found its solid old-world atmosphere congenial. The cable was from Howard Ziegler, chairman of the Philosophy Department at Lehigh University in Bethlehem, Pennsylvania, and requested me to get in touch with him. He and his colleagues were very interested in adding someone with my general qualifications as Assistant Professor in the department—a young P.h.D. trained in logic and philosophy of science, but with enough versatility to teach a wide range of subjects, and with some interest in the history of science. Ziegler was then chairman of the American Philosophical Association's placement committee, and had turned up my name in the inactive file, where it had rested since my job-seeking days of 1953, when my discharge from service was drawing near.

This invitation came as a bolt from the blue. But since I was close at hand, it seemed worthwhile to pursue the matter. And so I journeyed to Bethlehem by train a day or two later. When I arrived I was met at the Pennsylvania Railroad station by the entire department—all three of them, Howard Ziegler, Adolf Grunbaum, and Thomas Haynes. What impressed me as we talked around the lunch table in the dinning room of the Hotel Bethlehem was the evident enthusiasm about me on the part of all concerned. There was no sceptical reserve, no element of "go ahead and convince us that we should really want you" about the discussion. They were all actually *eager* for me to join them. I viewed this prospect, though wholly unanticipated and unprovided for, as altogether providential. While the salary was to be just half of my RAND salary (i.e., $5,500 as contrasted with around $11,000), the chance to return to academic life exercised a powerful attraction. As I journeyed back to Washington by train late that afternoon, I turned the matter over in my mind backwards and forwards, and did not see how I could refuse—given my fundamental commitment to philosophy and to academic endeavors. To be sure, I did not see my way clear to beginning at Lehigh that very fall; there were too many loose ends to tie up in Santa Monica. But I did think that I could manage an orderly transition of my affairs in time to begin at Lehigh in early January of 1967.

And so I flew back to Los Angeles with my head full of the plans and prospects of impending change. Uprooted from academic work in February of 1952, I felt that here at last was a spontaneous opportunity to resume—just five years later—the pursuit of what I had for most of my adult life regarded as my natural *métier*. It seemed to me that destiny was calling, and I decided to bring my RAND career to an end.

In the course of the Vietnam War the RAND Corp. became one of the bogeymen of the Liberal Left in American—a symbol of all that was reprehensible about intellectuals in the service of a warmongering establishment. (When I lectured in Oxford in the spring of 1974, one young participant told me of an American colleague who refused to attend because he heard that I had once worked for RAND!) Did I ever feel any qualms? In all candor I can say that I did feel some occasional twinges—but not many. My own work at RAND was, as described, largely concerned with matters of vulnerability and defense. Their upshot pointed towards the desirability of war-avoidance, and militated in a direction very much opposed to war-mongering. Moreover, I was too much of a realist to feel anguished. As long as nations maintain military capabilities—and in the present scheme of things it is not in the cards that they should soon cease to do so—they might as well conduct their affairs in this sphere intelligently, utilizing informed advice such as RAND was in a position to offer. The qualms that turned my away were not ideological but personal: a sense that "this was not for me." This sentiment was not yet (as of 1956) so strong as to impel me into an active pursuit of other possibilities, and indeed, might never have become strong enough to generate the requisite "escape energy" wholly by itself. But it was quite enough that, when an unexpected opportunity eventually presented itself spontaneously, I seized it eagerly.

As soon as I returned to California, planning got underway for the return "back East" (as Californians always say). The Bestor Boulevard house was put up for sale that summer, and we undertook an automobile excursion up the coast as far as Victoria, in British Columbia to make the most of the Pacific locale that was soon to be left behind. The house was sold in the course of this vacation and some temporary rental arrangement made thereafter. During that fall I wound up my affairs at RAND, and by the end of the year everything was ready for the transcontinental drive to Bethlehem.

I sometimes wonder whether, had fate not extricated me from RAND, I might have become "trapped" there for good—quite outside of what I think of as my natural habitat in philosophy. I regretfully surmise that the answer is a definite *yes*. As I look back on it, I see that there was nothing inevitable about my reentry into philosophy. I could readily have settled inextricably into research and administration in RAND or some comparable "think tank." With the passing years the prospects of return to Academia could have become ever dimmer. When I see people who have gone this route, the sobering thought comes to mind that "there but for the grace of God go I."

I thought (and still think) that I had managed to learn many things during the two and a half years at RAND—things about human nature, about the workings of institutions, and about the ways of life in a domain outside the academic sphere. Although RAND itself was a rather peculiar organization, I learned something about practical affairs from some of the many very practical-minded people in its employ. Above all, I learned to work with other people and absorbed the significance and the technique of teamwork and collaboration. (The result has been that no contemporary in my field has published more collaborative studies than I, and that I have frequently been able to enlist my students as collaborators in my own work.) Then too there was the interest of first-hand experience of the rather different life-style afforded by Southern California. Writing with the benefit of over twenty years of hindsight I feel that the RAND experience provided some very useful bits of intellectual nurture.

Moreover, while RAND activities were clearly "beside the point," so to speak, from the narrower perspective of my philosophical career, I have never believed, from that time to this, that the two and a half years I worked in Santa Monica were wasted in this respect. For I acquired a number of philosophically valuable lessons. In particular, I learned to appreciate the interest and utility of empirical investigations in the social sciences—especially economics and social theory—for working ethics and social philosophy. My philosophizing in these fields has never moved at the level of arid abstraction that was almost universal in the 1950's and 60's, when any taking heed of the empirical realities was all too frequently seen as ill-suited to "doing philosophy" in the proper, *a priori* mode. Without this public-policy oriented concern for the concrete social realities, various books of mine in applied philosophy, such as *Distributive Justice, Welfare*, and *Unselfishness*, would never have been written.

How did I assess RAND itself? On balance I would say that I had great respect for the organization. It had some extremely able and far-sighted leaders—preeminently including John Williams of Mathematics Division and Charles Hitch of Economics. It certainly had a wide and impressively competent array of talent in its employ in those times. As I saw it, RAND's main defect was its inability to bring these resources into a better focus. Some very fine work was being done by the organization (perhaps the best in its history), but its volume struck me as modest relative to the very impressive talents at the disposal of the enterprise. I suspect that to some extent the balmy climate, the beach-side site, and the "easy living" of Southern California tended to make lotus eaters of its staff.

Be that as it may, there were no regrets in my mind on that foggy California morning of January 4, 1957, when embarking on an eastward transcontinental journey in the same green 1954 Chevrolet which had crossed the country westward by train some two and a half years previously.

Nine

Lehigh University: 1957-1961

(Age 28-32)

ON REACHING Bethlehem, Pennsylvania at the end of my first and only coast-to coast automobile trip in early January of 1957, a few days were spend as houseguests in the Howard Ziegler's colonial-style residence near the center of town. Thereafter, a small but adequate apartment in a newish complex on the outskirts of town provided a new home.

It felt good to be "back East" again. Bethlehem was a thoroughly pleasant town. With a population of some 60,000, it was built on a rational, human scale—delightfully peaceful and old-worldish after the somewhat garish exoticism of Los Angeles. I was thoroughly pleased to resume academic life in such an attractive and liveable site. Things with a history have always appealed to me. I have a natural curiosity for background, and confronted with a new place or person or object I am always interested in the historical process that has led to the *status quo*.

Lehigh University was at this point a smallish institution, with roughly 2,000 students. Founded in 1865 by the munificence of a steel magnate, the university by now had some 1,000 undergraduates in engineering, along with roughly 500 liberal arts students, and 500 in the business school. (There was also a small graduate program mainly in the sciences.) Its diminutive Philosophy Department figured primarily in a "service" role, providing liberal-arts exposure to fledgling engineers and businessmen. The engineers in particular were able and hardworking students—if somewhat untutored on the humanistic side. It was a pleasure to teach them logic or philosophy of science, where the bent of their minds intersected with that of the subject.

At Lehigh I soon settled into the regular routine of a philosophy professor. As junior member of the department, I was called upon to teach a wide range of undergraduate philosophy offerings: logic, history of philosophy, theory of knowledge, and various special subjects (semantics, history of science). My duties during the initial years consisted of teaching four classes per term (each meeting three hours per week on a Monday/Wednesday/Friday or a Tuesday/Thursday/Saturday schedule). However, several of these classes were sections of the same course (usually two or three sections of logic), so that the number of distinct preparations was reduced. But while this "teaching load" was heavy (at any rate, by the standard of later times), I had little difficulty in combining it with a wide spectrum of other activities. In comparison with RAND's eight-hour day, this schedule afforded a new found freedom. I managed to get on with some research on my own, and with such outside efforts as the study of Arabic (of which more anon). All in all, I was happy and proud to be a member of the academic community once again. And I was delighted to be back at philosophy, relishing the opportunity to let my mind run in paths traced out by the great thinkers of the past.

The President of Lehigh at this stage was Martin Dewey Whittaker. He struck me as stuffy and unimaginative (an impression which, based as it was on rather casual contacts, may well do him injustice). His favorite anecdote—one heard it often from his lips—was the story of the man who had once given him the wise counsel: "Never explain your decisions! One generally reaches the right decision for the wrong reasons, and if you explain your reasons you will probably be talked out of them and the decision as well."²⁹ Whittaker apparently clung to this principle in and out of season, a fact which hardly qualified him as an ideal of academic leadership.

As far as I could see, the brain of the University's administration belonged to Harvey Neville, its Vice President. A loyal old Princetonian and an able chemist, he provided the institution with academic leadership and sense of direction. I emerged from my various dealings with him with an enhanced respect for his ability to combine dignity, courtesy, and helpfulness.

Howard Ziegler—the chairman of the philosophy department—was then just nearing the age of fifty. After undergraduate work at Franklin & Marshall College in his native region of Pennsylvania (he hailed from Reading), he had been trained as a Lutheran minister. But the ministry sat uncomfortably on his shoulders, and he gravitated towards academia, ultimately earning a Ph.D. at Columbia University with a dissertation on a tertiary American thinker (one Frederick Augustus Rauch). A person of many substantial capabilities, Howard was an excellent administrator—painstaking, hardworking, unselfishly mindful of the welfare of his subordinates, and heartily devoted to the effectiveness of the enterprise. Possessed of a friendly spirit and a good sense of humor, he labored unstintingly to advance the interest of Lehigh University and to enhance the quality of his department. Unusually effective in dealing with people at all levels—students, colleagues in other fields, and university officials—he conveyed to everyone with whom he dealt a concern for their well-being and care of their problems. He was a true Christian gentleman, and his strengths of character were matched by an attractive good humor and sweetness of temperament. His principal shortcoming was a certain sensitivity about his relatively modest abilities as a philosopher. Yet he handled this admirably. Many a department chairman would in such circumstances have sought security in mediocre colleagues. Not Howard! Dedicated to the good of the university, he went to great lengths to secure the services of really able people. And, fortunately, they respected him as a very superior person, greatly admired his flair for administration, and deeply appreciated the care for their welfare which he constantly manifested.

When I first met with Lehigh Philosophy Department for a luncheon "interview" at the Hotel Bethlehem in April of 1956, Adolf Grunbaum had already been a member of the department for some years, having come there for his first post after earning his Ph.D. at Yale in 1950. His career at Lehigh had been meteoric, a mere six years seeing him rise from a fledgling assistant professor to an endowed professorial chair. From the very first, Adolf's attitude towards me was one of great cordiality and helpfulness, and ever since I always ranked him among my very best philosophical friends. It had been largely due to his activity—both in the classroom and in the cultivation of personal relationships among his colleagues—that the Philosophy Department at Lehigh had achieved a substantial reputation among both the faculty and the students at the university. When I arrived in Bethlehem, Adolf's charming wife Thelma was pregnant with their (ultimately one and only) child—a little charmer called Barbara. We came to know the Grunbaums well and shared many Lehigh friends in common. Adolf was in those days laying the basis for work in the philosophy of space and time that was soon to earn him a world-wide reputation. Given the volatility of the academic profession in this era, I little thought when meeting Adolf in 1956 that he would still be my colleague some twenty years later. The collegial relationship between us has proved to be durable—and is invariably pleasant, owing largely to Adolf's great congeniality, kindness, and fellow-feeling. I have always admired him greatly, and am impressed by the unusual degree to which Adolf combines toughness of mind with sweetness of disposition.

The only other member of the Department of Philosophy at this stage was Thomas Haynes. He was an interesting and engaging person. Intelligent and articulate, he had a pleasant, outgoing, and thoroughly sweet-tempered personality. Then (in 1957) in his mid-30's, he combined a curious mixture of ability and ineffectuality. He was certainly an intelligent person who read and thought a great deal. But though he would talk of various creative plans, it soon became perfectly clear to anyone who got to know him even slightly that he would never discipline himself actually to bring to fruition any of the ideas and projects that enlivened his thought and conversation. His mode of outreach lay in the teaching of students: which he did most effectively, in the process evangelizing them with the 1920's era socialism he had imbibed in undergraduate days from some pupil of Elijah Jordan's, whose disciple he counted himself.

Outside the Philosphy Department, the Lehigh colleague with whom I had the closest ties was Carey B. Joynt, then (as now) chairman of the Department of International Relations. Carey was a shrewd and clear-headed Canadian Scots Presbyterian: solid and upright to the core—combining sound judgment and good sense with a twinkle of wry humor. I saw a good deal of Carey, both socially and professionally. We shared interests in the philosophy of history, and in the place of ethics in international affairs, and wrote some articles in collaboration, as well as a never published study of the place of morality in international affairs. Carey and his charming wife Anne helped to make the Lehigh period a delight.

Theodore and Marie Hailperin also stood high among the Lehigh people I came to know well. Ted was in the Mathematics Department at Lehigh and was a very able logician. Marie was a warm and charming person, and an excellent hostess. They had two attractive children, a boy and a girl, then just entering teenagehood. They lived in a functional little modernesque house off Pine Top Trail which they themselves had built. Even though Ted was somewhat hard to talk to, with the shyness and introversion not uncommon in abstract thinkers, the Hailperins were for me one of the real assets of the Lehigh academic community. (It was a loss felt keenly by everyone who knew her when Marie was struck down by cancer in the prime of life, not long after I had left Lehigh.)

The winter of 1957-8 was not a good one for me. During most of it I suffered from some sort of (undiagnosed) viral infection that left me in an enfeebled, run-down condition for several months. By the spring of 1958 this had passed off and I was as good as new. This illness had had a curious side effect. For almost a year after, I found it just about impossible to sit still in a room full of people—I was too jittery. I could not bear to attend such functions as concerts or lectures. This phenomenon mercifully faded away with the gradual restoration of physical vigor.

We soon tired of apartment living, and in the fall of 1957 purchased an antiquated but attractive Victorian frame house in an old residential area near the center of town (at 215 Wall Street). The house had definite attractions—especially its location which afforded convenient access both to the town and the university. But after a winter of struggling with the old coal-burning furnace we moved in the spring of 1958 to a convenient and modern Dutch-colonial style 3-bedroom house at 1815 Homestead Avenue. Located in one of the newer and more outlying residential areas on the northwest outskirts of town, this house was to be "home" for the rest of the time in Bethlehem.

The academic life offers an exceptional range of opportunity. One is "one's own master" and disposes of one's own time to an extent truly unusual in modern life (particularly since the summer months are altogether free). My return to the "groves of academe" thus proved to be a liberating experience. At RAND I had been caught up in the 9-to-5 regimen of a workaday routine. Now the long hours of each day spread out before me—most of them uncommitted. On even the busiest day, my university duties took up no more than six hours, and so I enjoyed the luxury of having discretionary time on my hands. Moreover, I did not feel drained at the end of the day as I had at RAND. I could work for a couple of hours in the evening, and did not feel a need for the soporific emptiness of television or light reading.

All in all, I was delighted to be back in academia. I taught a wide variety of courses during this period and was most pleased to reestablish contact with my old friends among the philosophers of bygone days. I found the contact with students most stimulating and gradually I made myself into an effective teacher.

Various writing projects now preoccupied my attention. The first took me back to an old love of undergraduate days—the Presocratic philosophers. In the early months of 1957, I wrote an essay on "Cosmic Evolution in Anaximander"[30] which combined this interest with yet another, the history of science. It gave me pleasure to be able to show just how sophisticated the ideas of this "primitive" thinker actually were. Writing this paper gave me more pleasure than any other piece of work I had done since my Princeton dissertation (which related Leibniz's philosophy to his science). My conjoint interest in the history of science and the philosophy of science was rather ahead of its time. The 1960's saw a general trend towards the co-cultivation of these fields—to the extent that HPS ("history and philosophy of science") is nowadays a well-established academic grouping. But in the 1950's this combination of interests was unusual.

I much enjoyed writing a paper entitled "Choice Without Preference." It led me down various historical byways that gave me a vista of the charms of working in the "history of ideas." I read this paper at the Fullerton Club (at Haverford College) in the fall fo 1958 and at the American Philosophical Association meetings in New York that December. Its success on these occasions helped significantly to promote the profession's growing perception of me as a capable young man.

I also branched out in other directions. After my father's death in 1952 I had inherited his correspondence with his cousin Oskar in Istanbul, where he had emigrated many years before. My father eventually became his last remaining link with the rest of his family, and when father died I took up this correspondence with "Uncle Oskar." Though I never met him, I felt a deep bond of affectionate kinship with the crotchety old gentleman. Since this contact was to have a substantial repercussion for me, it is necessary to say a few words about him.

Born in Stuttgart in 1883, Oskar Rescher pursued his university studies in Munich and Berlin, specializing in oriental languages. After taking his degree in Oriental Studies in Berlin around 1908, he habilitated as an academic at Breslau. He worked there as *Dozent* for some years, making annual forays to the manuscript collections of Istanbul, and around 1912 decided to take up residence in Istanbul more or less permanently. Remaining a German citizen, he was called up for military service in World War I, and served as censor for letters from Arabic-speaking prisoners of war. After the war he returned to Breslau as an Adjunct Professor (Ausserordentlicher Professor). Around 1925, he returned to Turkey, and became both a Muslim and a Turkish national during the 1930's. The years from 1920 to 1935 saw his happiest and certainly most productive period. His contributions to the studies of Arabic literary history gained him world-wide recognition. His scholarly influence was, however, greatly curtailed by adoption of a peculiar and idiosyncratic policy as regards publication. Around 1925 he gave up publishing in scholarly journals, and henceforth, to the dismay of his scholarly colleagues, all of his works were published privately by him in editions of from 30 to 50 copies and distributed only to favored recipients.

As World War II neared, Oskar's financial circumstances tightened: he had some money in Germany, but could not extract it under Nazi regulations. This forced him to accept positions far below the level of his capacities and attainments (e.g., after 1937 until the end of World War II he taught languages at the Military Academy of Ankara). He became an increasingly eccentric old man, given to writing German poetry with an Oriental flavor. He lived in a single room with some half-dozen cats to whose needs he catered more scrupulously than his own. He was a scholar of profound learning and vast intellectual resources, who, but for his eccentricities, would have won an outstanding place for himself in Arabic studies. He died on 26 March 1972—some 60 years after first making Turkey his home—and lies buried in one of those vast necropolises that punctuate the outskirts of Istanbul.[31]

My correspondence with "Uncle Oscar" was to have a far-reaching result for me. For I now became interested in learning what was involved in being an Arabist. So I bought A. S. Tritton's *Teach Yourself Arabic* and began to work through it. Soon I was forgetting old facts at the same rate as I was learning new ones. I then transferred to the didactically superior text of Kapliwatzky. But after a while I came to realize that what I really needed was a teacher.

And so in early 1958 I began to commute twice a week during term-time to Philadelphia on a Reading Railroad passenger service that then still linked these two cities, stopping at a half-dozen hamlets in between. My destination was the elementary class in Arabic conducted by Professor S. D. Goitein at the University of Pennsylvania. He was a scholar of the old school, trained in pre-war Germany and knowledgeable in a wide range of philological and literary matters. Long service in Palestine—first under the British as a school inspector, and then as Arabic professor at the Hebrew University—had reinforced his formidable competence as an Arabist. I enjoyed his classes, not only because they helped me with

Arabic, but also because of the quality of the man himself. My classmates were mostly Jewish youngsters who had studied Hebrew since childhood and were now pursuing Arabic—a closely cognate language—as part of Semitic Studies. This gave them a considerable start at learning vocabulary and grammatical paradigms. Here was I, a mature adult of thirty and a professor at an institution of higher learning, and yet I was by no means the best student in a class of college undergraduates. The experience was humbling but also helpful. As a teacher one deals with material that has become second nature through familiarity, and it is easy to forget the difficulties of the novice. My struggles with Arabic kept this difficulty before my mind and made me more sympathetic with the difficulties experienced by my own students.

Initially drawn to Arabic by curiosity, my interest soon took a more scholarly turn. For I came to realize that the Islamic philosophers of the middle ages had devoted much attention to my own pet interest, logic, and had done interesting work in this field, and yet their discussions were largely *terra incognita*, virtually untouched by modern scholarship.

I now began to work in odd moments at bibliographic compilations on Arabic philosophers—first on al-Farabi, and then on the Arabic logicians in general. I entered upon this bibliographic work for two reasons. Partly I thought that it would orient me in the field—to help me to gain a clear view of what had been done and what remained undone. Partly I felt that it would be a way of "paying my dues"—of making that contribution to the laborious routine of scholarship that could in due course earn a hearing from the specialist professionals for an outsider's work. While my proficiency in Arabic always remained sufficiently rudimentary to displease me, it was (in the early 1960's at any rate) adequate to enable me to do— over the next decade—a sizable amount of scholarship within various areas of Arabic logic that did not impose large philological demands.

One of the most rewarding results of my Arabic studies of this period was the restoration of a polemical tract by Alexander of Aphrodisias, an important Aristotle-commentator who flourished around 200 A.D. This text, long lost in the original Greek, could be restored in an Arabic translation. For by outrageous good luck it was possible to unite two incomplete manuscripts, one from Turkey, the other from Spain, the former containing the first half of the treatise, the latter its second half, with enough overlap to put the unity of the text beyond doubt. After considerable delays in publication, the treatise was published in Pakistan with the Arabic text edited and translated in collaboration with Michael E. Marmura of the University of Toronto, an ideally patient and cooperative co-worker. (The opus has the distinction of bearing by far the longest title of any book I am connected with—*The Refutation by Alexander of Aphrodisias of Galen's Treatise on the Theory of Motion.* [Islamabad, 1965].)

During these Lehigh years, I also wrote a steady stream of scholarly papers on a wide range of strictly philosophical topics, perhaps a dozen each year. What I now regard as my most important philosophical paper of the Lehigh period was the *Philosophical Review* essay on "Belief-Contravening Suppositions."[32] This paper proved to be a very fruitful foray. It opened up the lines of thought leading towards my subsequent work on hypothetical reasoning, and on systems-oriented epistemology.

My papers of this period manifested a diversified mixture of interest—in symbolic logic, in the history of philosophy (especially Aristotle, Leibniz, and Kant), in subjects like futurology and forecasting methodologies, and in some aspects of Arabic studies. Now around thirty years old, I was unwilling or unable to settle down to one particular speciality. (Even now, twenty years later, I keep more irons in the fire than most.) In fact, I believe this is why philosophy had such an appeal for me—it can accommodate, nay even to some extent demands a diversified spread of interests and competences. Nevertheless, I realize that many-sidedness exacts a price. For it is virtually impossible in the circumstances to polish one's skills in any one field to the fine edge of accomplished expertise. My colleagues who specialize in logic know the field better than I do, those who specialize in ancient philosophy know its texts better, and so on. It is only as a philosophical *generalist*—a combiner of many skills—that I could qualify as in any way outstanding. I am almost always satisfied with this, though there are also times when I feel pangs of discontent.[33]

As the 1950's came to a close, I undertook some writing projects of a larger scale. I turned my efforts at scholarship in Arabic philosophy towards the preparation of a general account of *The Development of Arabic Logic* (not completed until 1963 at Pittsburgh and published by the University of Pittsburgh Press in 1964). And at the invitation of St. Martin's Press I began work on an *Introduction to Logic* for beginning students (also completed in Pittsburgh and published in 1964). I also collaborated with Carey Joynt on a short monograph on ethical issues in international relations. (We submitted it unavailingly to two or three publishers—the time was not ripe for this theme, which came to flourish only in the post-Vietnam War era). These various forays provided my first experience at writing books for publication.

Throughout the Lehigh years I was professionally active not only in writing but also in other ways. I began to participate actively in the annual meetings of the Eastern Division of the American Philosophical Association. In December of 1957 I gave my first such paper at the Harvard University meetings, and in December of 1958 at the Columbia University meetings I presented the "Choice Without Preference" material, as mentioned above. In the spring of 1959 I served as external examiner for graduating philosophy students in the Honors Program at Swarthmore College. Growing recognition was attested by invitations to job interviews at various places, culminating in offers of assistant professorship at Cornell in 1958 and an associate professorship at Yale in 1959. In the meantime, I had been promoted to a tenured associate professorship at Lehigh in 1959, two years after arriving on the scene. My stature on campus—and in the philosophical profession—had grown rapidly during the first two years following my reentry into the academic world.

As I think back, I find it alarming that the move to Lehigh—so decisive for the whole course of my life—was something fortuitous. The thought of that telegram from Howard Ziegler is always a forceful reminder for me that there is no rational orchestration to the flow of things in the affairs of life—it is just a matter of "one darn thing leads to another."

Only with my appointment at Lehigh at the age of 28 did my life's course get safely placed on its proper track. This process of getting well settled into one's career is almost invariably a time of trial and tribulation. When one reads a biography, it often seems that its subject was led by a series of sure steps to that destined line of endeavor which was to prove his ultimate life's work. But a closer look generally shows that this impression is very much mistaken—a person's younger years almost invariably include a period of false starts and indecisive trials, a time of an anxious contemplation of alternatives, of zig-zag motion in ultimately aborted directions and abrupt turning-points. At such times, things could have eventuated in any one of several ways. My early life included at least three such critical junctures: when completing high school—could my family afford to have me go to college?; when completing college—should I go on to do advanced study in mathematics or in philosophy?; in the period after my military service—would I turn up a suitable post in philosophy or would I settle permanently into some RAND-like career? Each of these episodes were crucial forks in the road, and each could conceivably have led to a totally different eventuation. Not until the Lehigh appointment at the age of 28 did it become a settled matter that I would earn my livelihood as a philosophy professor—despite my having opted for this alternative when I chose graduate work in philosophy seven years previously.

Throughout the period of residence in Bethlehem we attended the local Quaker meeting (Lehigh Valley Monthly Meeting). At first it met in the assemblyroom of a private school in Allentown, but plans were just getting under way for the construction of a meeting house, and in due course a plot of farmland on the Bath Pike was purchased for this purpose. Here—some three miles north of the city-center—was erected the new meeting house, which was inaugurated in early 1961, just before I left Bethlehem. Overall, I attended this meeting for some four years, and it came to mean a great deal to me, counting many fine individuals among its members. I served as one of the overseers after 1959, and thus had the chance to see at close range the inner workings of a Quaker "parish." Perhaps this glance behind the curtain took away some of the magic. But I did continue to read widely in the literature of Quakerism and obtained a reasonable familiarity with its history and theology.

The condition of my marriage had undergone various changes in the course of these years in Bethlehem. The first months were a time of settling in—of making and remaking housing arrangements, of forging new social contacts, and of becoming active participants in the Quaker meeting. As was usual with our relationship, change and novelty in external circumstances produced an easing of inner pressures. But with the return of normalcy and stability, there came once more a heightening of those tensions between Frances and myself which made our life together difficult. Eventually there was little save the force of habit to hold our marriage together. However, a decisive change occurred in the spring of 1959 when it transpired that we would soon become parents. The situation was now transfigured, and tensions eased in the wake of yet another lapse from "normalcy."

The arrival of Elizabeth on February 20 of 1960—well after any hope of having a child of our own had been abandoned—worked a great change. A new and very precious person had entered upon the scene and a new situation had been created. In any case, our marriage, with all its various ups and downs, had endured for almost a decade. Perhaps in the now-altered circumstances it would hold together for good?

During her stay in the hospital, Frances had contracted a staph infection, and so I mainly cared for Elizabeth during the first weeks of her life. Partly, perhaps, because of this we were always very close throughout her infancy. From the very first Elizabeth and I were very close. She was a bright child who learned quickly. (Her first word, "car-car," applied to a passing automobile, was uttered when she was only ten months old.) The pleasure of parenthood was perhaps all the keener for coming well after all hopes had been abandoned. Circumstances thus intervened once again to put the strains and stresses of a difficult marriage into the background.

Throughout this Lehigh period, I still maintained the umbilical cord of a RAND consultantship. Each summer I would spend some four or five weeks in Santa Monica, working at some short-term project—sometimes in the entourage of Olaf Helmer, sometimes on my own. As best I now recall, some of my ideas on futuristics and social forecasting were a product of these efforts. Partly, I tended to view the RAND connection as "insurance" of a sort, in the event that my return to academic life were somehow to prove abortive. More importantly, I valued the opportunity to keep alive some personally rewarding and intellectually stimulating contacts (especially with Olaf Helmer, Norman Dalkey and several others).

The presidential election of 1960 was my first experience of politics as seen from a vantage point within a university faculty. True to my Republican allegiance, I backed Richard Nixon. In doing so I placed myself within a minuscule minority on our campus, which reflected the overwhelming tendency towards the Democratic party among American academics. My collegues never ceased to pontificate with facile assurance about the superiority of their choice, but this only served to confirm my doubts. The favored fallacy of intellectuals everywhere is to overestimate the external bearing of their superior talents and training within their professional specialties. All sight is lost of a point I have always taken as self-evident, that common sense and a certain "rustic faith" in the traditional values are our best guides in the affairs of life.

At some point during the Lehigh years, I discovered the novels of Anthony Trollope. I cannot recall the specific occasion, but I do remember that I began with *Barchester Towers* and *The Warden*. Thereafter I wandered more or less randomly through the enormous corpus of this charming and uncannily insightful Victorian novelist. I am deeply grateful to this tireless writer for the many pleasant hours his labors have given me.

As the terms at Lehigh succeeded one another in the annual cycle that makes the academic a kinsman to the farmer, I settled more and more deeply into the grooves of campus life. The seasonal succession of academic rituals was a notable feature of life at a small university: the regular pattern of social activities at the start and end of each academic year, the great end-of-year gathering of the whole faculty to honor the year's crop of retirees. Participation in the academic processions at the Fall and Spring commencement exercises was at that time compulsory for members of the Lehigh faculty. I must have sat through some ten commencement addresses. The medium does not lend itself to the production of significant results. Though these were usually delivered by eminent people, I do not retain the least recollection of the content of any of those addresses, and cannot recall the name of even a single individual who delivered them.

During 1959 Adolf Grunbaum had been negotiating with the University of Pittsburgh, at first with a view to his becoming Chairman of the Philosophy Department. After he declined this offer, it was succeeded in the spring of 1960 by his being offered the Andrew Mellon chair in philosophy. Adolf accepted this post, and moved to Pittsburgh during the summer of 1960. He soon impressed the Pitt administration with the desirability of securing my services. Negotiations began that fall which—after my also declining to serve as chairman—led to my acceptance in late 1960 of an appointment as Professor of Philosophy, to commence in the next academic year.

The timing of my return to academic life had been extremely propitious. With the late 1950's, a decade of rapid expansion came upon higher education in America. New institutions sprang up and old ones expanded greatly. The resulting shortage of qualified faculty created unprecedented opportunities for rapid advancement. I was a paradigm beneficiary of these circumstances: my career from fledgling assistant professor to acceptance of a full professorship was compressed into a four year timespan. By dint of luck and serious effort, the "lost time" of the years in the U.S.M.C. and at RAND had been made up. Various interruptions and detours notwithstanding, I had been able to establish my claim to a full professorship at a major university at the still relatively young age of thirty-two.

The spring term of 1961 was thus to be my last at Lehigh University. In May of that year, the house on Homestead Avenue was sold and a move across the state to Pittsburgh undertaken. I looked forward eagerly to the challenges of this transplantation to a larger and more active academic environment, which offered, in particular, the chance to participate in the training of graduate students. Yet I did not leave Lehigh without mixed feelings. Bethlehem was a pleasant, comfortable place in those days—a small but eminently liveable town. And I had been able to make many good friends in my brief time at Lehigh. All the same, there was no alternative to responding to the challenge of ampler opportunity.

Ten

Pittsburgh: The First Years, 1961-1966
(Age 32-38)

U PON ARRIVING in Pittsburgh in May of 1961, our first residence was a rented red-brick town-house on St. James' Terrace (No. 5313) in the Shadyside section, which had been found by Thelma Grunbaum. It was compact and convenient, and we were soon comfortably settled in. Although my post at the University did not formally commence until September, I began to acclimate myself there. I put in order my large, pleasant office on the 8th floor of the Cathedral of Learning, and began to organize my teaching and writing in this new setting.

After some months of readjustment, househunting began in earnest. It issued late in 1961 in the purchase of 200 Tennyson Avenue, a handsome, 1910-vintage, five-bedroomed brick house in the Schenley Farms area, no more than a three minute walk from my office.

Pittsburgh itself took some getting used to after the quiescence of Bethlehem. While it has many pleasant residential streets, it has rarely managed to separate them sufficiently from vehicular traffic, except in the suburbs. Almost nowhere in town is one secure against the sound of cars and buses. At the same time, the city has many attractive features. Its downtown area—hemmed in by rivers—is a conveniently compact area for shopping and affords some very good stores. There is ample music, the Pittsburgh Symphony in particular being a splendid resource. The museums, public libraries, and parks are very good. And above all, from my point of view, the University of Pittsburgh is a great asset of the place.

It had not always been so. At this time in the early 1960's Pitt was undergoing the revolutionary transformation inseparably associated with the name of Edward H. Litchfield. Recruited in the 1950's from the deanship of the Graduate School of Business and Public Administration at Cornell, he was commissioned by Pitt's trustees—the great men of the Pittsburgh power structure, especially Richard King Mellon and Alan Magee Scaife—to transform the University of Pittsburgh from a streetcar commuter college into a significant academic institution. A battery of Mellon Professorships and Mellon Fellowships were created, and over a period of seven years commencing in the mid 1950's some 70 millions of Mellon dollars flowed into the treasury of the University. Great things were done and even greater things were projected. It was a heady and exciting era while it lasted, but it soon came crashing down in ruins, and the reasons for this lay in the personality of the man who stood at the center of it all, Chancellor Litchfield. He was too driving and Napoleonic a personality to reach an easy accommodation with the power brokers of Pittsburgh's moneyed establishment. A classic drama ensued in the clash between a volatile object and a stable mass, a clash in which Litchfield ultimately came to grief.

The Vice-Chancellor, Charles Peake, whom Litchfield had recruited from a deanship at the University of Michigan, was an academic administrator of unusual quality because of his keen dedication to the furtherance of academic values. I knew him too late in his career to get a clear view of his merits as a professor of English, but as Vice Chancellor he devoted himself with buoyant enthusiasm to the support and advance of scholarship at the University. He was active in the recruitment of good scholars and supportive of those already there. He was always accessible and ready to help an academically concerned department or individual support this cause. He was certainly a good friend to the Philosophy Department, whose ascent into a position of national stature was only possible because of his tireless support and unstinting aid.

The (acting) chairman of the Philosophy Department at this point was Oliver Leslie Reiser. Born in 1898, Oliver was now a pleasant and easy-going, somewhat other-worldly elderly gentleman. He had entered the service of the University in 1926, before my own birth, and was drawing near to retirement. Neither Adolf Grunbaum nor I were willing to take on the chairmanship, since our own work was making demands that could not be subordinated to administrative duties, and so Oliver continued in office for a time as acting chairman. This state of affairs was not without its problems. Oliver was a person of many attractive qualities, being a widely read philosopher and able teacher. But he was totally ineffectual as an administrator. He was thus quite unfitted to the needs of the moment. In particular, he simply could not (or would not) take on the unhappy work of weeding out the lame ducks with which the department had become encumbered over the years so that the process of rebuilding could proceed. These people were his associates and colleagues—he would do nothing to displease or displace them. However understandable this sentiment, it seriously depressed Oliver's stock in the eyes of the new-model administration of Litchfield and Peake. He was never offered the chairmanship, and while he seemed to accept this without rancor, his wife resented it on his behalf, and put an end to his social relations with the rest of his colleagues as a result.

The recruitment of a new chairman was a priority task to which Adolf Grunbaum and I put our minds. Various efforts had already been made, but all had proved abortive and it was time to tackle the problem afresh. Adolf suggested an idea which I supported enthusiastically—that we should recruit Kurt Baier, who was then the philosophy chairman at the Australian National University in Canberra. Because of the distance involved, this had to be done without the usual formalities of an interview, but with Charles Peake's energetic support the effort was pushed through by correspondence to a successful conclusion. In the Fall of 1962 Kurt joined the Pitt department, a development which proved to be a stroke of good fortune for our common venture.

Kurt had been born in Vienna and had finished his legal training at the university there. In the wake of the *Anschluss* he had fled to England as a refugee, and during World War II moved on to do military service in Australia. After the war he returned to England for an Oxford D. Phil. and then took up an academic post in Australia. There his academic career had prospered, and he had acquired an attractive and gifted wife, Annette, a native New Zealander who was also a very able philosopher. A man of much charm and good humor, Kurt was an adept administrator who brought an urbane efficiency to the affairs of the department and with Annette's help did much to enliven the personal contact among its members.

It was a good time to have a capable hand at the helm. The people of limited ability—or less—who populated the department at this stage had to be encouraged to move on their way. And various opportunities were waiting to be seized. In particular, great rumblings were shaking the Yale department, and some very able people were sufficiently disgruntled to be willing to leave. Within a three year period, we recruited four Yale philosophers; first Nuel Belnap and Wilfrid Sellars (1963), then Jerome Schneewind (1964), and finally Alan Ross Anderson (1965). This rapid accession of strength went a long way towards making the department into one of real distinction.

The most formidable of our Yale acquisitions was Wilfrid Sellars. Born in 1912 and then just past fifty years of age, he was now entering upon the period of his greatest philosophical creativity. A stimulating teacher and pleasant colleague, he possessed a somewhat labyrinthine personality that made personal closeness difficult. But I have always admired Wilfrid as an immensely gifted philosopher and value him as a prime asset of our department. Periodically we lunch together to commune about departmental affairs (always at the Pittsburgh Athletic Association in Oakland, his invariable luncheon haunt). We generally see eye-to-eye on ends and usually on means as well.

The team of Anderson and Belnap afforded Pitt a potent resource in the area of logic. Alan Anderson was a logician of great creativity and insight—and a thoroughly delightful person to boot. His student, Nuel Belnap, was more involuted and complex, but could also manifest great personal charm. He too was a logician of formidable capabilities. Alan and Nuel worked well together, making a smooth transition from the master-student relationship to collaborative colleagueship. Despite their enthusiastic commitment to somewhat idiosyncratic logical doctrines, they have maintained an open-minded accessibility to their colleagues of different persuasions.

The mid-1960's also saw the arrival of Richard Gale on an NSF postgraduate fellowship, together with his charming Japanese wife, Maya. A fellow of infinite jest, Richard soon found many friends in the department (as well as one or two no less enthusiastic detractors). We persuaded him to stay on—at first temporarily and then as part of the permanent establishment. Concealing a deep and vulnerable personality behind a veneer of surface conviviality, Richard has, over the years, been one of my good friends in the department. I regard him as a philosopher of deep dedication and very substantial ability.

I soon came to realize that I had been fortunate in entering into academic work at a good time. The administrators of the old school—men whose view of the world had been formed during the hardships of academic management in the 1930's—were moving towards retirement by the late 1950's and the cheese-paring attitudes of that difficult era were giving way to a new era of expansiveness. While Lehigh was still to some extent caught up in the trammels of this old ethos, Pittsburgh under Litchfield had moved well beyond it. It had become an institution willing to back academic values in a forward-looking spirit, expending administrative time, effort, and resources on strengthening even so abstruse a subject as philosophy.

As to my own work, the first order of business after settling at Pitt was to clear the decks of unfinished projects left over from Lehigh days. And so I now completed *The Development of Arabic*

Logic (a "Cook's tour" of medieval Arabic work in this field), and finished the *Introduction to Logic* which was begun at Lehigh. I wrote a small book on *Hypothetical Reasoning* to develop and extend the lines of thought begun with the "Belief-Contravening Suppositions" paper of 1959. Moreover, I now reached back to Princeton days and carried out my long-standing plan of writing a book on Leibniz, drawing on some of the materials developed in my doctoral dissertation. Almost overnight I changed from a writer of papers into an author of books.

During this period I came to occupy myself more extensively with symbolic logic and a steady stream of work in this field now began to flow from my pen. My attitude towards this subject was of a somewhat unorthodox slant. For I never looked on logic as an accomplished fact—a field fully formed and merely in need of systematization and exposition, but saw it as an unfinished and malleable discipline to be reworked and restructured for the sake of its applications. I always gravitated towards those logical issues and areas that were of potential utility for the elucidation and treatment of philosophical issues, and viewed logic not just as a self-contained discipline, but as a tool for the accomplishment of extralogical tasks.

In the spring of 1963 the philosophy department was ejected from the Cathedral of Learning. We had been sharing the eighth floor with the Computing Center, but now they were entering a phase of growth in personnel and equipment. It came to a choice between moving this center at a cost of thousands or of moving the philosophers and their handful of books. Needless to say, the finger was pointed at us. We were offered the seventh floor of the old Schenley Hotel across from the Cathedral, which had been used as a dormitory, but now, with the completion of the new tower residence halls, was being refurbished as the Student Union. And here I acquired as my office the very pleasant panelled Southeast corner room which I occupy to this day, and which has been an element of stability amidst many changes in the circumstances of my life.

Our main common effort during my first years at Pitt was devoted to building up a good graduate program in philosophy. And in this respect the move to Pittsburgh more than lived up to expectations, for the chance to teach graduate students was a highly profitable and enjoyable experience for me. Beginning in 1961 with a virtual *tabula rasa*, with little on hand by way of students, traditions, or instructional curriculum, we now forged a strong program. But we were enthusiastic and determined—and lucky in that some of the very best students we ever graduated came during those early years—Brian Skyrms, Ernest Sosa, and Bas van Fraassen to name only a few. The chance to associate with really able young workers in one's academic field is a uniquely rewarding and stimulating experience. (To speak of "teaching" them would be misleading, for the process of instruction is in such cases reciprocal.)

By the middle of the 1960's, as the department expanded, it developed a program of philosophical training that was as good as any in the country. Various studies of academic quality—in particular those of the American Council on Education—now began to indicate Pitt's philosophy department to be one of the top three or four in the U.S. Not only did we have an outstandingly able faculty, but we worked well together in an effective collaboration for the benefit of the program as a whole. As an enthusiastic member of the team, I myself strove to make an effective contribution to this effort—in instruction, in program design, in recruitment efforts, in setting and maintaining a high professional standard, and in promoting the visibility of the department not only through my own work, but also in founding the *American Philosophical Quarterly*.

Late in 1962 word was circulated at Pitt that the Chancellor was eager for the Universtiy Press to expand its list of scholarly journals, confined in those days to two or three somewhat frail entries. I had long realized that the number of philosophy journals was not keeping pace with the rapid expansion of personnel and activities. After some exploration, I thus proposed to the University the founding of a new scholarly journal in philosophy, and the result was the organization in 1963 of the *American Philosophical Quarterly* to be published by the University of Pittsburgh Press in a large double-column format (borrowed from the *Journal of the American Oriental Society*). This plan prospered, and publication commenced in 1964. The reception of the enterprise was favorable from the very outset, and everything went along swimmingly until the journal was suddenly plunged into a struggle for its very existence in early 1965. For the University now sank into the abyss of a financial crisis whose steady unfolding led to the departure of Chancellor Litchfield. Drastic economies were introduced into the operations of the University Press, and in consequence, Frederick Hetzel, then—as now—its Director, decided (sensibly in the circumstances) to withdraw the Press from journal publication and to concentrate its reduced resources wholly on books. Suddenly and unexpectedly the APQ was left high and dry without any publisher. The University turned its back on the journal, and I found myself saddled with the task of providing for its continued existence.

Rapid measures were called for, and after various consultations the problem was resolved in a most happy way when the Oxford publishing firm of Basil Blackwell—which already issued such reputable philosophy journals as *Mind* and *Analysis*—agreed to take the journal on. The negotiations with their managing director, Henry Schollick, evolved smoothly, and the journal went ahead most satisfactorily under these new auspices. By the time of its 10th anniversary in 1974, its subscribership had climbed above the 1,600 mark. All the indications are that in the initial decade of its existence the APQ (as it is generally known) has managed to establish itself as one of the very best philosophy journals in the English-speaking world.

For me personally, the editorship of this journal has been a mixed blessing. On the one hand, success of my literary brainchild has been a source of satisfation. On the other hand, I have also had to pay a price. The fact that I annually manage to displease some 300 colleagues with rejection slips has meant inevitable failure whenever my name has been put forward for candidacy for any genuinely elective office in professional associations. Colleagues to whom one has said "No" apparently welcome the chance to reciprocate. Over the years I have occupied positions of considerable responsibility and trust in such organizations, but always by way of essentially appointive offices.

During this period I did a modest amount of miscellaneous reading wholly outside the domain of professional duty, averaging perhaps one book a month. To some extent this was sheer entertainment or escapism—a matter of relaxation and "breaking the circuits" of my official lines of thought. But half of it—the reading of autobiographies, biographies, and biographical novels (in particular Anthony Trollope)—had a utilitarian aspect in providing grist for the philosophical contemplation of the structure of human life and the condition of man—an interest not unconnected with my eventual decision to write these pages.

The presidential election of 1964 was the first occasion on which I broke my usual allegiance to the Republican party—to vote *against* Barry Goldwater (rather than *for* Lyndon Johnson). I quite mistakenly gave credence to the propaganda—blared with mindless unanimity throughout the media—that pictured Lyndon Johnson as the personification of sweet reasonableness and peacemaking in contrast to Barry Goldwater's warmongering. As it was, the nation got Goldwater's policies behind the screen of Johnson's machiavellianism.

My position in national politics has always been straightforward. In my teens, I felt that FDR could do no wrong. He was the leader in power in a country that had opened its doors to my family at the time of our emigration from Germany, and stood in the role of our host-in-chief as it were. Thereafter, I came, during my twenties, to favor the Republicans, thanks to the counterproductive intervention of Capt. Stevenson of the U.S.M.C. in the 1952 presidential campaign. While my commitment to this party was by no means total, I judged that the Republican party leaders, on balance, possess a greater acumen in military and international affairs, and I have always felt that this was the area that really counted. A misstep in domestic policy or economic affairs might cause discomfort, but one in international affairs might get us all killed in this nuclear age.

A highlight of this period was the opportunity to pay a week's visit to Istanbul in September of 1964. This visit had a very special purpose: to examine at first hand a particular Arabic manuscript on which I had been writing in connection with my study of the 4th figure of the syllogism.[34] I stayed at the Hilton Hotel and had a relatively pleasant time of it, apart from a stomach upset induced by one foray outside the orbit of European restaurants and sleep-deprivation due to a Turkish-style rock-concert extending far into the night at some nearby soccer stadium. Working in the Aya Sofya Library was a fascinating experience—and also a culturally broadening one, seeing that my omission to pay *baksheesh* to the library attendant led to my manuscripts becoming "lost" on the second day of my labors. (A kindly scholar in the library soon put me straight.) My great uncle Oskar's honorary niece, Dr. Ayla König, gave me guided tours of Istanbul and its environs (including the principal Bazaar, the offshore islands, the Sultan's palace, etc.). Oskar himself was away in Ankara—I suspect out of a purposeful reluctance to meet his remote relation and old correspondent face to face.

Around this time, I entered into a collaboration with the economist Herbert Simon of the neighboring Carnegie Mellon University. I had known Herb since RAND Corporation days, and should perhaps have described him as a polymath rather than an economist because of the impressive manysidedness of his talents and abilities. Together we wrote a paper on "Cause and Counterfactual," ultimately published in *Philosophy of Science* in 1966. The paper combined in fruitful symbiosis longstanding ideas of Herb's about causality with my own work on the epistemology of counterfactual hypotheses. I regard it as something of a model instance of interdisciplinary collaboration.

During this period my marriage went through a pattern of deterioration along by now familiar lines. At first, the business of resettling in a new environment, making new friends—and above all raising an infant daughter—had, as was usual with us, improved matters by providing external outlets for internal tensions and frictions. But gradually, as normalization proceeded and our lives settled into a stable pattern, all the old difficulties surfaced once again, and the 1963-65 period saw a continuing intensification of these pressures. As a new academic setting released new energies and activities in me, Frances wrapped herself up ever more tightly in a cocoon of disapproval and resentment towards my work. By mid-1965 the situation had deteriorated to a point where I felt that even the hackneyed though telling argument that a married couple must remain together "for the sake of the child" no longer mattered. I have long puzzled over what impelled Frances into the ever-recurrent paroxysms of bitter discontent and recrimination. In retrospect, I can only conjecture that she was psychologically unable to share a husband with requirements of a professionally demanding career.

This created an impasse. For twenty years, life's course had been shaping me step by step into a productive professor of philosophy. Even if I had wanted to reorient myself—which I did not—there is little I could have done about it. It became increasingly clear that no tolerable *modus vivendi* could be reached. By the summer of 1965 I had come to a settled resolve that there was no alternative to separation.

Shakespeare's *Hamlet* drives home the lesson that it is one thing to recognize a step as necessary, but something else to carry it out. Repeated trials showed the futility of trying through discussion to work out an agreed plan for "a parting of the ways." There was nothing for it but to take matters into my own hands by a unilateral step. One day in September of 1965 (virtually fourteen years to the day after our marriage in 1951) I simply did not return home after work, but moved into a room in the Webster Hall Hotel, having left behind a note to explain what was happening. This set up a flurry of activity—interviews with a teary Frances, the well-meant intervention of friends, and so on. But the situation was suddenly transfigured by Elizabeth's breaking her arm in a bicycle accident. We were reunited in the hospital, and I then returned to the Tennyson Avenue house, determined to pave the way for a more orderly break. The next few months were difficult—the less said of them the better. But in March of 1966 I finally and decisively betook myself to a one-bedroom, furnished apartment in the Ruskin Apartments near the Cathedral of Learning in Oakland.

I had not anticipated the extent to which the depression and discouragement that goes with an upheaval of this sort create a destructive cycle. A man accustomed to life in domestic circumstances—a wife (however problematic), child, and dog, a house with garden and neighbors—cannot but feel painfully lonely in a small empty apartment. Above all, I missed Elizabeth intensely. Then just six years old and starting her school career in the first grade at Winchester Thurston School in Shadyside, she was a charming little girl at a really delightful stage of development. Though I never really doubted the rightness and necessity of my move, there is no doubt that the spring of 1966 was for me a time of distress and anguish of spirit. I simply lived on from day to day, clutching tight to my work as a sheet-anchor that provided a much-needed element of stability and balance in my life. Had there not been the absorption of my work to sustain me, I might well have broken down. During these difficult days, my old friend Adolf Grunbaum gave me moral support in a way that meant much to me and for which I shall always be grateful.

I lived in the Ruskin Apartments that summer, but in August 1966 moved to a pleasant two-bedroom apartment in a large stone house at 920 College Ave. in the Shadyside section of town. I furnished the place with things bought very inexpensively in second-hand stores and "antique" shops. The process of homemaking helped to lift the fog of depression.

It is pointless to give more than a bare outline of the melancholy process of the ultimate dissolution of the marriage. In the fall of 1966 a separation agreement was arrived at with difficulty, and in the spring 1967 a property settlement was worked out, which was followed by the formal divorce in July of that year. The settlement was financially ruinous for me: the Tennyson Avenue house and all its contents and accoutrements save for a few scraps of furniture became the property of my former wife, together with the whole of our savings, making a literal (if belated) truth of the marital promise "with all my wordly goods I thee endow." Also, a sum which at that stage exceeded half of my after-tax income from the University was to be paid for alimony and child-support for the next fourteen years. On top of that, I had to pay a total of $4,000 to square the lawyers on both sides, a colossal sum, as it then seemed to me, which I had to borrow since all existing assets had gone into the property settlement. Considering my resources at the time the burden was crushing. But I assumed it without hesitation and without dismay, seeing it as the only feasible way of putting an intolerable situation behind me.

A common quip has it that the only divorce worth having is an acrimonious one. (If there's any good feeling between the parties, what's the point of divorce?) But the lever of acrimony must find some *point d'appui*. Tragically, it was Elizabeth in the present case. I made no difficulties whatever about property or finances. Frances got whatever she and her lawyer saw fit to ask for. But the human element was more problematic. Frances was adamant on one point—there was to be no sharing of Elizabeth, no visitation rights, no access to her at all. I could not bring myself to accept this, and sought remedy in the courts. The wheels of justice ground slowly, and Frances fought every inch of the way. The hiring of lawyers and psychologists was the least of it. What I felt most keenly was the extent to which the child herself was pressed into service in this battle. For years I labored as best I could under the straightjacket of the occasional weekend visits I was able to extract through the legal process. I struggled to create some spark of intimacy and good feeling, but gradually I could sense the ebbing away of any shred of affection on my daughter's part. This erosion of my once-happy relationship with Elizabeth has been a source of much distress to me over the years.

This period of the ending of my marriage was certainly a time of pain, trial, and tribulation. Fortunately, the inexorable passage of time slowly led me back to a more cheerful outlook and restored normalcy to my attitudes and my social relationships.

One useful distraction during this difficult time was a collaborative research project on "Technology and Values"—a philosophical inquiry into the impact of technological change on human values sponsored by the Carnegie Corporation of New York and International Business Machines Corporation who, in the ethos of the time, wanted to do something humanistic. (A decade later they would have sponsored a television program!) After trying in vain to interest philosophers at other institutions in so "applied" a venture, they came to Pittsburgh late in 1964, and persuaded the Department to take this on under the joint direction of Kurt Baier and myself. We organized the effort during the 1965-6 academic year, and eventually carried it through to a reasonable conclusion. The results of the inquiry were put into print in the book *Values and the Future* issued by the Free Press (in 1969—after much delay). An unqualifiedly positive assessment of the project is doubtless unwarranted, but it was at any rate, a beginning—a pioneering foray into little-charted territory.

As Kurt Baier and I devoted part of our efforts to this project, we used the opportunity to bring some interesting visitors into the department as teaching replacements. On this basis we profited from the presence of some of the more venturesome spirits of European philosophy. I myself particularly enjoyed the visits that I. M. Bochenski of Freiburg and G. H. von Wright of Helsinki made in Pittsburgh in this connection.

For myself, the principal product of the "Values Project" (as we called it) was the writing of a little book on *Distributive Justice*—my first substantial venture into social philosophy—which tried to unravel a knotty tangle of economic issues often obscured by political passion. Its clear and dispassionate attention to matters of practical policy stood (so it seemed to me) in favorable contrast to the abstract generalities of most moral and social philosophy during the 1960's.

Apart from work on the values project, the bulk of my professional attention during this 1961-1966 period focused on two not wholly unrelated, but still very disparate fields: the work of the Arabian logicians of the middle ages, and certain topics in symbolic logic. The half-dozen books I produced during these years are (if I myself may say so) not without merit, but nevertheless strike me in retrospect as afflicted with a certain shortcoming implicit in the very subject-matter to which they devote themselves. As late as the mid-1960's, something held me back from working creatively at the center of philosophy itself rather than merely nibbling around its edges. Only the calming atmosphere of a more settled existence ultimately encouraged me to sustained work on centrally philosophical issues.

The first phase of my life in Pittsburgh thus ended in dissonance. On the professional side I had managed to accomplish work that now secured me a place in the top stratum of academic philosophy. On the personal side, however, there was a state of unsettlement that could—conceivably—have blunted my potential as a creative scholar. Begun in hopefulness, this period closed in a condition of despondency and darkness of spirit, a condition that only passing time and changed circumstances could erase.

Eleven

Pittsburgh: The Years of Change, 1966-1971

(Age 38-42)

THE 1966-67 academic year saw the beginning of a new phase in the unfolding of my professional career. For now, as I was approaching my fortieth year, a decade after resuming academic pursuits at Lehigh in 1957, my stature in the profession had prospered to a point where the University of Pittsburgh saw fit to accord me the distinction of designation as "Research Professor." But the horizons were not unclouded. The affairs of Pitt's Philosophy Department were reaching a crossroads.

After five years of service as departmental chairman, Kurt Baier was eager to resume writing and teaching. Since the most senior professors, who held "special title" appointments—Adolf Grunbaum, Wilfrid Sellars, and now myself—were deemed exempt from this service, the Executive Committee of the department, after due deliberation, recommended to the dean that our colleague Alan Ross Anderson be invited to serve as chairman. This invitation—made with my own enthusiastic support—was in due course extended, and so it came to pass that Alan served as chairman from 1967 to 1970. But his tenure of this office was not without problems.

Able logician and fine person though he was, Alan was not cut out for administrative work. Early harbingers of the medical problems that brought him to a premature grave at the age of 48 in 1973 were already causing him difficulties. This left him with little patience for the minutiae of academic management. He tended to leave to others (often secretaries) the myriad small details whose proper handling makes for a well-run operation—without adequate supervision and with sometimes unfortunate results. Departmental affairs suffered visibly from the lack of a clear administrative focus. On the other hand, Alan was a fine scholar, a delightful colleague, and a man of truly superior quality—as was shown by his fortitude in the face of the cancer that ultimately laid him low. I had great liking and respect for him—and indeed had been a prime instrument in his recruitment to Pittsburgh.

The absence of a firm hand at the helm unfortunately brought many centrifugal forces into play. And this occurred at just the wrong time. For this was a period of stress and challenge—the era of Vietnam-connected student unrest across America's campuses.

The war in Indo-China had been on my mind ever since the days of my Marine Corps service. Towards its end, in 1953, an old-line sergeant harangued us as follows. We draftees who were about to be released ought not to think that we were saying good-bye to the Corps for good. The efforts of the French in Indo-China were failing, and the U.S.A. would have to go bail them out. We would soon be back in the Marines to assist in this enterprise. So prophesied the old sergeant, and I suppose one must give him credit for long-range vision. But, fortunately for me and my contemporaries, Ike did not see the matter in the same light, and entry of American soldiers into this conflict had to await the administrations of his Democratic successors. But then as our involvement grew, something occurred for which my own generation, reared in the attitudes of the Second World War, was quite unprepared—the tide of political disaffection compounded with self-serving distaste of personal inconvenience that swept over America's youth in the late 1960's. The graduate schools were filled in those days with people who entered the academic arena to escape the draft and avoid "the real world" rather than because they felt any calling to the professional work in teaching and research. But in taking refuge in academia, they did not leave behind their disenchantment with the existing order of things and their desire to "reform" it to their liking. Fortunately, we at Pitt experienced only relatively mild manifestations of these phenomena, but even what little there was quite sufficed to be both dismaying and eye-opening. The malign developments of this period, and the fervor of its ongoing assault on academic standards and values in the name of the politics of liberation, cannot be explained short of invoking the mechanisms of mob psychology. No observer of the academic scene in those days could ever again feel unmixed confidence that the era of "revolutionary excesses" was safely confined to the historic past.

In 1970, however the Philosophy Department's affairs began to look up. In the fall of that year Gerald J. Massey succeeded to the chairmanship. Jerry was a highly conscientious and efficient administrator, and it was reassuring to sense a firm hand on the wheel once again. It took about two years to erase fully the disorientation and loss of morale that had come to infect the operation. But in time the sense of common purpose and collaborative effort that had characterized the department in the years of Kurt Baier's chairmanship was again restored—now in the more difficult circumstances of a much-enlarged department, one now of twenty-four faculty members as compared with the dozen of the mid-1960's. We were most fortunate to find a person of Jerry Massey's superb administrative talents at exactly the moment when we needed this.

Among the offerings I taught during this period, the most regular repeaters were courses on Leibniz, on Kant, on the theory of knowledge, and on the theory of induction and confirmation. All told, my teaching at Pitt has been pretty evenly divided between undergraduate courses and graduate courses, and I think they have been pretty evenly successful as well. During the hey-day of the era of the "student unrest" of the 1968-69 period, I acquired the repute of being a hard-liner, because I strongly supported the maintenance of examination requirements and was in general opposed to the then-rampant assault on all established academic standards in the name of *liberté, egalité, fraternité,* or whatever. For a time (roughly 1968-1971) this impeded my rapport with some of the graduate students, but, happily, the wind changed with the gradual restoration of an ethos more oriented towards learning than societal transformation.

The cloud of the academic turmoil of the late 60's had its silver lining when Wesley Wentz Posvar came to Pitt from the Air Force Academy to be our new chancellor. Less driven and less flamboyant than Edward Litchfield had been, he was also far more approachable and had his feet more firmly planted on the ground. Buoyant and positive in outlook, he had a real dedication to the academic venture, and was able to exercise a cheerful and calming influence upon the turbulent waters into which he had sailed. Coming at the end of a period of over-rapid growth, his administration has seen ongoing efforts to maximize opportunities in times difficult both economically and politically—particularly since a university must nowadays come to terms with pressures emanating from the wider community of which it is a part. An academic administrator has many constituencies, and is a servant to many masters. It is no small compliment to say that Wes Posvar has managed to walk this difficult and wobbly tightrope for years on end without ever falling off.

The 1967-68 academic year also proved to be a turning-point in my personal life. I had known Dorothy Henle since 1961, when Oliver Reiser and I interviewed and hired her as Administrative Secretary for the Philosophy Department, a year or so after she had initially come to the University of Pittsburgh to work in the Fund-Raising Office. With the establishment of the *American Philosphical Quarterly* in 1963, she had become my Editorial Assistant for the journal. For years she had been part of the familiar, virtually unnoticed stage-setting of my workaday world. But now, in the altered condition on my life that ensued upon the breakdown of my marriage, I gradually began to take notice. We sometimes played tennis at the Chatham College courts and attended an occasional symphony or movie together. As 1967 moved on, we saw more and more of one another. Dorothy was a charming, vivacious, and delightful young lady—endowed with an impressive degree of personal warmth and outgoing sociability. I was soon head over heels in love with her. In July of 1967 my divorce was finalized, and by the end of the year Dorothy and I were engaged. A new and much happier era of my personal life was inaugurated.

At around this time I began to attend Sunday services in St. Paul's Cathedral in Oakland. Dorothy was a committed Catholic and it seemed sensible that we should join in worship. I cannot honestly say that I was drawn to Roman Catholicism on strictly theological or doctrinal grounds, although the theatrical dimension of the mass did evoke some response in my traditionalist nature. With each passing year since the iconoclastic time of adolescence, I have come to feel more strongly about the positive role of the traditional forms—that of worship included—in the shaping of a well-ordered and civilized life. To be sure, matters of doctrine or dogma never stirred me deeply. There are many ways to God, and I cannot believe that He is greatly concerned about the particular route one chooses. The Quaker deemphasis of matters of ritual (which I have always found congenial) itself seemed to prepare me to regard such matters of form as relatively unimportant, and so paved the way to acceptance of a highly ritualized religion.

On February 10, 1968 Dorothy and I were married in a small, private ceremony at her brother's Penn Hills home. At first we continued to reside in the small but comfortable apartment at 920 College Avenue where I had been living since the summer of 1966. It was the middle of term-time at Pitt and we did not have a real "honeymoon." But late that April we set out to spend the summer in Europe. After a brief visit in Helsinki, we proceeded to Oxford for the Trinity Term (late April through late June), where I conducted a seminar on imperatives jointly with R.M. Hare. We lived in Iffley at the just-completed Beechwood Flats apartments belonging to All-Souls College. In the course of our stay we came to like Oxford very much indeed. So much so, that we made the resolution—soon to be put into effect—of returning regularly to Oxford in the summers.

After the end of term we took a week's holiday at Hastings—some of it at the television set watching the Wimbledon tennis-matches, but also making touristic excursions to Rye, Salisbury, Bath, and other spots of interest. In July we set out for the Continent in our ancient green Hillman car, crossing the channel on the Air Ferry. First we visited my German relations in Hagen, and then set out on a circuit of lectures at various German universities, which enabled me to keep in touch with various German academic friends, including Albert Menne in Hamburg, Günther Patzig in Göttingen, Lothar Schäffer in Tübingen, and Wilhelm Totok in Hannover. Finally we spent a restful and very happy few days at Hinterzarten in the Black Forest. This was my first really extensive visit in Germany since leaving in 1938, and it took place under ideally pleasant circumstances.

Upon returning to England we stayed in London from late July to early August, combining tourism with my work at the British Museum on the Arabic manuscript by al-Shirwani that was eventually to be the core of my 1975 essay on temporal modalities in Arabic Logic.[35] In early August we returned to the Continent, making a trip up the Rhine by steamer from Mainz to Switzerland. There we stayed for a few days at Basle and then proceeded to the 13th World Congress of Philosophy in Vienna.

In early September we returned to the apartment on College Avenue in Pittsburgh. We now began househunting in earnest, for as the summer drew to a close Dorothy was just giving the early indications of pregnancy. We looked at almost a hundred houses all over the eastern section of Pittsburgh, but at last found an attractive, 1920's colonial-style brick house at 1200 Sheridan Avenue in the Highland Park section of Pittsburgh, which we bought in December of 1969. The house is compact yet roomy (with five bedrooms). Its three-storied layout is very conveniently arranged, and even before there were children we never felt that we rattled about the place. The location is in some ways less than perfect—Highland Park is rather far out from town, the University, etc.—but the house itself and its neighborhood have been thoroughly satisfactory. At any rate, it is here that we reside, live, and raise our family down to the present writing in 1974.

The neighborhood—as it eventuated—was one of the real assets of the place. There were the Dickson Shaws across the way, who are the most pleasant and helpful neighbors imaginable; the Charles McGuires, whose daughter Vickie was for several years our babysitter and twice accompanied us on summer visits to England; the Samuel Passafiumes, whose mother Mimi lives a couple of blocks away and has for many years been a much-appreciated babysitter; and others as well. The human element is critical to the pleasantness of a residential area, and these neighbors have unquestionably made Sheridan Avenue a good place to be.

Having known very straightened circumstances in the impressionable first years after my family's emigration to the U.S.A., I have generally been prudent with money, doing without whatever I could not afford to buy outright, so as to avoid burdening the future with the debts of the present. But the years after the financially crushing divorce settlement of 1967 saw me become increasingly careful in money matters. I came to realize that drastic measures would be needed if I were ever again to stand on firm financial ground. A rigid frugality gradually remedied the situation and rebuilt my shattered finances. Much credit also belongs to Dorothy, who is a good manager and, while not a penny pincher, avoids anything approaching extravagance. I hope against hope that my children can learn to be sensible about money without acquiring this quality—as I myself did—in the hard school of real impoverishment.

A succession of part-time visiting professorships—at Temple University during 1968-9, and the University of Western Ontario after 1970—were helpful in rebuilding the family exchequer. (Our regular subsequent excursions to Oxford would almost certainly have been impossible without them.) Moreover, these academic visits were very useful to me in other ways. They enabled me to try out some lecture materials of a more experimental sort than might have been convenient on home ground, and various books of mine went through their trial-runs on such occasions.

With the passage of the years I learned one valuable lesson: one must not sit back in life and await the development of favorable openings and opportunities—one must strive to *make* them happen, working to cultivate and develop them. (For example, I could well have waited until doomsday for the editorship of a major journal to come my way had I not simply set to and organized the *American Philosophical Quarterly* in the early 1960's.) To be sure, there must be opportunities, but these are usually so seminal as to be unrecognizable unless one is on the look-out. Good things are less likely to come to those who only sit and wait than to those who bestir themselves towards their realization. The wise man, said Plautus, shapes his own fortune (*Sapiens ipse fingit fortunam sibi*), which may be a bit optimistic, but undoubtedly indicates what he should at any rate *try* to do.

Dorothy and I moved into the Sheridan Avenue house in January of 1969 just in time to prepare the nursery for occupancy. With the birth of Mark in April of that year and of Owen in November of the following year we were no longer a "couple" but a *family*, with two active and lively little boys. Aging is a centrifugal process. Youth is self-centered, but with the passage of years and the accumulation of experience there comes a gradual externalization of concern to embrace one's children and family connections. The arrival of Mark and Owen reoriented the pattern of our existence. There is no denying that the boys are sometimes a source of vexation and often a source of anxiety, but they are priceless enrichments of our lives.

I always sought a close interaction with my children, even when they were very little. I did my share—perhaps by the prevailing standards of the day more than my share—of feeding, diapering, and baby-minding. And of course as the boys grew up and could be played with and read to, we became very close indeed. A close relationship with one's children is surely among the most satisfying experiences of life.

Mark and Owen are active, bright and engaging little boys and a continuing source of pleasure and satisfaction to their parents. Few things in life give me greater joy than when one of the boys does something that makes me proud of him. I offer up a daily silent prayer for the success and for the happiness of my children, and to thank a kindly fate that has endowed them with the health, vitality, and charm they possess so abundantly. Their bodies require constant care and nurture and their minds amusement, stimulus, and information. It is difficult to know what to set down on paper about this sort of parental involvement—the reader will either have a good idea through his own experiences or will think the whole business rather bizarre.[36]

In the fall of 1967, around the time when Dorothy and I became engaged, her sister Jacqueline married Peter F. Brown. The holder of a physics Ph.D. from Pitt, Peter is bluff, sociable, easygoing, and thoroughly good-humored. At that time he was employed at Bettis Laboratories, the nuclear research division of Westinghouse Electric Corporation. But he was not happy there, and in 1969 he took on a post as Assistant Professor in the Physics Department at Duquesne University. Dorothy was always close to her sister, who is in every way a delightful person. And so, as was only natural, the Peter Browns became a fixture in our lives, and our boys have made good friends of their daughter Alicia (b. 1970).

In August of 1969 the Browns accompanied us to Los Angeles for what was to be my final visit to RAND—now accompanied by baby Mark, born in April of that year. We spent some three very pleasant weeks, living in Brentwood amidst the old-time splendor of the "Villa Katzenstein"—a pre-war California-Spanish mansion, once the habitation of some movie mogul, but now belonging to a family of this name. We did a good bit of tourism in Southern California (Disneyland, Marineland, Santa Barbara, etc.) At RAND, interest had by this time shifted increasingly towards domestic affairs, and some of the themes I thought about on this occasion ultimately found their way into my book on *Welfare*.

In this connection, one public event of the late 1960's came home to me personally in an unlooked-for way. Ever since leaving RAND's employ in early 1957, I had been carried on their roster of consultants and had made occasional short visits to "keep in touch." Now, however came the time of the Pentagon Papers scandal, when Daniel Ellsberg leaked to the *New York Times* a top secret Defense Department study of America's Vietnam War policies which he had illicitly copied while on a consulting visit at RAND. This shook the RAND Corporation to its foundations. Harry Rowan, its new President, who in my day at RAND had been a minor planet to Albert Wohlstetter's sun, was now sacked, and everything was revamped—especially in the sphere of security. In rapid sequence the security clearances that gave consultants access to classified materials were first downgraded from *Top Secret* and then suspended altogether. It became clear that the relationship would be completely nominal, and I decided to terminate it. The RAND connection had, in any case, become of lessened interest to me since the departure of Olaf Helmer in the mid-1960's.

Colonial Williamsburg began to be a regular feature of our life at this stage. We first visited there in late 1969—again with baby Mark in tow. Almost every winter since we set off on the eight hour drive to Colonial Williamsburg for a sort of mid-winter break in routine. We stay in the old-world comfort of the Williamsburg Inn, eat at the various colonial taverns, relax, rest, sightsee, and enjoy the off-season quiescence and old-world charm of this historical treasure-spot. The very uniformity of this experience: the helpful personnel of the Inn, the table-service of the "young gentlemen from the college of William and Mary" in the various public houses, the historic buildings, the Governor's Palace and its gardens, are all woven as ongoing threads into the fabric of our lives. (I pen these very words at one of the card tables of the Inn where I have often worked at my philosophical writings as well.) More than any other factor these visits awakened an interest in antiques, an interest that was to be pursued actively during our visits in England.

In 1968 I had the pleasure of editing a *Festschift* for my old teacher and friend Carl G. Hempel. It gave me much satisfaction to be able to acknowledge in this way my debt to someone I greatly admired and who had on various occasions been so helpful to me—who, indeed, from my earliest days as a philosopher had provided the role-model for a professor in the field.

In the early 1970's, work on issues of moral and social philosophy in the U.S.A. turned away from the abstract formalistic and linguistic concerns of the two prior decades, and addressed itself increasingly to the more substantive issues. Philosophy once more descended from its ivory tower to deal with those sorts of public policy concerns that preoccupy people in "the real world." The field of "applied ethics" sprung up and became fashionable. But while American academic philosophy arrived here in the early 70's, I myself was already on the scene in the mid-1960's, the book on *Distributive Justice* (1966) being a case in point here. The fate of my 1969 paper on "The Allocation of Exotic Medical Lifesaving Therapy" also exemplifies this early arrival. When medical ethics became popular among philosophers in the 1970's, it was one of the few things in print on the subject and thus, intrinsic merit aside, was reprinted and anthologized more often than anything else I ever wrote—I am aware of ten reprintings within some six years. (The enthusiastic reception of this paper rather discouraged than pleased me, because it drove home the not wholly welcome lesson that a philosopher gains easy access to people's attention only when he tells them what they are predisposed to listen to.) The book on *Welfare* which I wrote in 1970-71 was a later instance of this same tendency to philosophizing about issues of social concern. Its insistence that the best welfare program is a healthy economy is a lesson of the depression years that was seemingly forgotten in the America of the euphoric postwar years.

As the decade of the 60's drew to its close, I had attained a firm psychological base of operations. I had climbed the greasy pole of academic advancement to the pinnacle of a special professorship. My family life was securely established through my marriage with Dorothy, the arrival of our first child, and our getting settled in our own home. These developments released new wellsprings of creative energy. Now forty years old, I had become a person of matured judgment and matured professional abilities as well. Sensing all this, I felt (no doubt subconsciously) that the time had come for me to undertake a work of larger scale than heretofore.

The timing for such a venturing forth was propitious. The period after the First World War had seen the diffusion of a more and more narrowly constricted view of the task of philosophy. The methodologically "hard" areas of philosophy, logic, the philosophy of mathematics, and the philosophy of science, were in; the methodologically "soft" and more speculative areas, metaphysics, substantive ethics, and social philosophy, were out. The spread of the logical positivist ideology so trenchantly articulated in A. J. Ayer's *Language, Truth, and Logic* typifies the culmination of this narrowing of views. Though I was myself largely reared in the ethos of this perspective, it gradually dawned on me that the mission of those of us who began to be active in philosophy after World War II was to reverse this impoverishment of our subject by the inter-war generation. Our task—as I saw it—was to work for a widened conception of the field, to effect broader synthesis, and to restore active concern for the historic problems of the traditional range of philosophical deliberation. We were to restore a concern for wholeness and system—not by abandoning the penchant for exactness and detail of the pre-war generation, but by fusing detail into meaningful structures, combining the older yearning for system with the new passion for exactness. It was thus to be our job to use the exact methods and rigorous standards of the inter-war generation as instruments for renewed assault on the "big issues" of the field that had figured importantly in the historic span of philosophical theorizing.

More than any other creative intellectual discipline, philosophy has a special relationship to its past. Its task, to be sure, is not one of syncretism, of preserving and restructuring the tradition for its own sake. But it can always draw enormous profit from the work at hand by exploiting the ideas and arguments and visions of the tradition as a storehouse of tools for the accomplishment of these present labors. The basic issues of philosophy are perennial and crop up in a renewed, reacclimated guise in every era. And attention to the ways our predecessors have dealt with them is a resource of inestimable value in the accomplishment of our own work.

I was thus led to take a rather different view of the technical preoccupation of the minutiae of formal analysis which had come to the forefront in the postwar years. It seemed to me that the passion for the detailed analysis of small-scale side-issues was getting out of hand. The situation was reminiscent of that of the simpleton who explained that he was looking for his purse on this side of the road because, while he dropped it on the other side, there was better light over here. All too often, philosophers were using their technical instruments on those issues of detail congenial to their application, rather than concentrating them on inherently important matters. Technical questions became preoccupations in their own right, rather than because of any significant bearing of the central problems of the field. Those who followed in the footsteps of Moore and Russell and Carnap often lost sight of the real problems—as these masters never did. I viewed this tendency with increasing distaste, and felt that while detailed technical studies were indeed indispensable, their utility was purely instrumental, and lay wholly in their bearing on the large traditional issues of the field. Accordingly, when

I now addressed myself to technical issues in logic and value-theory and philosophical history, I did so not for the sake of their intrinsic appeal, but only where I saw a prospect of wider philosophical significance and a capacity to provide useful building blocks for larger structures.

This constructive orientation was important for me. In general, philosophers tend to fall into two classes: there are those who see themselves as *destroyers*, revolutionaries, demolition experts, removers of rubbish. The ancient sceptics exemplify this tendency, as do the Humean empiricists, and the logical positivists of the present century. On the other hand, there are the *builders* whose approach is conservative and who seek to secure and consolidate rather than to abolish received truth, with the key issues posed by questions such as: "What validates our standard logical procedures—or our moral judgments, or our cognitive claims, etc?" Like Leibniz or Kant or Hegel, the builders too call received ideas into question, but with the very different positive aim of validating rather than destroying them. And while they too see the need for a new start (all serious philosophers do!), their orientation to the tradition is not one of abandonment but one of exploitation. It is certainly this latter, constructive and reconstructive school that commands my own allegiance. Scepticism, negativism, and nihilism may be a natural reaction to broken promises, but the risks of disappointment are surely preferable to the counsels of despair.

In any event, after 1968 the pattern of my philosophical work changed. For one thing, I stopped working on the history of Arabic philosophy (especially logic), thus putting an end to a venture commenced about a decade before. To be sure, I did not abandon my medieval Arabic concerns wholly without regret. But I had done pretty well everything I could readily do with the limited resources at my disposal. (I also sensed that my philosophical colleagues were utterly indifferent to this work, and some among them actually hostile to it—unthinking partisans caught up in the anti-Arab ethos of Near Eastern strife.)

I now became increasingly preoccupied with mainstream philosophical issues of epistemology and metaphysics, and my philosophical work gradually came to assume a more continuous direction and a more systematic aspect. The series of books that emerged so readily from my pen in the years after 1969—beginning with *The Coherence Theory of Truth*—were a systematic development of ideas launched during the just-preceding period and represented the culmination of lines of thought that originated at that stage. The fundamentals of methodological pragmatism were implicit in the last chapter of *Many-Valued Logic* (written in 1967; published in 1969). The imputational theory of lawfulness and the thesis of the mind-dependence of possibility go back to my essay in the *Festschrift* for C. G. Hempel (written 1968; published 1969), and this idealistic approach to natural philosophy was further developed in *Scientific Explanation* (written 1968-9; published 1970). These writings marked a turning point in my development as a philosopher.

I recall well how the key ideas of my idealistic theory of natural laws—of "lawfulness as imputation"—came to me in 1968 during work on this project while awaiting the delivery of Arabic manuscripts in the Oriental Reading Room of the British Museum. It struck me that what a law *states* is a mere generalization, but what marks this generalization as something special in our sight—and renders it something we see as a genuine *law* of nature—is the role that we assign to it in inference. Lawfulness is thus not a matter of what the law-statement *says*, but how it is *used* in the systematization of knowledge—the sort of role that we impute to it. These ideas provided an impetus to idealist lines of thought and marked the onset of my commitment to a philosophical idealism which teaches that the mind is itself involved in the conceptual constitution of the objects of our knowledge.

My drift towards idealism was largely impelled by the realization, driven home through studies of the history of science, that scientific discovery is not a matter of "reading off what is writ large in the book of nature," but is the result of *interaction* between the mind and nature. This interactional process is such that the contribution of our strictly mental contrivances is every bit as significant to the overall result as that of "the real world" we are concerned to study. What we call science is an intellectual process in which we *construct* a frangible picture of nature using conceptual materials of our own devising, materials which inevitably bear the imprint of their mentalistic origins. The articulation and development of this idealistic perspective became the governing principle of my philosophical labors, providing a unifying focus for my longstanding fascination with the question of how the human mind comes to cognitive terms with the world it lives in.

There now evolved what has become my characteristic method of book-writing. At any given time, I have three books in hand—one that is essentially completed and is just being polished and refined, one that is actually in progress of being written, and one that is only in prospect and for which I am merely gathering ideas and materials in a jumbled file of jottings, notes, and references. This last-named item is of enormous utility. It means that when serious work on a project commences, I do not face a *tabula rasa*, but can virtually assemble a first draft out of preexisting materials. This tripartite method has served me well, and I can recommend it unreservedly to anyone who has a large writing project in hand.

This turning of my work into a systematic direction yielded, over the six years beginning with 1968, a rapid succession of books which (I could sense) put my reputation as a creative philosopher on an entirely different footing. In any case, the year 1970 turned out to be the *annus mirabilis* of my professional career. In January of the year, Dorothy and I journeyed to an ice-cold Chicago, where I was awarded an honorary doctorate of humane letters by Loyola University at a small but impressive ceremony where Hans Küng and C. P. Snow were also among the awardees. This development seemed to me surprising and unmerited, and yet at another level perhaps intelligible as a gesture of pluralistic outreach from a thoroughly Catholic institution towards a younger philosopher (not yet to be classed as an extinct volcano) who combined analytic predilections with a sincere commitment to *philosophia perennis* and a pronounced sympathy towards traditional values and human concerns. The year also saw my designation as University Professor of Philosophy at Pitt, and my being awarded a Guggenheim Fellowship. The University Professorship in particular marked a change in my status. Instituted at Harvard in the administration of J.B. Conant, it was the aim of such professorships "to free a few particularly distinguished scholars form routine duties,"[37] with the idea that no more than one percent of the faculty of the institution is to qualify for such recognition. At the relatively young age of forty-two I had completed the climb to the top rung of the professorial ladder.

A new sensibility came upon me in the wake of these developments. Having now attained a place of some prominence in the profession, I felt that I had to live up to it by producing the sort of work one would expect of somebody in such a position. I saw my professional advance less as a reward than as a challenge.

The 1967-71 period was thus a time of innovation in my life: a new family, a new atmosphere in my department, a newly enhanced standing in my profession, and a new spirit in my work. I had entered into this period from a slough of despond; I left it with a sense of personal and professional security and a hopeful outlook towards new worlds to conquer. The old saw that "life begins at forty" is often mocked, but in my own case there was a grain of truth to it.

Twelve

Pittsburgh And Oxford: 1971-1974
(Age 42-46)

DURING BETHLEHEM days I once remarked jokingly at a cocktail party that nothing worthwhile was to be found in Pennsylvania west of Lancaster. A friend replied: "The people of Pittsburgh would certainly resent that!" And so, as fate's little ironies would have it, I was not only to move to Pittsburgh, but have now (1974) lived here for over a dozen years, have married a Pittsburgh girl, and am in the process of raising a family of little Pittsburghers. I am destined, to all appearances, to pass the rest of my life in this bridge-laden city. And I have grown sufficiently fond of the place to view this prospect, if not with unalloyed joy, at any rate quite without dismay. Pittsburgh has many assets as a community, and there is much about the place that is thoroughly likeable. In particular, Pittsburgh is a sensible place, where people tend to have a realistic, down-to-earth set of values, and where the traditional American work-ethic is still very much alive. It is a congenial environment in which to live and to do one's work—be it physical or mental.

The University, of course, ranks high on my list of Pittsburgh plusses—its Philosophy Department above all. By the late 1960's, our reputation had become secure as one of the very best departments in the country. And unlike most, we were a harmonious group, interacting well with each other and transacting our business in a spirit of mutual friendship and helpfulness. To be sure, the period of rapid growth that typified the era of Kurt Baier's chairmanship of the department was now over. But this itself was fortunate, since we now had assembled a faculty of some two dozen, as large a size as is compatible with functioning as a coherent unit. There is no question in my mind that Pittsburgh is a good place for a philosopher.

All the same, one thing that makes living in Pittsburgh pleasanter is the chance to get away for some months in summertime—the unique advantage of an academic career. In this regard, a major change in the pattern of our lives occurred in early 1971 with the leasing of 100 Victoria Road, Oxford, a brick row-house typical of the urban England of the Edwardian era. The acquisition of this house laid the basis for a new pattern of life, with summers regularly spent in Oxford. At this writing in the autumn of 1974, we have completed our fourth visit there, and this arrangement has worked out most happily. It is greatly relaxing and restorative to have each year a period of relief from the Pittsburgh routine—and from the Pittsburgh summer heat. In June of 1973, however, our English domicile was transferred to 6 Cunliffe Close, a compact modern townhouse in a brand-new development located on the former site of the Greycotes School. Closely proximate to the Summertown shopping area, the house is also within convenient walking distance of the city center, being situated off Banbury Road at a distance of just over a mile from Carfax. Its garden (of whose designing I am rather proud) is sufficiently straightforward that it is not too strugglesome to keep it in good appearance.

As a residential setting, North Oxford is thoroughly pleasant but in one way dissapointing. It is surely one of the most attractive and best preserved Victorian suburbs in existence, with its variety of large handsome brick and stucco homes in every style—from neo-Gothic to neo-Georgian—that was popular towards the close of the last century. But its potential is sadly unrealized, for the charms of the place are spoiled by an aura of scruffiness. Far too often the houses are ill maintained and the gardens are ill tended. Absentee landlordism is the root of the trouble. Many of those splendid old homes are òwned by colleges. Some have become offices. Others are rabbit warrens of student accommodations. Some are rented to college fellows in a misguided paternalistic concern to spare academics the vexations (and benefits) of home ownership. North Oxford amply illustrates the principle that a property not in the hands of an owner-occupier is a property that is neglected.

A link to the University has come to be forged in the course of these Oxonian visits. The Sub-faculty of Philosophy has invited me on each occasion to give a series of lectures on topics of my choosing. And so during each Trinity (Summer) Term of this period, I have presented, in preliminary form, the substance of a book on which I was currently working.[38] This chance to float my trial balloons before a capable and critical audience—generally containing several other visiting academics—has proved very helpful.

It is somewhat difficult to articulate the charm Oxford has for me. Part of it lies in those dreamy spires and castellated college structures that do credit not only to their long-gone builders, but to those who strive nowadays to preserve the physical appearance of this ancient university. Part of it lies in the manifest commitment to academic excellence that pervades every corner of the place. Part of it lies in a near-Quixotic dedication to old ways—to ceremonious pomp and the maintenance of tradition for tradition's sake. Everywhere one finds manifestations of a commitment to scholarly values expressed in ways sometimes charming, sometimes silly, but always impressive to those who themselves hold such matters dear. The Enceinia ceremony is an academic exercise that encapsulates all this to perfection—timeworn Chancellor, blasé honorees, Latin citations, academic humor, and all.

Regular features of routine in our Oxford summer create a pleasurable continuity: the "trooping of the colors" for the Queen's birthday celebration and Wimbledon tennis on the BBC; lunches at the Royal Sun (a charming old Inn on the road to Woodstock that produces a delicious *quiche Lorraine*), an occasional dinner at the expensive but excellent Restaurant Elizabeth opposite Christ Church or at the inexpensive but pleasant La Dolce Vita in Summertown. Such occasions make a repetitive design in the fabric of experience that always give one something to look back upon—and forward to.

Oxford and its surroundings are immensely appealing and especially well suited to the interests and needs of a philosopher. The setting is also congenial to our entire family. Over the years Dorothy has made many friends and the boys have many playmates. Here too we have more time to entertain guests and visitors—activities which, though we enjoy them, are not easily fitted into the busier Pittsburgh routine. Our theater-going seems principally to transpire during summers, with Shakespearean trips to Stratford on Avon or attendance at the New Theater of the Oxford Playhouse for its London-bound trial-balloon productions. We also manage to take in some three or four films each summer, many of them children's productions that we share as a family.[39]

Another favorite diversion is tourism, with a special focus upon houses of historical interest, for over the years I have acquired something of an amateur interest in architecture—especially domestic architecture. We have managed to inspect a fair proportion of the many "stately homes" on display within 30 miles of Oxford. This interest in historic houses forms part of a wider interest in history and in historical artifacts. Some time each summer is devoted to antiquing in the Oxford area. We regularly participate in auctions (especially those conducted by the estate agency firms of Buckell & Ballard at the Horse Fair in Banbury and Victor Side in St. Hugh's Church in Woodstock). And we search through a regular circuit of antique shops. (Some favorites are Phyllis White's small shop in Stanton Harcourt, and various establishments in Oxford, Burford, Moreton-on-the-Marsh, Henley, etc.) Gradually we have managed to acquire an interesting assortment of miscellaneous items, and our Oxford house has a bit of the museum about it.

In Oxford I do not work at peak efficiency. The adrenalin does not pump quite so hard in the somewhat enervating atmosphere of the Thames valley. For this very reason my mind can range somewhat more freely there—it works well on issues of strategy while perhaps dealing less effectively with matters of tactics. In Oxford I tend to work at sketching large projects whose detailed execution is more effectively handled in Pittsburgh. There is the leisure to do things the more pressured pace of Pittsburgh does not admit of—to ruminate, to let the drift of thought wander loosely down the byways of personal affairs and professional concerns, and so to gain a fresh perspective on things.

Dorothy, too, has her own cluster of favored activities in Oxford. She takes tennis instruction at the Norham Gardens Tennis Club, participates in some of the activities of the University Newcomer's Club (nowadays not as a newcomer, but as an "old hand"), and she does brass-rubbing at miscellaneous churches in the area. Periodically she goes on a shopping trip to London. And then, of course, there are the various activities we do together: tourism, antiquing, entertaining, etc. Dorothy is a person of much enterprise and energy—active and outgoing—and life with her is a constant source of happiness.

The months we spend each year in England mean much to me. It is a refreshing change to live in the cultural framework of a cognate yet distinctively different society. I find our English cousins by and large congenial—particularly those of the older generation. There is, perhaps, less bonhommie than in America, and people tend to keep a bit more distant from others. (The lower noise-level of talk in restaurants, busses, and other public places is one rather striking token of this.) But it did not take me long to become persuaded that English people do not deserve their reputation for reserve and unapproachability. To be sure, they generally do not thrust themselves forward with a pretence of "Hail fellow, well met!" joviality. But they seldom fail to answer friendliness with friendliness, and almost invariably go out of their way to be helpful to strangers. Except for the occasional eccentric academic—whom, after all, one can meet anyplace—I have seldom found that friendliness goes unreciprocated in England.

I am repeatedly surprised at the standard of living of academics in the United Kingdom. Like most British workers they are substantially less well paid than their colleagues in continental Europe and in the USA. And yet their lifestyle is generally comparable. No doubt this is in part because a very high proportion of them are married to professional spouses. Given their attachment to the good things of life—annual holidays in the Mediterranean sun, children at private schools, imported wines, and the like, one cannot help being struck by the frequency with which English academics talk socialist cant from the comfortable vantage point of a bourgeois household. To an unabashed partisan of bourgeois values like myself, this seems downright hypocrisy. If a middle-class lifestyle is worth living and prizing, it is surely also worth defending in the sphere of ideology and political discourse.

Academics the world around are cut from much the same cloth and have many common interests and points of contact—their colleagues not least among them. If the old saw is true that servants talk about *people* and the gentry about *things*, then academics are servants. This is especially pronounced in England, because British academia is a relatively compact and tightly knit society—much like a small town. Everyone knows everybody and wants the latest word on their doings, and preferably their misdoings and mishaps. (This is particularly reinforced by the unwritten law of Oxford colleges that one does not talk shop on social occasions.) Oxford dons, to be sure, tend to have a somewhat insular outlook—as though everything worth happening happens in Oxford. To my surprise, academics in England are even more given to self-indulgence and self-advertising than here. (Only there is it standard operating procedure to line one's invitations up on one's mantlepiece for all the world to see that one is being asked to the Vice Chancellor's reception or the Provost's tea.)

Throughout my visits in Oxford the fellows of Corpus Christi College have taken me unto themselves as a visiting member of their Senior Common Room. An Oxford college is a most delightful sort of club. To be sure, as a dedicated family man with a ménage of his own in Oxford, I only eat in College once in a blue moon. But I often use the reading room, and often work in the Medieval setting of the picturesque old library. Having a foothold in college makes all the difference in helping an academic visitor feel part of the Oxford scene, and I am very grateful to Corpus for its courteous hospitality, which has meant a great deal to me over the years. All in all, Oxford affords an environment where a philosopher can feel especially at home, because it is so clearly a place where the things that matter to him are thought important.

My oldest Oxford friend is R. M. Hare, the White's Professor of Moral Philosophy. I first met him around 1964 when he came through Pittsburgh to give a lecture. When I planned my sabbatical visit to Oxford in 1968, he arranged for us to do a lecture-course on imperatives together, and it was he who introduced me into his college (Corpus Christi), thus establishing a relationship of long-term standing. A fine scholar and clever philosopher, he is a gentleman of the old school, and I have come to be quite fond of him, and of his very charming wife as well.

Jonathan Cohen of Queens College, who works in philosophical logic and language theory, and Ron Harré of Linacre College, who cultivates the philosophy of science, have also been among my closer Oxford contacts. Both are nonstandard but yet by no means unusual Oxonian types, Jon as the cultivated cosmopolitan metamorphosed into a bookish English country squire and active protector of rural England, and Rom as the returned Colonial (from New Zealand) out to show those stay-at-home fogies some new-world vitality. Hettie, his vivacious wife, is something of a good-natured one-member fan club for Rom, who in her eyes is a peerless doer of fine and admirable deeds. They are a sweet couple.

Another person I see much of around Oxford is David Taylor, who is in charge of journals in the publications department of Blackwells and has managed the *American Philosophical Quarterly* for this firm since it arrived there in 1965. Dorothy and I have known him ever since our Oxford "honeymoon" of 1968, and we like him much and enjoy his company. A graduate of Queen's College, Oxford, David is a chorister at Christ Church and an enthusiastic Latinist, which especially endears him to me. He is also an amateur playwright of considerable dedication and ability. (In 1975 I attended the opening night performance of his splendid comedy, *Ghengis Khan*, put on by the boys of Christ Church Cathedral School.) David is a person of unusual qualilty and versatility.

Yet another of our good friends in Oxford is Mr. William Sumpter, the gardener who first came in the summer of 1971 to take care of our Victoria Road garden. A World War I veteran then in his early 70's, he had retired as gardener at St. Edward's School some years ago, but was glad to take on a part-time job, and answered our advertisement in *The Oxford Times*. He lived nearby, in Hernes Road, and would come by on his bicycle once a week to cut the lawn and manicure the garden. A charming, dapper, little pink cherub of a man with a delightful sense of humor, he endeared himself with the boys, whom he persisted in calling "Master Mark" and "Master Owen." Shortly before we sold the Victoria Road house in 1973, he was forced into retirement by circulatory difficulties in his legs. We continue to stay in touch with him and call on him and his very nice wife regularly during our Oxford visits. "Pop" Sumpter, as he came to be known around our house, is a point of contact with an older type of English workman, cheerfully class-conscious yet totally selfassured—a type now on the verge of extinction.

All in all, then, the Oxford connection has greatly enriched my life and widened my horizons. Such longish visits abroad create a certain detachment from the surrounding bustle. One is able to view things—both locally and "back home"—with some detachment, and gains a fresh and broader perspective on human affairs, by no means useless experience for a philosopher.

During the 1960's, I became increasingly active in international activities in philosophy. I came to hold various offices[40] and attended various meetings of international scholarly organizations, visiting Helsinki in 1962, Jerusalem in 1964, Vienna in 1968, Bucharest in 1971, Cambridge in 1972, and Berne in 1974 in this connection. My service as Secretary of the Logic, Methodology, and Philosophy of Science branch of the International Union of History and Philosophy of Science (an organ of UNESCO)—an office I held during 1969-1975—was particularly interesting. The post was no sinecure, for the Secretary stood at the hub of the enterprise, and all the business of this active international scholarly organization passed through his hands. (I was most fortunate in this regard in serving with two immensely helpful and cooperative presidents: Sephan Körner of Bristol and Andrzej Mostowski of Warsaw.)

It required considerable diplomacy to keep the organizational ship sailing smoothly along amidst diverse personal rivalries and international frictions. (Scholars can be every bit as primadonnaish as singers!) Handling interpersonal complications with reasonable adhesion to Sir Robert Walpole's principle of *quieta non movere* (roughly—"let sleeping dogs lie!"), my main accomplishment lay in furthering the division's proper work through a lively program of conferences and colloquia. During my tenure of office the organization grew substantially in numerical strength and in professional activity, so that I have at least the satisfaction of feeling that my period of service did more good than harm. But I found it fascinating to see how deeply the passions of academics could be aroused by stakes of negligible size and how engrossed people could become in jockeying for position in a situation in which there was in fact no real power to be jockeyed for.

I was active on other fronts also. In 1971, I organized *The Journal of Philosophical Logic*. I negotiated the inauguration of this journal with the firm of Reidel in the Netherlands and recruited my former student Bas van Fraassen as its initial editor. I take some justifiable pleasure in the success of this journal in the short course of its history. More importantly, however, the year 1973 saw the tenth anniversary of publication of the *American Philosophical Quarterly*. My literary offspring had not only survived its first decade, but has in its brief history managed to establish itself as a leading philosophy journal. I must confess that I am thoroughly pleased with its success.

During the 1968-1972 period I managed to regularize my relationships with publishers. My earlier books had appeared under a variety of imprints, but step by step I developed a closer and more continuous relationship with two publishing houses. For one thing, I became friends with Fred Hetzel, the able and enterprising director of the University of Pittsburgh Press, who had come to Pitt from Williamsburg a few years before. Initially the Pitt Press had published all my books on Arabic philosophy, thanks to Fred's interest, but there now came a transition to some of my regular philosophical work. The publication of three books over a six-year period confirmed this ongoing relationship: *Essays in Philosophi-*

cal Analysis (1969), *Welfare* (1972), and *Unselfishness* (1975).

In the course of my Oxford visits I also became friends with Jim Feather, the Managing Director of the publishing branch of Blackwells and a most knowledgeable and perceptive publisher. After completing his studies in Oxford, Jim was initially a newspaperman, but he soon made the transition into academic publishing and transformed Blackwells from a small-scale operation into a major publishing house. Blackwells had been publishing the *American Philosophical Quarterly* since 1966, but in 1971 we also reached an understanding as a result of which a steady stream of my own books has been issued by this house (*Conceptual Idealism*, 1973; *The Primacy of Practice*, 1973; *A Theory of Possibility*, 1975; *Methodological Pragmatism*, 1976). With both Fred and Jim, there has been a mixture of business and personal contacts, and it is striking here (as elsewhere) how greatly the element of personal relationship tends to smooth the conduct of business affairs. I consider myself fortunate to have two such conscientious and congenial publishers to deal with.

My philosophical horizons also continued to expand. I now launched a systematic study of two movements I had heretofore neglected: the Hegelian tradition and American pragmatism (and especially Peirce). Particularly in their stress on dynamic and evolutionary considerations in the validation of thought, both of these major figures of modern philosophy were to prove of substantial importance for the work of the "Pragmatic Idealism" trilogy (*Conceptual Idealism*, 1973; *The Primacy of Practice*, 1973; and *Methodological Pragmatism*, 1976) that I wrote during this period. This work led to my increasing commitment to an idealism based on the conception that our conceptual tools reflect a predisposition to view the world in a way that takes human thought and action as its model and sees the integration of human functioning as the paradigm of a "natural system."

Teaching has always been the center of my work-life, and during this 1971-74 period I taught a wide variety of courses. In time, my teaching interests came to focus on three areas: the history of philosophy, metaphysics, and the theory of knowledge—especially scientific knowledge. (My writing has run along just these same tracks.) As the years moved on I came to see myself, in relation to my students, as the diplomatic representative of a foreign civilization representing in their midst some of the great philosophers of the past, and especially some of the now-gone greats or near-greats whom I have known personally and whose work had, in one way or another, exerted some influence on my thinking—Rudolf Carnap, A. C. Ewing, W. T. Stace, and others.

I have never taken the role of a remote Herr Professor towards my graduate students. Yet I also never sought to be their "buddy," nor enter into a first-name relationship (as some younger faculty members began to do in the latter 1960's). Rather, I have tried to be their collaborator, their senior partner or colleague in an association of peers. I felt I had things to teach to my students not only about the substance of philosophy, but about the spirit in which philosophical work is done and what it takes to be a philosopher—a serious concern for the issues, a deep desire to get things straight, a willingness to work, and a preparedness to put aside any affectations or pomposities that can get in the way between the task to be done and the person who is to do it. Except for a time during the heyday of student activism in the 1968-1970 era—when battle-lines were drawn on an ideology largely based on age—I always had excellent relations with the great bulk of our graduate students. Whenever former students of mine do good work, I am as proud of it as of my own.

In the course of the 1970's, I began to be increasingly active on the philosophical "lecture circuit" as invited speaker at departmental colloquia, at conferences and congresses, etc., visiting campuses throughout the country—and making various visits abroad as well. During the four years of this chapter I presented two dozen major invited lectures in the U.S.A., and eight in Europe, an average of six *per annum* in the former category and two in the latter. Increasingly I gained confidence and developed a "style" for performances of this sort, and they were generally successful.

The year 1970 inaugurated another enlargement of the scene of my professional activities. My friend Robert Butts, an able philosopher whom I had known since Lehigh days, when he was at Bucknell, had become chairman of the philosophy department at the University of Western Ontario in London, Ontario, Canada. At his initiative, I was invited to offer a course during the 1970-1971 academic year in the form of occasional visiting lectures. This invitation was renewed on a number of subsequent occasions. I would commute by air to Canada one Wednesday every other week during term to give a course for graduate students. These trips were somewhat demanding—I would set out from home before 7 A.M. and return to Pittsburgh at around 11 P.M. But this ongoing link with an active department largely staffed with able young people was a source of stimulus and satisfaction. The philosophy students at "Western" were able people—and very pleasant too. Some of this lecturing I did in Canada during this period was by way of contribution to the routine teaching work of the department, but in the main I used these lectures as a sounding board for work in progress; for example, *The Coherence Theory of Truth, a Theory of Possibility*, and *Unselfishness* were all presented in such lecture-courses. This link to "Western" faded away after Bob Butts put the chairmanship aside in 1973, but while it lasted it provided me with useful stimulus.

Along similar lines, I gave a series of lectures at the Catholic University of America during the spring of 1972. I was pleased to have the chance to learn something of the inside workings of this fine institution and to get to know Jude Dougherty, the enterprising head of its School of Philosophy. This visiting arrangement proved of value to me in affording an occasion for polishing yet further the materials of my Oxford lectures that eventually issued in *Conceptual Idealism*.[41]

Some visits that did not happen also deserve mention. It has long been my desire to go "down under" to see something of New Zealand and Australia. Twice I had made all arrangements for an academic visit in New Zealand—in 1968 in Auckland and in 1975 in Dunedin. Both visits were cancelled for the same reason: Dorothy became pregnant—with Mark on the earlier occasion and with Catherine on the later. Perhaps the fates intend this particular ambition of mine to go unsatisfied.

Throughout the 1970's I maintained a steady interest in the philosophy of Leibniz, writing, on average, one paper every two years on related topics. I participated regularly in national and international Leibniz congresses and conferences, and became an active member of that small international fraternity of members who interest themselves in the wide-ranging thought and multifarious doings of this great man. Over the years I have remained a dedicated Leibnizian, though, to be sure, I am not a Leibniz-scholar in that mode of total commitment which typifies the European philosophy-historians of the old school.

Gradually I have gotten to know Leibniz well, not only as a thinker but as a person. I have learned, bit by bit, a good deal about his life and times and about the people amongst whom he labored. And repeated visits to Hanover have made me feel thoroughly at home among the few remnants of that much smaller town with which Leibniz was so thoroughly familiar.

As Leibniz himself so clearly illustrates, the work of a scholar or scientist has the unusual aspect that only a part of him belongs to the institution that has him in employ. In the main, his vocational identity and loyalty belongs to the professional guild of which he is a member by virtue of the discipline he cultivates. On the whole, he knows his remote fellow specialists—in philosophy or chemistry or whatever—better than his extradisciplinary colleagues in the institution they serve in common.

Even today a disciplinary guild of academic colleagues forms a truly international fraternity that largely transcends political and cultural boundaries. The productive scholar or scientist can walk into a laboratory or department in his field at virtually any university or research institute in any corner of the globe and take up almost instantaneous friendships with others of extensive common interests and acquaintanceships. Here is a continuing heritage of that international fraternity—then ecclesiastical—which created the university system of the middle ages. Physicians, lawyers, and sundry other professionals, all nowadays require for practice a certification governed by law, whose validity is consequently circumscribed by political boundaries (which operate down to the state level in the U.S.A.). The university teacher—be he a research scientist or a humanistic scholar—can take his Ph.D. in hand and ply his trade in any corner of the world where a university is desirous of his services. The political divisions of national boundaries are almost irrelevant in the practice of an academic profession. The academic belongs to what is perhaps the only truly supranational professional confraternity that has survived the rise of nationalism in the modern world.

Nevertheless, in my own case internationalism has its limits. To be sure, I have lived a quarter of my life outside the USA (the initial decade in Germany and the equivalent of a year and a half in England during this 1971-75 period). The most influential among my philosophical teachers (Hempel, Stace, Ushenko, Urmson) were European imports, and my general outlook in philosophy is throughly international. Of my leading philosophical heroes (Plato, Aristotle, Leibniz, Kant, Hegel, Peirce) only one is an American. Nevertheless, I unhesitatingly view myself as a specifically American philosopher—for three reasons: (1) the methodology I favor is a fusion of analytical techniques with historical concerns, an approach characteristic of the tradition of those modern American philosophers I admire most (from C. S. Peirce to C. I. Lewis and W. V. Quine); (2) my philosophical ambience in terms of close personal and professional contacts runs heavily towards my American colleagues; and (3) the tenor of my philosophical thinking is oriented markedly towards pragmatism, which is generally—and, I think, rightly—regarded as the quintessentially American philosophy. Just as the language I speak best is an American English that no one would for a moment mistake for the British or Australian versions, so the philosophy I write is characteristically American.

This is perhaps the place to say a word about what becoming, nay, *being* an American has meant to me. It has, above all, meant belonging to a confident people—proud, capable, compassionate, and, above all, resourceful: a people of buoyant, can-do spirit that has always been glad to make room in its land for those willing to put their shoulders to the wheel of the world's work, encouraging them to make something of themselves, with a pat on the back for those who succeed and a helping hand for those who, through no fault of their own, cannot do so. Americans, I have always felt, are a people who can walk tall on the streets of other nations, confident that they represent a country that has not only the power but the moral quality that compels respect. At a banquet given late in his reign by William IV of Great Britain in honor of the American minister of the day, the king (with characteristic eccentricity) diplomatically declared that it had always been a matter of serious regret to him that he had not "been born a free, independent American, so much did he respect that nation, which had given birth to Washington, the greatest man that ever lived." I can see exactly what he meant, and feel thoroughly pleased that in my own case a kindly fate has seen fit to remedy the defect of the accident of birth. Wherever I detect traces of the American spirit of practicality and common sense and optimism and idealism in my personality or in my philosophical work, I welcome it with pleasure.

In youth and middle age one tends to think of oneself as immortal. Death, like other catastrophes, only befalls other people. The realization that one's days are numbered is neither pleasant nor easy. (It shocks me to think that when Spinoza was my age—now 46—he had been dead for over a year.) In 1973 I experienced for the first time a bout of serious health problems. In the middle of August I had a text-book attack of appendicitis in Oxford. I diagnosed this myself, and drove myself, Dorothy accompanying, to the old Radcliffe Infirmary, where this was swiftly confirmed. It was an acute case, and within two hours they had me out of the operating theater where a capable lady surgeon had removed the troublesome organ. I spent several rather pleasant days recuperating in the private room which had fortunately fallen to my lot in the hospital, then returned to Cunliffe Close to prepare for the return to Pittsburgh a week or so later. But I continued to have stomach pains. I attributed this to normal post-operative developments. However, a few days after our return to Pittsburgh, at Jerry Massey's start-of-the-year party for the newly incoming students, these pains became very severe. I returned home and began bouts of vomiting. That evening Dorothy drove me to University Presbyterian Hospital, where I came under the care of an able professor of surgery at Pitt's medical school. It transpired that my gall-bladder had gone badly awry (so badly that gangrene had set in). Unfortunately, during the operation the anesthetist's breathing tube managed to traumatize one of my vocal cords which remained paralyzed some six weeks afterwards, leaving me in a condition where I could only whisper. (For a time, I wondered if I would ever again lecture normally.)

These medical troubles led me to realize that if some more serious medical disturbance had removed me from this scene, my children would know precious little about their father himself and nothing about his antecedents. And I felt keenly that in this event they would be losing a part of the awareness of their identity and thus a part of themselves. I resolved that they should not sustain this loss if it lay in my power to prevent it, and this was the origin of the biographical notes whose weaving together has resulted in the present book.

With each passing year I derived deeper satisfaction from my growing family. Children present an ever-changing panorama of challenges—and rewards. In Pittsburgh, Mark (b. 1969) and Owen (b. 1970) have both attended St. Edmund's Academy, a fine private boy's school located in the Squirrel Hill section of town. Mark began there in the nursery class for four year olds in 1973 and Owen in 1974. They continue there at this writing (1975), with Mark in the first grade and Owen in the kindergarten. They both enjoy the school and have profited a good deal from its caring and competent nurture. Their thriving baby sister Cathy (b. 1975) will no doubt attend the (coeducational) nursery school there one day.

A word should also be said about the boys' education experiences on the other side of the Atlantic. The Squirrel School in Oxford—where they began attendance at three years—is an unusual school, by American standards at any rate. It is run with a loose but kindly rein by Miss R. S. Bell, the spinster daughter of an erstwhile Oxford professor. Its home is a pair of old, large, rambling, late Victorian houses on Woodstock Road (off Rawlinson Road). The physical plant is plain and somewhat run down. But the staff is dedicated and the children are well taught in a caring and thoughtful atmosphere. Mark attended the Squirrel for part of every year during 1972-1975 and Owen was a year later in joining him there. They have enjoyed themselves there, and I feel that the school has done very well by the boys. In nine weeks or so at the Squirrel School in

Oxford during the summer of 1974, Mark (then five) learned to read very well, and he does so now (early 1975) avidly and quite on his own.

Upon retiring from her job at Westtown School in 1971, my mother stayed there for a time, but in 1972 moved to a small flat overlooking the sea at Illetas in Mallorca. There we had a pleasant visit with her in the summer of 1973. She for her part much enjoyed her visits with us in Oxford, and in the fall of 1974 she moved into our house in Cunliffe Close. She seems to enjoy Oxford a great deal and has made many friends there. She is quite active—in the Ferry Center (the neighborhood center in North Oxford) and at Oxfam, where she does a good bit of volunteer work in the little shop on Oakthorpe Road in Summertown. Mother's presence in Oxford means that our English visits also offer a chance for the boys and their grandmother to spend time together, to the immense pleasure of all concerned.

On another front, however, familial affairs stand in a less rosy condition. Until the summer of 1971, Frances and Elizabeth continued to reside in Pittsburgh. I was thus enabled to preserve not, to be sure, a close and cordial, but at any rate a regular contact with Elizabeth. However that summer, after she had completed her Library Science degree at Pitt, Frances moved to Hanover, N.H. to take up a post in the library of Dartmouth College. She now refused me any visiting privileges at all, and so I had to pursue the matter in the New Hampshire courts, which entailed various visits to the handsome new red-brick courthouse at Grafton, N.H. This process dragged on until well into 1972, but in the end I was granted the meager satisfaction of one weekend visitation per month. Beginning in October of that year, I availed myself of this regularly, except during the summer months when we were away in England.

These visits went off pleasantly enough. Air New England's diminutive propeller-driven de Haviland biplanes provided a reliable though bumpy service from Boston to Lebanon, N.H. The Hanover Inn was a most pleasant place to stay and the town and its environs (especially Woodstock) afforded many interesting targets for father-and-daughter tourism. But the contact between us was now too occasional for close cordiality to be maintained in the face of the psychological pressure upon Elizabeth of her mother's hostility towards me, which—contrary to expectation—did not diminish with the passage of time.

In January of 1974 Frances and Elizabeth removed to Brighton, near Rochester, N.Y., where Frances took up a post in the library of the University of Rochester Medical School. This time there was no legal contest—my entitlement to monthly visitation was treated as a tacitly acknowledged fact. But as best I could tell, Brighton was not so pleasant locale for Elizabeth as Hanover had been, and she now seemed even tenser and less at ease than before. The passage of time brought nothing better than a continuance of the strained relationship between us which had been developing over the years—all of my wishes and efforts to the contrary notwithstanding. I know that I love Elizabeth with deep fatherly affection and would like to share her happiness and sorrows and be able to play some constructive role in her life. Perhaps someday when she is older it will become possible. "Where there's life, there's hope."

In the meantime, life goes on. In recent years I have done much traveling by air. I spent the bulk of this time on various writing projects, and so would estimate that a nontrivial fraction of what I wrote during these years was written aloft, the equivalent of a modest sized volume at any rate. The confined space of the cabin, the security against the telephone or other interruptions and the gentle hum of the jet engines all conduce to concentration. And the idea that a fixed but limited period is available for getting something done provides a useful impetus to "get on with it." (I write these very words at an altitude of some three miles on an Allegheny Airlines flight from Buffalo to Pittsburgh enroute home from a Canadian visit. My quota of work for this trip having been accomplished, I am devoting the residual time to these biographical notes.)

For the most part, however, we live a very home-oriented life, with house and children at the center of our horizon. Bit by bit, a good deal of work was done on the Sheridan Avenue property, both in the house and in the garden. The gradual introduction of various antiques and artworks has made this house a very pleasant dwelling. With the approaching completion of the sixth year of occupancy in

January of 1975, I will have lived longer in this house than in any other during my adult life.

A word about diversions seems in order. One of my major pastimes is reading, primarily in English history and biography. (During the 1971-75 period I waded through the entire *Oxford History of England*.[42]) Watching television is another favored leisure activity—even more prominent than pleasure reading in terms of time devoted to it. Drama is easily my favorite (especially the BBC serializations on the order of *The Forsythe Sage, The Early Churchills,* or *The Pallisers*—some of which we saw as U.S. imports, some during our Oxfords visits), but I also enjoy the spy series (*Secret Agent, Man from Uncle*) and detective series (*Cannon, Ironside*). Then too we maintain an interest in the more traditional art forms as perennial season subscribers to the Pittsburgh Symphony and the Pittsburgh Opera Society.

A brief further word regarding my development as a philosopher. For a long time my work in this field followed the wind-drift of inspiration and interest. I would become intrigued by some issue, have an idea about it, and work it through to some reasonable conclusion. As a result my earlier productions—though manifestly competent—have the somewhat disconnected and scattered aspect of a series of *pièces d' occasion*. As I think of it from this perspective, it astounds me that I did not hit my stride as a systematic philosopher at work on coherently connected topics until the age of nearly forty. Since I had found my way to philosophy well before I was twenty, and had earned the Ph.D. at the tender age of twenty-two, it has never occured to me to think of myself as a late bloomer. And yet I have come to the reluctant recognition that only during my forties—when mathematicians and physicists are often already past their productive prime—did I begin to turn out the sort of substantial philsosphical work that can, even remotely, lay claim to some scintilla of significance.

Thirteen

Retrospect: 1975
(Age 47)

THIS BOOK must stop, despite the continuation of life's steady flow in interesting new developments. Among these was the birth of Catherine Ann Rescher in April of this year (1975), enriching our progeny with a feminine dimension. New intellectual horizons have also opened up. *Methodological Pragmatism* (completed in 1974) awakened a concern for the evolutionary dimension of human knowledge. And *Scientific Progress* (begun in 1974) furthered my interest in the historical dynamics of the growth of science and technology—a development stimulated by rereading *The Education of Henry Adams*. Yet, though a life story written in the midst of events does not end, it must be brought to a close, lest it metamorphose from an autobiography into a diary.

What then, of a synoptic overall assessment? Aristotle says that one cannot tell whether a life is genuinely satisfying until after this life has ended. And this is basically correct. As long as life continues, the prospect of an all-spoiling catastrophe is everpresent. Still, however vulnerable a judgment made in mid-journey may be to being upset by unforeseen developments, some attempt in this direction seems called for.

There is first of all, the fact that my life has unfolded during an era of war. My impressionable teens were lived in the shadow of World War II. My young manhood traversed the time of the Korean War, which occurred during my twenties, and saw many of my contemporaries killed or wounded. The Vietnam War crept along its malign path during my 35-45 decade. All these conflicts touched my life in different ways, but most fortunately none prevented its running a relatively normal and undisturbed course. Living in an era of war, I have been able to grow up, marry, raise a family, and develop a professional career in a manner largely untouched by these cataclysms. I have dared to try to live a peaceful and productive life in an uncertain and destructive world—and think myself extraordinarily fortunate that this has been possible.

As I review the three decades of my adult life in writing these pages, the question inevitably arises: "Am I content with the course of things?" I feel there is no alternative but to give an affirmative answer. On the personal side, my wife, my children, and my friends are a source of much happiness for me. And I enjoy my professional life thoroughly, and derive satisfaction from its varied activities: writing, teaching, lecturing. The chance to work at a subject of such inherent fascination as philosophy is of inestimable value to me. A person who can find constant pleasure in living through his allotted role in life's drama is lucky indeed. I do not say this with smug self-satisfaction, but with genuine amazement at my undeserved good fortune.

I would not deny that on occasion I have done things that I regret—acts of thoughtlessness or unkindness, deeds done or things said in moments of impatience or irritation. But I have never idly and malicioulsy inflicted injury on another: my main faults have been those of thoughtlessness rather than of malevolence. (If the newspapers can be trusted, I have not sinned very much as the world goes nowadays.) Still, these errata—such as they are—are my sins, and it is only proper for me to feel ashamed of them, as I indeed am. I shall certainly not catalogue them, but it would be fatuous to omit an explicit avowal that I have my full share of human failings. I want to stress that, content though I am with my *fate*, I am far from being altogether satisfied with *myself*. For one thing, I certainly would like to be more companionable and outgoing, instead of being rather shy and reserved and self-contained. But one does not select one's personality. One discovers gradually and partially what it is, and, for the most part, learns to live with it—though perhaps one may, here and there, manage to effect some (generally small) improvement.

Both as a person and as a philosopher I have generally gone my own way—without much regard to current trends and fashions. The editor of a scholarly journal soon learns that one simply cannot please everyone. But it is a hard lesson to learn that one can offend people—deeply and mortally—not necessarily by *doing* anything, but merely by what one is, by *being* a person of a certain sort. There is, as Spinoza clearly saw, something deep in each of us that wants and needs others to be like ourselves, and failure to answer to this need in others is readily taken by them as a personal affront. All the same, with regard to the petty conflicts and intrigues astir in any professional community, I have generally taken the olympian view that life is too short—and work too important.

One characteristic aspect of my outlook on life is the substantial irrelevance for me of the *avant garde* thinking and the sophisticated cant of the day. A great part of the productions of "twentieth century culture" in the field of art, literature, and ideas strikes me as rubbish. My ruling interests, tastes, and values are largely those of an earlier era. Most of the books I value (historical works aside) and most of the thinking I esteem, were available in the antedeluvian days preceding the First World War.

In philosophy, too, most "modern thinking" leaves me cold. My allegiances and doctrinal sympathies lie with the great figures of the past—although the intellectual tools I use in argumentation and analysis are those of the present. It would be a caricature—with its typical mixture of truth and falsity due to exaggeration—to say that much of my work in philosophy represents an attempt to deal with philosophical issues of my grandfather's day with the approaches and methods of my contemporaries. (The value of the history of philosophy is—as I see it—much heightened by the fact that so much contemporary work in the field is just plain dull.)

To be sure, a thinker may well pay a penalty for such lack of trendiness—by not being *of* the time, he may fail to be *for* the time as well. But then it seems to me that a serious philosopher cannot ever truly be a "child of his time." He lives too much in the thought-world of other days, of Plato and Aristotle, Descartes and Leibniz, Kant and Hegel, Mill and Peirce. His co-workers are not his contemporaries at all, but the great thinkers of days past who have brought grist to his mill. Like most scholars in humanistic fields, a philosopher is fundamentally a member of his intellectual tradition and only superficially a member of his own biological generation.

The demands of the work are such that one cannot be a philosopher but a few hours each day—perhaps four or five at the very most. The rest of the time one is an ordinary person—husband, father, citizen, colleague, teacher, editor, administrator, or whatever—filling one's day with the ordinary activities of workaday existence. And the issues of one's *happiness* in life rests ultimately on these, the ordinary-life concerns that affect all people. The teaching of Epicurus was not far off the mark: the surest path to contentment lies in schooling oneself to take pleasure in the commonplace and prosaic stuff that comprises the fabric of everyday life.

In conducting life's affairs I have by and large been a rather conventional person conducting a rather conventional existence. By nature I tend to be not so much a conservative as a conservationist. My concern for preserving the good is more intense than that for remedying the bad. I can suffer fools—readily, even if not gladly—but towards bohemians I feel an instinctive antipathy.

I have nothing but contempt for those who expect the world to rearrange itself for their convenience and to reshape its whole system to facilitate their eccentricities. "If you want to 'step out of line,' then be prepared to accept the penalty without whining about it" has always seemed to me to be perfectly reasonable advice. I am not saying that the rules are perfect—far from it. But I tend to dislike those who want them changed simply for *their own* convenience, rather than on the basis of a disinterested and realistic view of the general good. I do not care for those who think and act as though the rules were made for other people, and have always detested the Bloomsbury Syndrome—the penchant of intellectuals to think themselves a superior breed exempt from the rules and proprieties that hold for lower-cast mortals. The Bloomsbury people had no resistance to the virus of the dangerous delusion that the world revolved about themselves—they smugly mistook their narrow and pampered world for the *real* world.[43] Among human failings, I find more tolerable those that reflect self-doubt than those that reflect arrogance. (As a person, I much prefer Hamlet to Faust.)

Over the years I have managed to accomplish various things in philosophy in which I take satisfaction. In early 1975, the editors of the big German encyclopaedia *Brockhaus* decided to include a short article on me, and invited me to indicate what I saw as my main professional contributions. I listed the following in reply: (1) The elaboration of a system of idealistic philosophy within the framework of the analytical tradition; (2) The development of a theory of inductive reasoning and scientific method based on the coherence theory of truth; (3) Contributions to the systematization of various philosophically oriented applications of symbolic logic (modal logic, many-valued logic, temporal logic, the logic of assertion, and others); (4) Contributions to the development and criticism of utilitarian ethics (especially in relation to distributive justice); (5) The rediscovery of the work of medieval Arabic logicians on the theory of temporal modality. It is a reputable record for someone still in his forties.

Lord knows, I have had my share of discouragements and disappointments. Consider one small example. I once entertained hopes of being invited to write the article on *mantiq* (= logic) for the new edition of the *Encyclopedia of Islam* that is now in progress, feeling that I have done more—and more interesting—work on Arabic logic than anybody else at this stage. Still, this invitation never materialized, perhaps because of the professional cliquishness of Islamists towards an outsider. Viewed with detachment such disappointments may seem small, but one does not feel them any less keenly for that—though to be sure, success in some areas is an anodyne for the pain of defeat in others. In any case, I have never allowed this sort of thing to affect my positive outlook and my determination "to get on with the work." Confident in my own mind that my philosophical efforts, whatever their shortcomings, have a core of merit and creativity, I have become independent of a need for approval. (Though I readily confess that whatever words of praise have come my way have always been welcome.) One of the tremendous advantages of being a scholar is that, unless one makes oneself a hostage to others by seeking their approbation, one need labor to please no one but oneself.

At any rate, I have managed to accomplish a good deal by way of publication. The over-all picture here is presented in the accompanying Table 1. (I hope that this Trollopian touch will be pardoned in a Trollope admirer.)

None of my contemporary colleagues in philosophy have written so prolifically. To be sure, from a material standpoint the result is distinctly unimpressive. If one excepts the *Introduction to Logic* textbook, the yield of the remaining 22 volumes averages some 2,000 copies sold and roughly $850 in royalties produced. A philosopher would certainly be ill advised to try to earn his bread with his pen. (As a supplement to an academic salary, the added income of roughly $2,500 per year was, however, not unwelcome.)

Why then all of these books?—to return to the question posed at the outset. At first there was, no doubt, a mixture of motives—self-education, the wish to "make a contribution," and perhaps some yearning for recognition as well. These factors initially led me into authorship, but gradually there was a change—the hardening of habit, the settling into a certain pattern of life, the process of becoming someone who writes philsophical books. The best answer I can give to the question is simply that a slow evolution saw my emergence as a habitual—even *addictive*—writer. In the course of time the writing of philosophical books became my avocation as well as my work and *Nulla dies sine linea* ("No day without a line") my motto.

Philosophical books are written for a wide variety of reasons: to dispel ignorance, to impress a faceless "them," to spread a gospel, to *épater les bourgeois*, and so on. Perhaps the most prominent reason is "to let off steam," to strike out at something that seems to us foolish or perverse. None of these were operative in my case. With

Table 1
THE RESULTS OF PUBLICATIONS THROUGH 1975

	Title	Publisher	Publication Date	Copies Sold	Royalties Paid
1.	Al-Farabi Bibliography	Pitt Press	1962	610	$ 40
2.	Al-Farabi's Short Commentary	Pitt Press	1963	960	180
3.	Intro. to Logic	St. Martins	1964	17,710	13,470
4.	Al-Kindi Bibliography	Pitt Press	1964	510	0
5.	Studies in Arabic Logic	Pitt Press	1964	860	290
6.	Development of Arabic Logic	Pitt Press	1964	1,020	250
7.	Hypothetical Reasoning	North Holland	1965	1,503	410
8.	Logic of Commands	Routledge & Kegan Paul	1966	3,320	290
9.	Galen and the Syllogism	Pitt Press	1966	850	0
10.	The Philos. of Leibniz	Prentice Hall	1967	5,960	1,490
11.	Distributive Justice	Bobbs Merrill	1967	5,390	1,730
12.	Temporal Modalities	Reidell	1967	1,038	300
13.	Studies in Arabic Philos.	Pitt Press	1968	890	610
14.	Topics in Philos. Logic	Reidel	1968	1,430	1,610
15.	Topics in Philos. Analysis	Pitt Press	1969	1,150	1,360
16.	Intro. to Value Theory	Prentice Hall	1969	6,470	1,780
17.	Many-valued Logic	McGraw-Hill	1969	1,540	1,500
18.	Scientific Explanation	Free Press	1970	2,010	1,690
19.	Temporal Logic	Springer	1971	1,260	1,040
20.	Welfare	Free Press	1972	2,030	1,200
21.	Coherence Theory of Truth	Clarendon Press	1973	1,730	1,650
22.	Conceptual Idealism	Blackwells	1973	910	460
23.	The Primacy of Practice	Blackwells	1973	940	470
	Totals			60,100	$31,880

me, one idea unfolded into another in a natural sequence of events, and writing was a way of working out ideas—a mode of learning. The evolution of my work is thus in large measure a matter of tracing out the half-formed implications of my own writings, a process of an increasingly explicit development of what was implicit before. The recognition of the limitations and imperfections of my earlier performances has acted as a constant incentive to their extension and improvement. This endows my over-all work with an *exfoliating* character, akin to biological growth, with later stages giving a more elaborate—and in some ways altered—structure and content to the earlier ones. Ideas (like books) take on a life of their own, and frequently one that lies only very partially in control of their nominal "author."

The pattern of my writing has had a cyclic structure, working in one area for a time, and then a second, and then a third, finally making my way round to the first again. In this way it has proved possible for me to keep up with a number of topics, managing (I hope) to strike a reasonable balance between superficiality and narrowness. A good philosopher, it seems to me, must be many-sided because the impetus to philosophizing is ultimately a search for systematic principles underlying the jumbled profusion of phenomena.

But what of that slippery issue of "success"? As I write these words, I am a man in his middle 40's—his productive prime. My professional career has unfolded with remarkable smoothness: a Ph.D. at 22 years, a full professorship at 33, the editorship of a major journal at 35, soon followed by a University Professorship and the achievement of substantial roles in various professional societies. In strictly careerist terms, I have come far: the secretaryship of a major international professional organization (the International Union of History and Philosophy of Science), membership in the major international academy of the profession (the Institut International de Philosophie), repeated invitations to lecture at Oxford, an honorary doctorate, and the incumbency of a distinguised professorial chair. Such tokens of "professional recognition" as can still come my way cannot add much to those I have already enjoyed.

Yet all this is essentially irrelevant for what has become the fundamental issue of my professional life. Many productive years presumably still stand before me, and the real question is: Just how far can I go, not in such careerist terms, but as a contributor to the work of philosophy itself? In each generation, only a modest proportion of philosophy professors manage to make some mark on the development of their subject—to effect some difference in the way in which, eventually, at least some of its practitioners do some of their work. The big question, as I see it, is whether—given health and luck—I have what it takes to establish myself as a philosopher belonging to this small but worthy band of significant contributors. Insofar as I am an ambitious person, it is in this particular direction that my ambition lies. This may well be a misguided, but it is surely not an ignoble aspiration. At any rate, I feel I have the capability within me, and if the realization of this felt promise eludes me for reasons of my own fault (rather than, say, because I am removed from this arena of action by a falling meteorite) then—quite regardless of any other "success"—I shall have failed by the one standard I myself accept as valid.

Gradually, I have acquired the vision of a system of philosophy geared to the idealistic tradition from Leibniz and Berkeley through Kant to Hegel and Peirce, with the German idealists on the left side, the English Hegelians on the right, and the American pragmatists to the front. (Subconsciously, perhaps, my being a German-American Anglophile is at work in motivating this fusion of traditions.) It has become my life's task—my "mission," if you will—to proceed with the exposition and elaboration of this philosophical perspective of a pragmatical idealism or idealistic pragmatism. The aim is to become clear about the import and the credentials of various sorts of human knowledge—above all in the sciences, in everyday life, and in philosophical reflection itself. The adequate comprehension of the character of these various realms of inquiry—especially of their mutual interrelationships—is the formative purpose of the enterprise. The system as I see it in my mind's eye is a substantial structure combining historical elements from the idealistic and pragmatic traditions with various original moves—a structure embodying traditional materials, but built up with contemporary tools of logical and conceptual analysis. Whether I shall have the requisite health, staying power, and creative impetus to carry this project to a reasonable state of completion, and how it will be received if and when completed, remain the big open questions of my professional life. This story thus ends *in medias res*, in the middle act of a life-drama that remains to be played out amidst the pervasive contingency of human affairs.

But "no man knoweth the hour . . ." What if my life were to end here and now? For one thing, I would not feel that I had lost out on a great deal. It has long struck me that there is a crucial difference between one's *chronological* life (in terms of mere years) and one's *cognitive* life (in terms of experience and learning), the latter being measured essentially in terms of the *logarithm* of the former. Experience, after all, is cumulative, and each new installment can only add its merely marginal increment of new lessons to the great body of what has gone before.[44] The resulting picture is set out in Table 2.

At this reckoning, someone who dies at my present age has lived only some two-thirds of his expectable *chronological* life, but has lived almost 90% of his expectable *cognitive* life. Accordingly, I feel that I have already gained the great bulk of what life has to give in terms of its lessons and experiences, its joys and its usable sorrows. To die now would not be to lose out on all that much. (To be sure, I would, abstractly speaking, greatly welcome the chance to acquire the rest, however modest its scope.)

Were my life cut short, one principal regret would be the loss of work. I feel that there are still a score or so of good books left in me. I would be saddened by the thought that the philosophical edifice I leave behind would be so grossly incomplete in relation to what I sense it could, would, and should be. Above all, however, would be the loss of familial companionship of my marriage with Dorothy and

Table 2
COGNITIVE VS. CHRONOLOGICAL AGE

Chronological Age	log(Age)	log(Age) as % of log 80	Cognitive Age (on basis of 80 year lifespan)
5	0.70	37	30
10	1.00	53	42
20	1.30	68	54
30	1.48	78	62
40	1.60	84	67
50	1.70	89	71
60	1.78	94	75
70	1.85	97	78
80	1.90	100	80

of the chance to see my children grow and develop. I reckon high the fortunes of those who live to see the children of their children.

I often brood about the fate of my children. Not that they have yet given me grounds for worry. But I want very much that they should make something of themselves in the world and yet be both good and happy into the bargain. The parents of children certainly give hostages to fate. Yet, even from a purely selfish standpoint, children are a great and good thing—with advantages greatly outweighing whatever sacrifices and anxieties their presence entails. They give one a stake in the future of the race. Without children, life is an empty and solitary affair—like playing chess with oneself. They add an element of interest and excitement that no substitute can adequately replace. Then, too, children provide a consideration which helps to make life meaningful—that there is someone to whom it matters over the long run what sort of person one is. And, of course, all of the egocentrism and "calculating" considerations are as nothing in the balance once the element of love and caring enters in.

Anyone who rightly reckons with the chilling insight that "You can't take it with you"—that we can carry exactly as little out of this world as we initially bring into it—is bound to recognize that it is right and proper to care for the quality of what one leaves behind. It gives me satisfaction to feel that I would leave a worthwhile legacy to my children: a caring nurture, a fairly good, or, at any rate, a not really bad example in the conduct of life, a modicum of financial security. Yet that possession which, more than any other, I would like to bequeathe to my children is one I cannot transmit to them, namely, good luck.

Kant repeatedly told his friends that no man in his senses would be prepared to live his life over again in exactly the same way. If the offer were made to me, I would not hesitate to accept it on these terms—though there are indeed many things that I would *prefer* to see altered. If the writing of these pages has done any one thing, it has helped me to realize just how fortunate a person I really am.

PART II

Ongoing Journey (1985)

TRANSITION (1985)

Two reasons impel me to take pen in hand once more to continue the story after an interval of ten years. One is the urging of some friends for an updating of the account. (They probably spoke only out of politeness, but I have been naive—or vain?—enough to take them at face value.) The other, doubtless more cogent, reason is that the old rationale still holds good, albeit in a lessened degree—the wish to preserve for my children some record of their family during the time when they themselves were too young for a knowledge of its affairs. Even in so quiet a life as ours has been, things do not quite stand still, and there have been various developments that deserve to be added to the record.

Fourteen

Squirrel Hill: 1975-1980

(Age 47-52)

IN THE later 1970's we moved our domicile from the rather suburban Highland Park district of Pittsburgh to the Squirrel Hill section, which is a small town unto itself, to all intents and purposes. As our boys, Mark and Owen, settled in at St. Edmund's Academy, our life had became increasingly three-concerned—home in Highland Park, work in Oakland, school in Squirrel Hill. The starting and ending times for the pre-school and regular school sessions were out of phase, however, greatly complicating the matter of transportation. Then too, after Catherine's arrival in 1975, the Sheridan Avenue house provided tight quarters. And so we now established contact with some realtors and began house hunting in a slow but steady manner. In the spring of 1977, one of the real estate agents with whom we were in touch drew our attention to the house at 5818 Aylesboro Avenue. Only two blocks away from St. Edmund's, we passed it frequently when taking the boys to school. We liked the house and arranged to buy it—delaying transfer of possession until our return from Oxford that September.

The Aylesboro Avenue house was a substantial brick residence, a typical townhouse for an American family of the pre-World-War I era. With ten principal rooms located on three floors, it had been in the possession of the Reismeyer family, from whom we bought it, since its construction in 1915. (The building-lot had been given to Mr. Reismeyer's mother by her father as a wedding present.) Built in the solid old Pittsburgh manner—with interesting woodwork and stained glass, it combined considerable charm with substantial comfort—as well as convenience because of its close proximity to the crux of Squirrel Hill's shopping area at Forbes and Murray Avenues. It is a comfortable family house and we settled in easily and happily. The location is most convenient for school, shopping, and the varied offerings of Squirrel Hill Village. And the daily drive from home to the University through the seasonal changes of Schenley Park is every bit as much a pleasure as a necessity.

Throughout the later 1970's we continued our annual summer migrations to Oxford. (It is remarkable that, at this writing in 1985, we have been proprietors of the Cunliffe Close house, bought in 1973, for longer than any other I have ever owned.) These Oxford visits have run a pretty uniform course—some lectures in the Sub-Faculty of Philosophy during Trinity Term (which runs until the end of June), a brief lecture visit to Germany or Austria during July or August, and some local tourism by way of day excursions. Then too there are such recurrent rituals as shopping in London, showing Pittsburgh visitors through Blenheim Palace, taking in a Shakespeare play at Stratford, and antiquing in the Cotswolds. A mixture of novelty and fixed routine, our Oxford visits have invariably been times of enjoyment and restoration.

Those Oxford summers offer a foretaste of retirement—I have no employment, no formal duties, no local obligations! As a "man of leisure" I can pursue my own activities at my own pace—which, for me, means a good deal of miscellaneous writing. Oxford gives me the chance to look at life as it goes on about me with a certain distancing: we live in the community but yet are not of it. This sort of disengaged existence also makes it possible to take a more detached and reflective view of one's own life, a circumstance not altogether without value for a philosopher.

Since we arrive well before the end of the English school year, our children also have some Oxford schooling. All of them attended the Squirrel School at the intersection of Woodstock and Rawlinson roads under Miss Bell's tutelage. Mark then attended the Dragon School for two summers, but subsequently changed over to Christ Church Cathedral School. Both boys then attended this institution year on year for the summer term—thanks to the cooperation of Hugh MacDonald, the benevolent headmaster—until their eventual graduation in the early 1980's. Catherine completed her Oxford schooling at age nine at St. Aloysius R.C. School on Woodstock Road. These schools not only taught the children various useful things but also provided them with friends to supplement their neighborhood playmates from "the close."

In early July of 1978, a month or so after we had settled into the Cunliffe Close house in Oxford, my mother left Oxford for a vacation in Freudenstadt in the Black Forest area of southern Germany where she had often visited with my father before the War. A few days after arriving there, she suffered a stroke that soon issued in unconsciousness. By the time I reached her it was already too late for any contact, and she quickly and quietly slid into death. I felt her loss deeply. Mother was my last surviving ancestor, and now on the eve of my 50th birthday—ready or not—I myself entered the ranks of "the old generation." It is never easy to lose a parent, and I still miss both of mine very much. After one attains the teen-age years, one no longer resorts to parents as confidants and consultants—one is too much concerned to assert one's independence from that sort of thing. But simply the knowledge that they are there, and available in time of need, is a comfort. And this is particularly so when those parents are people of as much savvy and common sense as mine were. I can well understand why the elderly are inclined to "live in the past," seeing that it is peopled with those one loves.

Throughout these years I continued to live in the past in another way as well, continuing my desultory but devoted reading of history and biography—perhaps some twelve or fifteen books a year. I made a point of reading material in German, French, and

Latin as well as English to keep my linguistic equipment from getting too rusty. The Japanese attack on Pearl Harbor was one topic on which I read a good deal. (It has always fascinated me. Being thirteen at the time, I remember well the events of that bleak December of 1941 when the affairs of my new-found world were revolutionized by America's entry into that assemblage of cataclysmic events conveniently grouped together under the label of "World War Two.") During this period I also read my way through all ten volumes of the California Press edition of Samuel Pepys' *Autobiography* and read huge quantities of historical and biographical material, particularly relating to the political and cultural history of England after the 18th Century.

During the latter 1970's our family situation assumed on a changed aspect. There were now three children each of whom makes a characteristic contribution to the fabric of the family: Mark as thoughtful of people and rather serious and intense, Owen as more easy-going and adaptive, Catherine, yet only five, as sociable and people-oriented. The children now began to be enjoyable not just as children but as people too.

In the winter of 1978, I decided to join the Pittsburgh Athletic Association—a club located across Fifth Avenue from Pitt's Cathedral of Learning, equipped with extensive facilities for exercise and athletics. The social side of the club had little interest for me, but its exercise facilities were something else. At mid-day I could cross the road, change into jogging clothes, run for a mile or so, shower, lunch, and be back at my desk—all within the confines of a single hour. For years now (1985) I have done this routinely for three days each week when I am in town—to the benefit not only of my physical condition, but also of my spirits—and my intellect as well, since I generally manage to read a page or so of Cicero at the lunch-table. An increasing facility at Latin has been one of my real satisfactions during my 50's, and I try never to let a day pass without at least reading a Latin paragraph or two from some Latin author, ancient, medieval, or modern.

Such a period of retreat from the world in the midst of one's workday is a useful balm to one's spirit, particulary when one is involved in administrative duties. When John Cooper left for Princeton in the spring of 1980 thus vacating its chairmanship, the Philosophy Department was plunged into a management crisis. At the urging of the department's Executive Committee, I agreed to fill in for one year, until some longer term arrangement became possible. I did this reluctantly, however, hesitating partly because of the inevitable interference with my own work, and in part because it struck me as anomalous that a University Professor—who *ex officio* stands outside the departmental framework—should play an administrative departmental role. Still, the Department that had been my professional "home" for some twenty years was in a bind, and I swallowed my reluctance in the interests of the common good.

During the period of my chairmanship (1980-81) I concentrated my attention on matters of staffing and personnel. And I managed to achieve three substantial successes in this sphere: I initiated and conducted the negotiations with the affluent mother of our late colleague Alan Ross Anderson which eventually resulted in her endowing a professorship in his name; I carried through to completion the process, inaugurated in my predecessor's administration, of recruiting Wesley and Merrilee Salmon to the university; I arranged for four promotions in the Department (Robert Brandom and John Haugeland to associate professorships, Alexander Nehamas to a full professorship, and Kurt Baier's redesignation as Distinguished Service Professor). Taking into account Nuel Belnap's eventual designation as Anderson professor, I thus succeeded during my brief tenure of the chairmanship to arrange for the promotion of one-quarter of my departmental colleagues. Seeing that the recognition of talent is the foundation of a good and happy department, I feel that my brief time of office was a very constructive period. During the next few years, serious but unsuccessful efforts were made to lure each of "my promotees" away from Pitt. My labors towards making these valued colleagues feel appreciated by the university were, as I see it, an important positive contribution to the department's continuity.

I was glad, however, that the period of my departmental chairmanship was mercifully brief. I am not so constituted as to get great satisfaction out of an administrative role. Dealing with them in a way that made me responsible for accommodating their interests did not always manifest my colleagues in the most favorable light. But the helpfulness of Marj Boyle, the Departmental Secretary, and the supportive efficiency of Linda Butera whom I brought along from the *American Philosophical Quarterly* to be my personal assistant certainly helped to make the job a more pleasant one.

One curious later development marred this period however. During my departmental chairmanship, one of my younger departmental colleagues (who shall remain nameless here) had vehemently opposed the appointment of the Salmons on grounds of Merrilee's involvement therein, whose abilities and merits he disdained. When this appointment nevertheless materialized, he was furious with those of his colleagues he held responsible for this supposed outrage—virtually the whole rest of the department, but especially the "ringleaders," myself preeminent among them since I had conducted the negotiations on the Department's behalf. He withdrew from Philosophy, ultimately transferring to another department. But an opportunity for creating mischief soon presented itself—this time in connection with my directorship of the Philosophy of Science Center. He had been a member of the Center for some time, but the term of his membership had expired, and the formalities of its renewal dragged out over some months, as administrative processes in academia often will. He chose to represent this delay as an aggression on my part, and launched complaints in various forums against my supposed assault on his rights and privileges. On three occasions over the next year I had to defend myself against his charges of administrative malfeasance—before a group of Center members, before a board of inquiry appointed by the Provost, and before a subcommittee of the Senate Committee on Academic Freedom and Tenure. My accuser obtained no satisfaction in any forum, since on each occasion I had little difficulty in rebutting his accusations of wrongdoing. His forays had no ultimate effect except to display the absurdity of his charges before an ever-widening group of colleagues.

All in all, however, things were brightening up at the university. A great change came over the climate of academia by the late 70's in comparison with the situation that had prevailed a decade earlier. It was a time of "normalization" of return to a more conservative and tradition-geared outlook. As the students' mode of dress became less exotic, so their behavior towards their seniors became less truculent. They even occasionally thanked one for services rendered rather than brusquely taking them for granted as no more than their due. Students—the graduate students especially—were now more serious in their studies and more friendly, alike towards their fellows and their elders. The era of neurotic distrust and baseless hostility to the older generation slipped unregretted into the past, and it became customary once more to proceed in a spirit of cordial collaboration—a development which redounded to the benefit of all concerned. This development pleased me particularly because I always liked teaching and enjoyed my personal interactions with students—particularly at the more advanced levels where a common interest in philosophical matters could serve as a bridge across the divide of years.

In politics my position has always seemed to me to be rather right of center. But with the sharply rightist turn of American political opinion in the Reagan era, my political persuasion took on a middle-of-the-road status once more. It is grounded in a deeply "bourgeois" attitude that regards the productive role of the middle class as the backbone of the country.

In a very small way I too have been an entrepreneur. I had launched the *American Philosophical Quarterly*—the APQ as it has come to be known in the profession—in the early 1960's as part of the ongoing expansion of academic activity in the U.S. after the end of the Korean War. Initially the University of Pittsburgh Press had been its publisher, but retrenchment in its activities in the wake of the University's financial crisis in 1965 led to its total withdrawal from journal publication. The journal then emigrated to Blackwell's in Oxford, where it flourished under the astute care of Jim Feather, the managing director of the firm. But after Jim moved to the U.S. in the late 70's, our relationship with Blackwell's deteriorated, and I resolved to repatriate the publication. It proved possible to work out a suitable arrangement with the Philosophy Documentation Center at Bowling Green State University in Ohio for their cooperation in the publication of the journal, beginning in 1981. The new arrangements with Bowling Green have been eminently satisfactory and the journal continues to thrive in a gratifying manner. I have always found the people at the "Doc Center" to be pleasant and cooperative in every way. Dick Lineback, its enterprising director, and Jerry Slivka, its business manager were good colleagues from the start and eventually became good friends as well.

My own philosophical research and writing continued to evolve in a constructive direction as well, with each successive year bringing along its quota of one or two books. I find it particularly helpful to set up at the end of each work-day the particular tasks that need to be accomplished on the next. Morning-worker that I am, this makes it possible to get off to a good start—without the impediment of having to stop and ponder at the very outset about what it is that one has to do next.

Arising sometime between six and six-thirty a.m., I manage to put in around an hour's work at writing before anyone else in the family gets up. But throughout the day I write in snatches, seldom spending more than one hour at any one sitting, and often just thirty or forty minutes. (Perhaps with age my attention span has grown shorter?) These brief writing-sessions will be interspersed with various other activities. But by the time I retire for my sleep-preparatory reading at around ten-thirty or eleven, I have managed to put in several hours of creative effort. To be sure, most of my work-time goes not to writing but to the more routine tasks of academic work—correspondence, editing, preparing for or engaging in teaching, etc.

I am particularly proud of my 1978 book on *Scientific Progress*, which argues (in what I deemed to be an original and rather insightful way) that the increasing technology-intensiveness, and thus the increasing costliness, of modern natural science is an inevitable feature of the problem-situation of scientific research. Such a use of philosophical perspectives to gain insight into a crucially important intellectual and practical area of human endeavor strikes me as particularly useful. I believe it was this book, perhaps via its subsequent German translation, that was primarily instrumental in my being awarded the Alexander von Humboldt humanities prize in 1983, and if this was indeed so, it represents one of those rather rare instances where what a creative scholar sees among his best work is also so deemed by others.

In any case, it seems fair to say that I have continued to grow and thrive intellectually because (and I really think *mainly* because) of my continued writing of books. These have given me constant occasion to learn new material, and extend my thinking into new directions. Setting oneself to meet new challenges is unquestionably something that makes life intellectually more interesting and rewarding. This is what my books have done for me and I am much indebted to them for it (to put it somewhat quaintly).

If I had to choose one key word to characterize the 1975-80 quinquennium, I would opt for *consolidation*. This period saw the continuation and accentuation of various well-entrenched aspects of my make-up. (At fifty, the leopard does not change his spots!) It was a time when my activities as a paterfamilias, as a teacher and scholar, and as a peripatetic academic with a variety of intellectual interests all extended themselves further along firmly preestablished directions.

Fifteen

Wanderings: 1981-85
(Age 53-57)

THE PHILOSOPHY of Science Center at the University of Pittsburgh dates from the 1960-61 academic year, which saw the arrival at Pitt of Adolf Grunbaum at its start and myself at its end, with Adolf serving as its Director and I as Associate Director during the early years. Eventually, as my term as the Philosophy Department's chairman was nearing its end in the spring of 1981, it was proposed that I should assume the directorship of the Center. I was reluctant to do so because of the primacy of my committment to research (and small enthusiasm for administrative work), but once again there were no easy alternative, and so my colleagues managed to prevail on me to serve in the interest of the common cause.

The Center now stood on the threshhold of a new phase of expanded activity made possible by a grant from the R. K. Mellon Foundation. Heretofore the Center had enjoyed the benefit of occasional postdoctoral visitors, but now it embarked on a systematic program to bring ten or more senior visitors to our campus each year, with at least five or six of these "Visiting Fellows" resident during every semester. This transformed the Center into a small-scale "Institute for Advanced Studies" in the general area of philosophy of science. Such an accession of philosophical talent, over and above the regular establishment of the departments of Philosophy and of History and Philosophy of Science, renders the University of Pittsburgh one of the most exciting places for philosophical study in the world, providing us with an impressive community of researchers in this field.

The Center's program of Visiting Fellowships created a change in my personal life in bringing to Pittsburgh a steady stream of old and new friends. I had known some of these visitors casually for many years (Joseph Pitt and Rolf George, for example), but others (Aristides Baltas, Paul Humphreys, Klaus Mainzer, Marcello Pera, Lorenz Puntel, Oswald Schwemmer, and Robert Toretti) I now met for the first time. In addition, the visiting fellowship program gave me the chance to get to know more closely several colleagues whom I already knew well. Special mention is due to Timo Airaksinen of the University of Helsinki, who combines congeniality with personal warmth and philosophical dedication; Robert Almeder of Georgia State University, a philosopher of great human warmth and outgoing friendliness; George Gale of the University of Missouri, a colleague of outgoing geniality and keen philosophical enthusiasm; and Jürgen Mittelstrass of the University of Konstanz, a scholar of energy, ability, and great personal charm. This widened and deepened contact with colleagues from many countries has been a source of great pleasure to me, for almost invariably our Center visitors have been not only able scholars but very nice people as well, and are not only colleagues but friends.

The directorship of the Center was made much easier for me through the aid of Linda Butera, whom I brought over from the Philosophy Department as my assistant. Her cheerfulness and efficiency—and her talent at being "mother hen" to the visiting fellows by solving their practical problems—has made managing the Center far more pleasant than it would otherwise have been.

With the Center's move from Thackeray-Mervis Hall to the Cathedral of Learning in the spring of 1984, we finally acquired quarters where our visitors could be accommodated in convenient proximity to the cognate academic departments. For me this move was a homecoming of sorts, since I now once again had an office on the 8th floor of the Cathedral, where my office had initially been when I came to Pitt almost a quarter-century before in 1961. (However, the Philosophy Department's move to the 10th floor of the Cathedral in 1982 had already returned my departmental office to this curious structure.)

December of 1985 saw a major conference to celebrate the 25th Anniversary of the Center. At the time of the anniversary, I enlarged the brief of Al Janis, who has been Associate Director for many years, and also brought my old friend Gerald Massey into the management of the operation as Associate Director for Academic Programs. Largely motivated by our enlarged activities, this augmented administration positions the Center for more extensive activities during its second quarter century.

One personally important eventuation was my formal reception into the Roman Catholic church in March of 1981. Since marrying Dorothy in 1968, I attended mass regularly and gradually slid into the status of an unofficial member of the congregation of the Oratory at the University of Pittsburgh. But Fr. William Clancy, the Provost of the Oratory, cast a friendly eye in my direction and encouraged me to formalize my status and offered his help in the process. And so in due course I enrolled in a faith which is not only personally congenial to me in its less authoritarian post-Vatican II conformation, but also makes for a united religious front within our family unit.

The children repeatedly ask, with ever-renewed puzzlement, "But dad, just what does a philosopher, do?" The answer is, basically, that he is a Cartesian *ego*—"a thing that thinks." His province is defined by the historic "big questions" of the nature of man, the character of our place in the universe, the ramifications of our interrelationships with one another, and the lessons of our experience in this "vale of tears." But of course while his fundamental concern is with these great matters, there is a vast proliferating host of increasingly localized and technical questions that must be addressed in order that one can properly deal with them. And it is largely with these more technical, subsidiary issues that philosophers nowadays deal (often, alas, forgetting in the excitement of their preoccupations to articulate those threads of linkage that bind their technical concerns to those great issues that constitute their reason for being.) The task of philosophy, then, is to clarify and sharpen our thinking about man's place in the world's scheme of things. Other branches of inquiry deal with matters of limited detail—the philosopher tries (or *should* try) to "put it all together"—to provide, as best he can, a look at "the big picture." To do this adequately, is, alas, a well-nigh impossible task, but here, as elsewhere in life, one ought simply do the best he can.

Throughout these years, Oxford continued to play an important role in our lives. We would migrate there annually in early June and remain until early September. I would usually give some lectures during Trinity Term and would then settle down to a mixture of research and tourism. Over time, a certain degree of local academic respectability has come my way—as Oxford lecturer, adjunct member of Corpus Christi College, and occasional reviewer for the *Times Literary Supplement.*.

Then too, I now began to make regular academic journeys from England to the Continent during the summers—especially to the German-speaking countries, where the academic year runs into mid-July. When in Germany I generally visit Hanover, that Mecca of Leibnizians. My Friends, Albert Heinekamp and Wilhelm Totok at the Nether-Saxon State Library are always most hospitable and keep me informed of the activities of the Leibniz Society. During this time too, I made something of a study of the history of Hanover in the time of Leibniz, among other things making my way through all four big volumes of Georg Schnath's *Geschichte Niedersachens: 1670-1814*. I also repeatedly visited Austria by way of participating in the annual Wittgenstein symposia at Kirchberg. In this way I have gradually broadened my acquaintanceship among European colleagues.

Attending professional meetings is a humbling but salutary experience. When anywhere from 300 to 3,000 professional colleagues are present, one realizes how small a fish in the pond one really is. Most work on issues one has never even touched oneself. And even those who work on one's own topics are often uninformed about one's work—let alone taking account of it in theirs! (I have long ago schooled myself to regard such failures as grounds for amusement rather than regret.) The chastening thought comes to mind that it would make little if any difference to one's profession if one vanished from the scene and one's work were "lost without trace." (The fact that others are in the same boat is of little consolation.) The most one can expect is the occasional encounter with someone who has profited from one's endeavors. And—alas, oh vanity!—how sweet it is to find that one has not labored entirely in vain.

With the passage of years, my philosophical work began to make a growing impact outside the U.S.A. The translation of some of my books into other languages was part effect and part cause of this development. *The Primacy of Practice* was published in Spanish in 1980 and by the time that *The Limits of Science* appeared in German translation in 1985, I had six books in print in languages other than English—including one (*Dialectics*) in Japanese. Discussions of my work now appeared in philosophical publications outside the English-language orbit with increasing frequency. Over the years I have been elected to several international academies: *The Institut Internationale de Philosophie* based in Paris since 1975, and the *Academie Internationale de Philosophie des Sciences* based in Brussels since 1984.

1983 brought a development that occasioned me great pleasure. The Alexander von Humboldt Foundation, which supports scholarship under the aegis of the German Federal Republic, awarded me its Humanities Research Prize. Some three or four of these are given internationally each year to humanistic scholars "in recognition of major research contributions in the humanities." This prize represents the closest approximation that we humanists have to the international Nobel prizes awarded to scientists (though is monetary dimension is substantially smaller). It carries with it an obligation to spend a period of time lecturing in German universities, and during 1984 I made several trips on the German lecture circuit, visiting universities in various parts of the country.

Of the various university towns I visited in Germany, I found Konstanz especially pleasant. The fact that Konstanz is an historically interesting and most scenically situated town certainly helps. But it is the human element that counts. The philosophy department of the university consists of colleagues who are not only highly able but personally most pleasant. A degree of personal collegiality prevails among philosophers there that is unmatched at any other German university I have visited. I am especially close to Jürgen Mittelstrass, whom I have known for a long time—and whom we tried unsuccessfully to lure to Pittsburgh on one occassion. Klaus Mainzer and Gereon Wolters are also among my particularly good friends there.

In consequence of this renewal of contact with Germany, I have resumed a much closer relationship with the use of the German language. My spoken German—which had been rusting away since my tenth or eleventh year—now received the benefit of extensive practice, and I now also began to do more reading in German than I had been accustomed to in recent years. To some extent my psychological outlook shifted as well, and I do not now see my German origins as belonging to the dead and buried past but rather as an enduring part of the fabric of my make-up. To be sure, I see myself as a "100% American," but as one who—like so many others—is the bearer of a national and cultural heritage in which he takes both interest and pride. In this regard, my preoccupation with the philosophies of Leibniz and of Kant—steadily maintained both on the side of teaching and on that of research—have provided a connecting bridge to the heritage of my ancestral country.

As I now think back over the twenty-five years of my association with the Philosophy Department at the University of Pittsburgh, one thing that strikes me is the stability of this work environment. Five of my twenty fellow professors there, a full quarter of them, have now been my colleagues and friends for twenty years or more: Adolf Grunbaum, Kurt Baier, Wilfrid Sellars, Nuel Belnap, and Richard Gale. This ongoing association represents a remarkable—and deeply appreciated—continuity and stability in a constantly changing world.

In surveys of quality in higher education, the Philosophy Department at Pitt nowadays scores in the top two or three. For the time being, at least, our reputation stands very high. Recognition of my own work has also continued to come my way. Honors bestowed on me include presidencies of the C.S. Peirce Society (1983), and the American Leibniz Society (1983-86). On various occasions my name has been put up in the contested elections of the larger philosophical societies (including Presidencies of our regional division of the American Philosophical Association, the Philosophy of Science Association, and the Metaphysical Society of America). But, for reasons already mentioned, I have never managed to succeed in such a contest and doubtless never shall.

Living in the "land of opportunity," an American academic confronts the question: "If you're so smart, why ain't you rich?" As of the time that I had my very first regular job—that meager instructorship in Princeton at the age of 23 in 1951—I have never suffered any lack of money and have always *felt* affluent. This is not because my resources were ample or my pay generous. Far from it! It was because I kept my wants modest and my expenditures small. Money is not important in itself—especially not for a philosopher!—but it has to be given some attention by those who have family responsibilities. The great thing is to have enough money to free one from worries about having too little and yet not so much as to lead one to worry about keeping it.

Over the years my financial condition improved markedly. It has always been my practice to "save for a rainy day"—to put by a bit from current university salary payments and—above all—to save the entire income from other resources—royalties, lecture honoraria, consulting fees, etc. By virtue of prudently conservative care, these savings have grown slowly but steadily. Only in recent years—with three children in private schools and family vacations becoming increasingly expensive—have I made some departure from this rigorous policy of savings. While I don't at all enjoy money management (philosophy is a lot more fun to think about), still I am not the sort of person who can walk away from responsibilities. And so like it or not I have had to become something of a financier.

Prudence and modesty alike combine to suggest the inadvisability of exposing our financial situation to "the envy or pity of strangers" (as Gibbon puts it). In this world, wealth is something relative; it's all a matter of whom one chooses to compare oneself with—whether prince or pauper. My own appraisal of my situation is this: that fortuitous circumstances have rendered me affluent to an extent that exceeds my (relatively modest) requirements—and perhaps my deserts. Yet the contingency of fate—the fragility of human arrangements for the good—can never wholly leave the mind of one who has, like myself, spent a part of his formative years in Nazi Germany. Amidst the most secure circumstances there is a low voice that whispers at the back of one's mind "Don't count on it! It could all come crashing down." It is, I suppose, a bit like surviving a dreadful fire or earthquake—worsened by the realization that catastrophes are caused not just by natural disasters but also by man's malice and folly.

But let me turn from such gloomy musings to the warmth of the domestic hearth and the affairs of my family. Both Mark and Owen had been attending St. Edmund's Academy in the Squirrel Hill section of Pittsburgh since their kindergarten days, and as the years passed by, we all became involved with the school—especially Dorothy who was a volunteer worker in its library and active in various PTA committees. St. Edmunds is unusual in that, being administered by a "corporation" made up of the parents of its current pupils, it also involves those parents in many aspects of the life of the school—ranging from transporting children on school excursions to organizing money raisers of ingenious and diversified kinds. In the course of time, I too became more involved in the school. I served on the search committee that recruited Sterling Miller in 1979 to serve as the splendid headmaster he has proved to be. I was elected to the board of trustees in 1980, and served as its Vice President during my second term (1983-85).

The main contribution I made to the life of the school in this connection was to serve as chairman of the committee that mobilized the decision to transform St. Edmunds from a boys school into a coeducational one and framed the policies and plans to put this change-over into effect. On close attention, it became clear to all concerned that no really constructive end was served by educating in a single-gender institution children of the impressionable years from three to thirteen who will have to go out to spend the rest of their lives in a two-gender world.

Having been a faculty member for almost all of my working life, it was interesting to see how the affairs of a school look "from the other side of the fence." Then too this was an occasion to get to know some interesting fellow Pittsburghers, such as my able board chairman David Smith, coming from walks of life removed from the academic—doctors, lawyers, bankers, and others of the "solid citizen" type who make a community hum.

But time marches on—and our children are all continuing to grow and develop. In the spring of 1983 Mark graduated from St. Edmunds. He is now (1985) an honors student at Central Catholic High School in Oakland, about to enter his junior year there, just sixteen years old and a bit taller than his father's six feet. He is currently passing through that "teen-ager" phase, which from a parent's point of view is surely the most trying phase of child-development. Owen (now fifteen) is also in the middle of this phase—though a bit less tryingly so, perhaps because, unlike Mark at his age, he has not yet "discovered girls." He is just starting his sophmore year at Shady Side Academy in distant Fox Chapel— described by one recent writer as "Pittsburgh's leading private day school,"[45] I know not with exactly what justification. He is performing pretty well in his studies, and also promises (once teen-agehood is safely traversed) to become a very fine young man. Cathy now aged ten, is an absolute delight in every way—thriving, vivacious, and thoroughly good natured. She has attended Ellis School in Shadyside since the first grade and is deservedly popular there. Educating three children in private-sector schools is not inexpensive (it presently absorbs roughly a quarter of my after-tax university paycheck). But it is worth every penny, since the atmosphere in these schools is more supportive than those in the public sector, so that academically minded parents have less of a struggle in counteracting unhelpful school influences.

As the children grew more mature, I found myself pushed increasingly into the parents' traditional dilemma—the tension between endeavoring to maintain control and simply "letting go"—between paternalistic interference "for their own benefit" and willingness to let them stand on their own feet. I am quite sure that I do not have the balance right. Yet not to worry. They are fine people, and I know in my heart of hearts that they will ultimately carve out a niche for themselves in the world. To be sure, it galls me when they don't "listen to reason" and accept parental direction in ways I know to be beneficial. But, alas, the lessons of life are ones that each person has to rediscover for himself—the extent to which we can transmit the instruction of hard-won experience to our progeny is very limited indeed. And so there are unquestionably times of annoyance and frustration during these years when the boys are passing through their teen-agehood with its skirmishes and uprisings. Fortunately, there are also those compensating times of love and fatherly communion.

In the earlier years of our marriage, we tended to take our week's midwinter vacation in Williamsburg in Virginia—a place I have really grown to love for its dedication to the excellences of a past era (a spirit that is bound to please someone dedicated to the history of thought). But in more recent years the children have yearned for "the beach," and so we have headed for Florida—Daytona or St. Petersburg. Everyone has a good time, except when they get too sunburned! A shady spot with book or workpad does just fine for me.

My television viewing has fallen casualty to increased activity on other fronts, reduced to something like one-third its former level. Partly this was because the newer programs appealed less to me as they became increasingly geared to the tastes of a juvenile audience. But the primary reason was the need to find some quiet time for my writing as the needs of the Center took up more of my office workday. Since I generally enjoy writing and actually find it relaxing, this exchange of television for work did not really exact a sacrifice.

One development of these years that has done much to brighten my life is the big change that has transpired in regard to Elizabeth. Virtually as of the day she moved away from home to live on-campus as an undergraduate at the University of Rochester in 1978, her relationship to me was revolutionized. She now became accessible, cordial, and downright friendly. In the summer of 1983 she even visited with us in Oxford, and we are now the best of friends. After completing her undergraduate studies at Rochester as an English major with much success, she made a false start at graduate studies, and "dropped out" for a while to become a substitute school-teacher. She is now back in graduate school in the English Department at Duke University in North Carolina, concentrating on the literature of the Victorian era, and doing very well indeed. Her general development, and in particular the turn-around of her relationship to me, has been among the really happy developments of the past decade.

In effect, I nowadays have four jobs: as teaching professor, as prolific author, as administrative director of the Philosophy of Science Center, and as managing editor of two professional journals. (All this in addition to responsibility for a family of five persons with two houses in different continents.) Someone less efficient and less organized than I could easily manage to make a full-time job out of each one of these tasks. Having already touched on the Center and on my writings, I shall confine my present comments to the other two jobs.

Thirty-five years—more than the one-third of a century generally reckoned as the span of human generation—have now elapsed since the time when I began my teaching career as Instructor in Philosophy at Princeton. Over that span of time one is bound to improve at a craft, and I am pretty sure that what I have lost in youthful ebullience has been compensated for by augmented competence. Certainly I enjoy teaching as much now as then—though I sometimes grumble about its getting in the way of my research. Though trite, it is nevertheless true to say that college professors are lucky to earn their living at something that is so enjoyable.

In terms of personal satisfaction, the journal editorships have also been well worthwhile. I speak in the plural, because with the success of the *American Philosophical Quarterly* I was emboldened to start a cognate publication focusing on the history of philosophy, the *History of Philosophy Quarterly*, publishing its first issue in 1984, just on the 20th anniversary of the launching of the APQ. This journal too has got off to a good start, attracting some 400 subscribers already in its second year. While the APQ has of course had to subsidize this new venture at the outset, there is little question that the new HPQ will in due course be able to stand on its own legs. Its favorable reception among academic colleagues has certainly been gratifying. I would not have been able even to think of such an expansion of publication activity had I not had the benefit of secretarial and editorial support of the very highest quality for my journal operations. But during 1982-83 there was Donna Williams, and since 1983 Christina Masucci, to provide the necessary support at a level of exemplary excellence. Still, a single person, however competent, could hardly have coped with the work had modern technology not come to our aid. The conversion of my editorial office to electronic word-processing in 1982 made possible a volume of correspondence and paperwork that would otherwise be unthinkable. (Even so, the volume of work we get done in our small office is totally unprecedented by university standards.)

Still, writing philosophy is a lonely enterprise: the writer of philosophical books in on his own. Some people are easily bored with their own company. (King Edward VII of England, for example, had this trait to the extent of a phobia, and just could not bear to be alone.) My own failing lies in the opposite direction. To read, to meditate, and—above all—to work my ideas out on paper is always a pleasure for me. What began as a diversion hardened into habit and ultimately perhaps even became a necessity.

These lines make me sound rather the "loner" and perhaps in my work-life this is indeed so. But not in my family life. I am deeply fond of Dorothy and enjoy her company very much. Whenever I return home, she is the first person I seek out, and I never feel that I am really at home until I have exchanged news of the events of the day with her. I greatly enjoy the familial things we do together. My life without her would be empty indeed. And in a different way this is true of the children as well, for as they mature in years they change in status from one's "kids" to one's friends.

To be sure, for a scholar there is always also that matter of the companionship of minds long gone. Dealing with them via their books has been my constant task—and pleasure. For me it has been an active exchange since I respond to their writings via my own.

Anyhow, my philosophical writing has gone on thrivingly. Each successive year has seen the appearance of a book or two with the agricultural regularity of spring lambs. After Jim Feather's departure from Blackwell's, my relationship with that firm eroded, and I have since had no regular publisher but have patronized a variety of houses, trying for a suitable publisher attuned to the character of each particular book—often a tedious venture. However something of a special relationship did develop with the University Press of America and with Jed Lyons, their enterprising Vice President and chief editor. He was instrumental in launching a "Nicholas Rescher Series" in 1983, which consists mainly of reprints of books of mine that had lapsed from print, but also includes several new titles. (It was Jed's interest in having this series include something of a biographical character that nerved me to the decision of including *Mid-Journey* in its scope.)

Edward Gibbon said that "an illiterate scribe may delineate a correct and elegant copy of penmanship, while the . . . (pages) of the philosopher or poet are most awkwardly scrawled in such ill formed and irregular characters, that the authors themselves, after a short interval, will be incapable of deciphering them."[46] This observation is right on the mark in my case. It generally takes months for a new secretary to master my handwriting. Despite Miss Ferber's efforts in the 4th grade, I never successfully managed the transaction from the rugged German school-script to rounded Palmer penmanship, and the result has vexed successive generations of secretaries laboring over my writings which, without exception, have always been produced in long-hand. With age my handwriting has, if anything, gotten worse.

The salient feature of my latter writings have been their concern for clarity not in handwriting but in ideas—above all for a clearer understanding of the nature of human knowledge—and scientific knowledge in particular. Just how are we to establish and consolidate such knowledge, and how far can we hope to press this project—these have been the main objects of my deliberations. I am particularly pleased with my book on *The Strife of Systems*, which the University of Pittsburgh Press published in 1985. It tries to develop a model for understanding the nature of *philosophical* inquiry along the sorts of line that philosophers of science have for decades been trying to develop for *scientific* inquiry. It is a rather ambitious attempt to characterize philosophical inquiry in systematic terms. Taking its point of departure from the 19th Century German tradition of study of the "cultural sciences" as exemplified by Herbart and Dilthey, it gave a picture of "how philosophy works"—of what the actual process of philosophizing is like—in clearer and more explicit terms than any other treatment I know of. The epistemology of philosophy has been an underdeveloped discipline for a long time now, and what pleases me is the sense that I have made real progress in this complex and difficult field. Since philosophy is not only my profession but also my love, it is gratifying to feel that I have been able to contribute towards a clearer understanding of how this discipline actually works.

In the Germany of the academic old regime of the era before World War I, it seems that every senior professor (*Ordinarius*) was expected to have a "system" of his own. I seem to have fallen into this mold, less by design than by happenstance. I am certainly not so vain as to think that my work will last. I fully expect my system to be every bit as obscure a century hence as is the case with those created by most of my predecessors of a century ago. I am not such a fool that it is for "lasting fame" that I have labored to produce all those pages, but simply for the satisfaction inherent in the work itself and for the enhanced understanding that these attempts at clarifying my ideas—at *self-education*—have brought in their wake.

Sixteen

Retrospect: 1985

(Age 57)

IN ROMAN times one became a *senex*, an old man, at sixty. But nowadays, when people generally live into their seventies and eighties, those who stand at the threshold of their seventh decade are still relatively young. All the same, when one comes to the obverse side of middle age, one enters a tendency to dwell increasingly on the past, seeing that one must now expect more experience to lie behind than ahead.

This tendency towards looking backwards has undoubtedly begun to make itself felt in my case. For one thing, I have resumed closer contacts with Germany, the land of my birth and my ancestry. For another, I have recently resumed acquaintance (only by mail, alas) with Philip Merwin, my old childhood friend of Beechhurst days, of whom I have fond memories, and whose correspondence is clearly that of a really nice person. And I find myself giving increasingly serious thought to the possibility of organizing a 40th Anniversary reunion in 1990 for the draftees who staffed the Marine Corps Institute in the Korean war years of 1950-55. (Who knows if this plan will go ahead, but the very fact that I am thinking of it seriously says something.)

"You can't teach an old dog new tricks." And yet I feel that I have changed and grown over the past decade. Not necessarily for the better. As a person I think I have become less naturally gregarious, and it takes increasing effort to keep in touch with people. I am not totally satisfied with this—I still want to maintain contact with others and to broaden my circle beyond those with whom "I go back a long way." But I have to work at it more than I used to do. These are things one cannot control—or can at best control in part. One simply has to take them in stride as they come.

Still, with the tightening of my social reach there is a broadening of intellectual outreach. Recently I have launched forth into fields quite new to me: the philosophy of religion (*Pascal's Wager*) for example, and metaphilosophy (*The Strife of Systems*). Perhaps I am compensating for diminishing flexibility as a person by enhanced flexibility as a thinker.

As one grows older, certain traits of character harden and become more pronounced; others tend to fade into the background. One becomes a better defined, more fully formed personality—but at the same time one that is a mere caricature of one's earlier self with certain particular features assuming a distinctive sharpness. Much of one's many-sideness fades away and one becomes less pliable but at the same time less flexible and versatile. Whether this is to the good or to the bad depends on the intrinsic quality of those particular characteristics that become predominant.

What is there to look forward to? For the near term, I certainly hope for a time of continuing productivity and enjoyment of the fruits of a productive life. Over the long term there is, no doubt, a period of decline and dissolution ahead, such being man's lot on earth. But even so, there is the other side of the coin. There is, after all, the compensation of seeing the children grow and develop and begin to make their place in the world. Then too there are my brainchildren—my books. It is pleasant to see them making *their* way in the world as well, occasionally meeting with appreciative attention. "A mere bauble"—perhaps; but one that cannot be entirely without value for a scholar.

At the start of his *Memoirs*, Edward Gibbon wrote: "In the fifty-second year of my age, after the completion of a toilsome and successful work, I now propose to employ some moments of my leisure in reviewing the simple transactions of a private and literary life." Though older by several years than Gibbon when he wrote these words, I cannot share his valedictory sentiments. My work has unquestionably not been as toilsome as Gibbon's—and certainly not as successful. Nevertheless, I feel that I yet have some good work left in me, bubbling away subterraneously in the hopes of finding its way out. My recent years have been a time of motion, both geographic and intellectual. During this period I have crossed the Atlantic four times a year, on average, and have carried on researches in a wide variety of philosophical topics. I certainly expect to cut back in the years ahead on physical journeys. But I hope and pray that the health and energy will be granted me to continue those interesting and rewarding mental journeys for many years, feeling, as I do, that I have some good books left in me yet, and that there is still much that I yearn to learn. May a kindly fate grant me this opportunity before the onset of that night where no man can work!

Meanwhile, the journey continues. "*Heureux qui, comme Ulysse, a fait un beaux voyage.*" It has been a good journey so far. But, alas, no journey can be characterized as altogether happy before it is safely completed. And who knows what lies ahead? It is my nature to be apprehensive—the early experiences of my life have made it impossible for me to face the future with a feeling of assured confidence. Yet, though lacking confident expectation, I look forward with a combination of gratitude for the past and hopefulness for what is yet to come.

And so I conclude these pages with the dots one traditionally uses in print to indicate the incompleteness of what is said....

—*Finis* though not yet the end—

Notes

Chapter one

1. See H. Bahlow, *Deutsches Namenlexikon* (München, 1961), under the entry "Resch" = "Rosch." The word occurs in Middle English in precisely the same sense, and the modern English verb *to rush* and adjective *rash* (= overhasty) are its direct descendants. The verb form is *raesen* = *to rush*, whence also the English *race*.

2. See the entry "Resch(n)er" in J.K. Brechenmacher, *Etymologisches Wörterbuch der Deutschen Familiennamen*, 2 vols. (Limburg a.d. Lahn, 1957). The name indicates a weaver of *Rasch* = *arr-sch*, derived from the city Arras—that is, a maker of tapestry wallhangings, known as "arras" throughout Europe, and highly popular as a wall-covering in the houses of the affluent in medieval and renaissance times. (Shakespearean villains are frequently found hiding " behind the arras.") On *rasch* = *arras* cf. Grimm's *Deutsches Wörterbuch*, where various data are also given for the equivalence *resch* = *rasch*.

3. Bahlow, *op. cit.*, under the entry "Rascher."

4. See T. Roscher, *Zur Geschichte der Familie Roscher in Niedersachsen* (Hannover, 1891).

5. Data from *Universal-Lexicon aller Wissenschaften und Künste*, Vol. 32 (Leipzig and Halle, 1742).

6. There is still one remaining topographic trace of their presence there in the name of an old country road, "Reschersfield Lane" (*Reschersacker Schnitt*) a few kilometers north of Zwingenberg, not far south of

Darmstadt. See the *Gazetteer to the Army Map service: 1:25,000 Maps of West Germany*, vol. III (Washington, D.C., 1954; Army Map Service).

7. See the *Dictionnaire historique et biographique de la Suisse*, Vol. V (Neuchatel, 1930), p. 394.

8. See the entries *Rascher* and *Raschar* in Vol. III of J. B. Rietstap, *Amorial général* (Lyon, n.d.). The Raschar's of Chur in Switzerland were ennobled in the 16th century. The Austrian Rascher's were made chevaliers in the early years of the 18th century. Their coats of arms are illustrated under the same entries in J.-B. Rietstap, *General Illustrated Armorial*, ed. by Victor and Henri Rolland (Lyon, n.d.), Vol. V (the French original appeared in Paris and The Hague in six volumes during 1903-1926).

9. The family is now extinct in Chur, but collateral branches are still extant in Zuoz and elsewhere in Switzerland. Rascher & Cie A. G. was once a major bookseller and publishing firm in Zurich (the bookshop having been founded in 1758 and the publishsing house in the 1880's). However, the Austrian branch appears to have died out.

10. A devoté of Lessing and admirer of *Nathan der Weise*, he did not see this step in the same light as his relations.

11. In the 18th and 19th centuries, people throughout Europe changed the styling of their names readily. The grandfather of John Stuart Mill was born a Milne, for example, and the Duke of Wellington's family exchanged Wesley for the more distinguished Wellesley.

12. These four half-siblings of my father's were Lina b. 1870, Alfred b. 1871, Ernest b. 1873, and Martha b. 1879.

13. She emigrated around 1890 to Denver, Colorado (where one of her brothers lived), apparently to extricate her sons Alfred and Ernest from the system of compulsory military service that had been established throughout recently unified Germany. She died at age 84 in 1925.

14. Its epitaph is written on the headstones of the family plot in Denver's Fairmount Cemetery:

Emil A. Gunsen	Joseph A. Gunsen	Lina Gunsen	Nanette Rescher
1842-1890	1845-1910	1856-1938	1841-1925
Lina Rescher	Alfred Rescher	Ernest Rescher	Martha Rescher
1870-1943	1871-1950	1873-1951	1876-1969

In moving to Denver, Nanette joined her two brothers, who had simplified the family name to Gunsen. Of her sons, only Alfred had sons; but both of these are now (1974) childless septuagenarians, and so the Rescher name stands on the verge of extinction in this branch.

15. See pp. 115-16 below.

16. There were also two daughters, Emma (b. 1860), and Julia (b. 1865). Of Emma I know little. A childhood illness left her in broken health; she never married and died in 1901. Julia married one Johann Fröhlich in 1885. They had four daughters, none of whom survived childhood save one, Irma, who was born some four months after her father's death in 1891. She eventually married but had no children.

17. Her brother Ludwig Haarburger touched my life more closely than most of my other distant relatives, because in 1958 I came into a small legacy of about $3,000 under a will he made in 1889. It struck me as amazing that anything at all should be left by 1958 to be inherited under a will made long ago by a man who died in 1903—notwithstanding the passage of several generations, two world wars, and the catastrophic inflation of the 1920's.

Ludwig Haarburger's wife Flora was half Jewish, a circumstance that was to bring home the most despicable aspects of the Hitler period. For while Ludwig himself had died in 1903, Flora survived long enough to end her days at great age in 1942 in the "concentration camp" at Theresienstadt.

18. Apparently thinking that the "roaring 20's" were designed for her benefit, Aunt Gertrude took three husbands in rapid succession in the course of the decade. Her first husband, whom she must have married at around 1921, at age 18, was Franz Siegele of Starnberg, a then well-known landscape painter. (See Hans Vollmer, *Allgemeines Lexikon der Bildenden Künstler des XX. Jahrhunderts*, Vol. 4 (Leipzig, 1958), p. 277.) He was, I take it, a charming but undomesticable man—a typical artistic bohemian. After divorcing him around 1926, Gertrude married again with a Herr Keuffele in Gersthofen, but this marriage ended in divorce after a matter of months. Gertrude's third husband, whom she married in the late 1920's, was a physician, Dr. Hermann Neussell of Gersthofen. He was a rather authoritarian type, and became an ardent Nazi. Gertrude divorced him around 1937—no doubt a sensible move—but she did not live to enjoy her restored independence for long. Becoming melancholy and despondent, she died a year or two later in 1939 (according to reports, of an overdose of sleeping pills made conveniently available by her hired lady companion, who had gained ascendancy over her, and had talked Gertrude into making a will naming herself as sole beneficiary).

19. By the terms of the convention of 1871, the troops of Württemberg formed the XIII corps of the imperial German army.

20. The Nazis had been particularly incensed by the acquittal of five defendents in the Reichstag fire trial in 1934. The crackdown on the judiciary proceeded apace thereafter.

21. To this present day (1974) there are still distant Landau relations in Goddelsheim, farming some much-reduced portion of the ancestral lands.

22. I can only recall my mother's sister, Luise, as the aunt of my young childhood, and so do not really know her well as a person. Around 1928 she married Erich Sander—a salesman or manufacturer's representative for some sort of metal-products. Their one child, Wilm, born in 1935, is the only first cousin I have. In 1964, Wilm married Karin Schröter whose family also hailed from Goddelsheim. They now (1974) have two children. Wilm has always remained in Hagen and works as a mechanical engineer in a metal-fabricating firm in Schwelm. His father Erich—an outgoing, personable, easygoing man of who I have fond childhood memories—died as a German infantryman fighting on the Russian front in 1943 or 1944.

23. Aunt Luise, my mother's sister, still lives in grandmother's old flat at this writing(1974). [And still does so in 1986.]

24. She long kept her youthful good looks. Throughout my boyhood, people took her for my "big sister"—somewhat to father's chagrin.

25. I myself had moved to Santa Monica in 1954. Mother came for a visit, and liked the place so well she decided to stay.

Chapter two
None

Chapter three
None

Chapter four
26. In those days, I even wrote some poems, of which one still remains—a sonnet written in 1945. I reproduced this juvenile production here not because I think it to have the slightest shred of merit, but only because it shows something about the sort of lad I was at this stage.

On Reading Aeschylus's "Prometheus Chained"

To a high cliff Prometheus is chained,
Which neither men not hostile gods do see.
His limbs by Vulcan's well-wrought chains are pained,
And his a myriad dreadful tortures be.
This is his punishment for giving aid
To man whose doom the god-king Jove had planned.

> And so by Vulcan's very able hand
> Fast to a Scithian rock his chains are made.
> Jove punishes with undeserved pain
> Those who his iron will do dare oppose;
> This harshness was unknown before his reign,
> Never before had gods endured such woes;
> But still great Jove might fail to reach his goal,
> For they who body chain, chain not the soul.

(From *Young America Sings: 1946 Anthology of New York City High School Poetry*.)

Chapter five

27. I missed membership in Phi Beta Kappa because there was not yet a chapter at Queens. More than a quarter-century later (in 1977), the University of Pittsburgh chapter made me an honorary member, a thoughtful step which pleased me greatly.

Chapter six
None

Chapter seven
None

Chapter eight

28. The high-water mark of his efforts along these lines were his books *Social Technology* (New York: Basic Books, 1966) and *Looking Foward: A Guide to Futures Research* (Beverly Hills: Sage Publications, 1983).

Chapter nine

29. Actually, the original author of this advice was Lord Mansfield, who thus counselled an inexperienced judge. See J.S. Mill, *System of Logic*, Vol. I, Bk. II, chap. iii, sect 3.
30. Published in *Studium Generale*, vol. 12 (1959), pp. 718-731, and reprinted in my *Essays in Philosophical Analysis* (Pittsburgh, 1969).
31. His grave memorial was erected by Dr. Ayla König, who was the daughter of his old (1920's) landlady. She practiced dentistry in Istanbul

and did much to care for Oskar in his later years. She supplied the materials for the biographical notice of Oskar prepared by Dr. Leon Nemoy for the *Yale University Library Gazette* in 1972 on the occasion of Yale's acquiring a part of Oskar's collection of Arabic manuscripts.

32. Vol. 70 (1960), pp. 167-196.

33. In particular, I wish that my knowledge of mathematics and physics were more solid, or again, that I knew far better than I do the languages (French, Latin, Greek, Arabic) which I have "learned" over the years.

Chapter ten

34. Ultimately published as *Galen and the Syllogism* (Pittsburgh: University of Pittsburgh Press, 1966).

Chapter eleven

35. See G. F. Hourani (ed.), *Essays on Islamic Philosophy and Science*(Albany: State University of New York Press, 1975), pp. 189-221.

36. I might just mention one of the little rhyme-cum-action jingles I concocted for their amusement during their infancy:

> In the middle of the night
> Slinks the purple hippadite
> Slowly creeping, slowly crawling
> Slowly 'round the corners grawling*
> On the hunt for little boys
> Whom it uses for its toys
> When those little boys it catches
> Then it pounces, grabs, and snatches*
> And with many fearsome grickels
> Then those little boys it tickles*
>   (*Accompany with suitable actions)

37. Compare G. B. Kistiakowsky's obituary of Conant in *Nature*, vol. 273 (29 June 1978), p. 794.

Chapter twelve

38. Thus in 1971 I lectured on "Idealism," presenting the core of *Conceptual Idealism* (Oxford: Blackwell, 1973). In 1972, my lectures on

"The Primacy of Practice" prefigured a book of that same name (Oxford: Blackwell, 1973), and my 1973 lectures on "A Theory of Possibility" outlined the book of that same title (Oxford: Blackwell, 1975). My 1974 lecture series on "Sympathy" ultimately saw the light of print as *Unselfishness* (Pittsburgh: University of Pittsburgh Press, 1975).

39. In quantitative terms, I would estimate that I nowadays (1973-1974) watch television for some twelve hours during the week, and average just under three hours per week of home-external forms of spectatorial entertainments like films and concerts (representing roughly two such outings ever three weeks). The sizable difference speaks volumes for the impact of television!

40. Secretary General of the International Union of History and Philosophy of Science and Secretary of its Division of Logic, Methodology, and Philosophy of Science (1969-1975); Chairman of the Finance Committee of the International Federation of Philosophical Societies (1973-78); Member of the Institut International de Philosophie (elected in 1971); Member, U.S. National Committee for History and Philsophy of Science (1969-1975); Member, Bicentennial Program Commission of the American Philosophical Association (1973-1976).

41. Published in 1973, but mainly written in 1970-1971. I have always been particularly fond of this book, seeing it as perhaps the first of my works as a fully matured philosopher.

42. In the course of 1974, which was a fairly typical year in this respect, I read:

> Robert Ensor, *England: 1870-1914 (Oxford History of England*, Vol. XIV).
> Kathleen Norris, *The Treasure and Uneducating Mary* [an anthology of her short stories]
> Mrs. Humphry Ward, *Sir George Tressady*
> Samuel Pepys, *Diary* [for 1660]
> Maria Knoll, *Sophia: Electress of Hanover*
> Ruth Jordan, *Sophie Dorothea* [of Hanover]
> Elizabeth Longford, *Wellington: Pillar of State*
> Alan Palmer, *Metternich*
> Charles Petrie, *A Historian Looks at His World*
> Ralph Barton Perry, *The Thought and Character of William James*
> Robert Adams, *Watership Down*
> James D. Watson, *The Double Helix*

I wish that this list of "general," work-disconnected reading were much longer, but am very glad it is at least this long.

Chapter thirteen

43. John Maynard Keynes alone took steps to inform himself about it, and the rest of Bloomsbury found it hard to forgive this peccadillo.

44. Thus fresh experience superadds its additional increment dv to the preexisting total v in such a way that its effective import is measured by the proportion dv/v. And $\int dv/v = \log v$. On such an approach, an increment to one's lifetime has a *cognitive* value determined on strict analogy with Daniel Bernoulli's famous proposal to measure the *economic* value of incremental resources by means of a logarithmic yardstick. (To be sure, man does not live by cognition alone, and many other factors must doubtless enter into an *overall* assessment.) ADDENDUM (1985): When writing the initial version of this book in 1974, I deemed myself to have discovered the principle of the merely logarithmic growth of knowledge through experience. In fact, however, the sagacious Edward Gibbon anticipated it in his *Memoirs of My Life*: "The proportion of a part to the whole is the only standard by which we can measure the length of our existence. At the age of twenty, one year is a tenth perhaps of the time which has elapsed within our consciousness and memory: at the age of fifty it is no more than a fortieth, and this relative value continues to decrease till the last sands are shaken out by the hand of death."

Chapter fourteen
None

Chapter fifteen

45. David E. Koskoff, *The Mellons* (New York, 1978), p. 411.
46. Edward Gibbon, *Memoirs of My Life*, (Harmondsworth, 1984; Penguin Library Edition), p. 63.

Chapter sixteen
None

Name Index

Adams, Robert, 225n42
Airaksinen, Timo, 202
al-Farabi, 117
Albritton, Rogers, 64
Alexander of Aphrodisias, 117
Alles, Günther, 23
Almeder, Robert, 202
Anderson, Alan Ross, 128, 139–40, 195
Aristotle, 118, 168, 175, 178
Artin, Emil, 63
Austen, Jane, 65
Ayer, A. J., 149

Bahlow, H., 219n1 & n3
Baier, Annette, 128
Baier, Kurt, 127, 137–9, 141, 156, 206
Baltas, Aristides, 202
Beddell, John, 30–1, 42
Bell, R. S., 170, 193
Belnap, Nuel, 128–9, 195, 206
Benes, Vaclav, 68
Berkeley, George, 183
Bochenski, I. M., 138

Bohnert, Herbert G., 51
Boswell, James, 12
Boyle, Marj, 196
Bradley, Omar, 63, 100
Brandom, Robert, 195
Brechenmacher, J. K., 219n2
Brown, Alicia, 147
Brown, Jacqueline Henle, 147
Brown, Peter F., 147
Buckley, Thomas Floyd, 31–2, 42
Butera, Linda, 196, 202
Butts, Robert, 165–6

Colden, Cadwallader, 59
Callaghan, William, 51
Carnap, Rudolf, 51, 102, 150, 165
Church, Alonzo, 62–4, 70, 92
Churchill, Winston, 80
Clancy, William, 203
Clarke, Jack, 44
Cohen, Jonathan, 161
Cohen, Leon, 52
Colden, Charles S., 59
Cole, Barbara, 73
Cole, James L., 64, 73

Collbaum, Frank, 101
Conant, J. B., 153
Cooper, John, 194
Cope, T. Freeman, 52
Couturat, Louis, 65-6
Curl, Herbert, 88

Dalkey, Norman, 100, 122
Davidson, Donald, 51
Descartes, René, 48, 63, 178
Diels, Charles, 44-5
Dilthey, Wilhelm, 214
Disraeli, Benjamin, 65
Dumas, Alexander, 38, 43
Durant, Will, 48, 52
Drakert, Joan, 55

Edward VII, 212
Eilenberg, Samuel, 56
Einstein, Albert, 76
Eisenhower, Dwight D., 84, 87, 90
Ellsberg, Daniel, 147
Ensor, Robert, 225n42
Esterowitz, Harry, 40
Ewing, A. C., 165

Fay, Cornelius Ryan, 55-6, 65
Feather, James, 164, 197, 213
Feller, William, 68
Ferber, Miss, 30-1, 213
Fielding, Henry, 61, 65
Fischer, August, 9
Ford, Lester, 100
Fox, Colonel, 72
Frankenheimer, John, 43
Franklin, Benjamin, 68, 88
Fraassen, Bas von, 131, 63
Freud, Sigmund, 56
Fröhlich, Irma, 221n16
Fröhlich, Johann, 221n16
Fröhlich, Julia, 221n16

Gale, George, 203
Gale, Maya, 124
Gale, Richard, 129, 206
George, Henry, 42, 56
George, Rolf, 202
Gibbon, Edward, 91, 213, 217, 226n44 & 46
Goethe, J. W. von, 12, 41, 48
Goheen, John, 52
Goldsmith, 12
Goldwater, Barry, 84, 133
Grelling, Kurt, 76
Grote, Gunther, 23
Grunbaum, Adolf, 104, 112, 123, 127, 136, 138-9, 201, 206
Grunbaum, Barbara, 112
Grunbaum, Thelma, 112, 125
Gunsen, Emil A., 220n14
Gunsen, Joseph A., 220n14
Gunsen, Lina, 220n14

H., Jean, 55, 67-8
Haarburger, Flora, 221n17
Haarburger, Ludwig, 221n17
Hackenberg, Beatrice, 43
Hackenberg, John, 43
Hailperin, Marie, 113
Hailperin, Theodore, 113
Hare, R. M., 161
Harman, Gwen, 89
Harman, Walter, 89
Harré, Hettie, 161
Harré, Rom, 161
Hauff, Wilhelm, 23
Haugeland, John, 195
Haynes, Thomas, 104, 112
Hebel, Johann Peter, 41
Hegel, 151, 168, 178, 183
Heinekamp, Albert, 204
Helmer, Maggie, 99-100
Helmer, Olaf, 99-100, 101-2, 122, 148

Hempel, Carl G., 48, 52, 58, 75, 148, 152, 168
Herbart, J. F., 214
Hetzel, Frederick, 132, 163
Hitch, Charles, 107
Hoffman, Banesh, 52
Holmes, Sherlock, 43
Hourani, G. F., 224n35
Humboldt, Alexander von, 205
Humphreys, Paul, 202

Ihrig, Gwendolyn, 75
Ihrig, Judson Lamour, 75
Isar, Leopold, 5
Isenberg, Arnold, 52

Janis, Allen, 203
Johnson, Lyndon, 84, 133
Jones, C. Maury, 89
Jones, Miss, 30
Jordan, Elijah, 113
Jordan, Ruth, 225n42
Joynt, Anne, 113
Joynt, Carey B., 113, 119

Kahn, Herman, 101
Kant, Immanuel, 118, 151, 168, 178, 183, 185
Kemeny, John, 76
Keuffele, Herr, 221n18
Keynes, John Maynard, 226n43
Kistiakowsky, G. B., 224n37
Knag, Charlotte, 40, 48
Knoll, Maria, 225n42
König, Ayla, 134, 223n31
Körner, Sephan, 162
Koskoff, David E., 226n45
Küng, Hans, 153

Landau, Adele Kämper, 14–5, 20
Landau, Johannes, 13–5

Landau, Karl, 13
Landers, Richard, 37
Landau, Wilhelm Heinrich Ludwig, 13–5
Leibniz, G. W. von, 4, 65, 69, 118, 151, 166–8, 178, 183, 207
LeMay, Curtis B., 100
Lessing, G. E., 220n10
Lewis, C. I., 168
Lieber, Lilian, 41
Lindbergh, Charles, 100
Lineback, Richard, 198
Litchfield, Edward H., 126, 132, 142
Longford, Elizabeth, 225n42
Lyons, Jed, 213

MacArthur, Douglas, 101
MacDonald, Hugh, 193
Maier, Wolfgang, 23
Mainzer, Klaus, 202, 206
Mann, Miss, 41
Mansfield, Lord, 223n29
Maritain, Jacques, 62
Marmura, Michael E., 118
Marx, Karl, 56, 101
Massey, Gerald J., 141, 203
Masucci, Christina, 212
McCarthy, Senator Joseph, 85
McGuire, Charles, 144
McGuire, Vickie, 144
Mellon, Richard King, 126, 201
Menne, Albert, 144
Merwin, Donald, 31, 42
Merwin, Philip, 31, 42, 215
Mill, John Stuart, 178, 220n11, 223n29
Miller, Sterling, 208
Mittelstrass, Jürgen, 202, 206
Moore, Frederick B., 98, 150
Mostowski, Andrzej, 162
Myers, Richard, 55

Nehamas, Alexander, 195
Nemoy, Leon, 224n31
Neumann, John von, 79, 100
Neussell, Hermann, 221n18
Neville, Harvey, 111
Nixon, Richard, 84
Nölle, Dieter, 23
Norris, Kathleen, 225n42

Oates, Whitney, 68
Oppenheim, Paul, 75

Palmer, Alan, 225n42
Passafiume, Mimi, 145
Passafiume, Samuel, 145
Patzig, Günther, 144
Peake, Charles, 126-7
Peirce, C. S., 102, 164, 168, 178, 183, 207
Pepys, Samuel, 194, 225n42
Pera, Marcello, 202
Perry, Ralph Barton, 225n42
Petrie, Charles, 225n42
Pitt, Joseph, 202
Plato, 168, 178
Plautus, 146
Posvar, Wesley Wentz, 142
Puntel, Lorenz, 202
Putnam, Hilary, 76

Quine, W. V. O., 51, 168

Rascher, Albrecht Heinrich von, 4-5
Rauch, Frederick Augustus, 111
Raymond, Jack, 101
Reagan, Ronald, 197
Reiser, Oliver, 142
Rescher, Adolf, 6-8
Rescher, Alfred, 6, 220n12 & n14
Rescher, Catherine Ann, 166, 170, 175, 191, 193-4, 209
Rescher, Dorothy, 142-44, 146-7, 153, 158-9, 166, 169, 184, 203, 208-9, 212
Rescher, Elizabeth, 121, 134-7, 171-2, 210-11
Rescher, Emilie Haarburger, 7
Rescher, Emilie Isar, 5
Rescher, Emma, 6, 221n16
Rescher, Ernest, 220n13 & n14
Rescher, Erwin Hans, 7-13, 24-5, 35, 91
Rescher, Frances Short, 73-5, 96, 102-3, 121, 134-7, 171-2
Rescher, Gertrude, 7-8, 221n18
Rescher, Julie, 6
Rescher, Lina, 220n12 & n14
Rescher, Mark, 146-7, 166, 170-1, 191, 193-4, 208-9
Rescher, Meta Anna Landau, 9-12, 14-17, 20-25, 193
Rescher, Nannette Gunzenhausen, 6-7, 220n14
Rescher, Nehemias, 3-6
Rescher, Oskar, 7-8, 115-6, 224n31
Rescher, Otto, 7-8, 20
Rescher, Owen, 146, 170, 191, 194, 208-9
Riétstap, J. B., 220n8
Ritter, Irmgart, 21
Rolland, Henri, 220n8
Rolland, Victor, 220n8
Roescher, Johann Jakob, 4-5
Roscher, T., 219n4
Roscher, Wilhelm, 4
Rowan, Harry, 147
Russell, Bertrand, 63, 65-6, 76-7, 150

S., Lorna, 55
Sabbathé, Miss, 30
Salmon, Merrilee, 195

INDEX

Salmon, Wesley, 195
Sander, Erich, 222n22
Sander, Luise Landau, 14-5, 222n22 & n23
Sander, Wilm, 222n22
Savage, James, 102
Scaife, Alan Magee, 126
Schäffer, Lothar, 144
Schiller, J. L. F. von, 41
Schnath, Georg, 204
Schneewind, Jerome, 68
Schollick, Henry, 132
Schopenhauer, Arthur, 48
Schröter, Karin, 222n22
Schwemmer, Oswald, 202
Scoon, Robert, 92
Sellars, Wilfrid, 128, 139, 206
Shaffer, Jerome, 68
Shaw, Dickson, 144
Shehadi, Fadlou, 64
Short, Henry Howe, 74
Siegele, Franz, 221n18
Simon, Herbert, 134
Simpson, Florence, 96
Skyrms, Brian, 131
Slivka, Gerald, 198
Smith, David, 209
Smollet, Tobias, 65
Snow, C. P., 153
Sosa, Ernest, 131
Spencer, Herbert, 65
Stace, Walter Terence, 62-3, 165, 168
Stebbing, Susan, 99

Sterne, Laurence, 12
Stevenson, Capt. Charles, 84, 133
Stevenson, Robert Lewis, 38
Störtebekker, Klaus, 14
Sumpter, William, 162
Szathmary, Arthur, 63

Tarski, Alfred, 97
Taylor, David, 161
Thompson, Frederick B., 96-8
Toretti, Roberto, 202
Totok, Wilhelm, 69, 144
Trollope, Anthony, 122, 133
Truman, Harry, 88

Urmson, James O., 71, 168
Ushenko, Andrew Paul, 48, 63, 168

Walpole, Robert, 163
Ward, Mrs. Humphry, 225n42
Watson, James D., 225n42
White, Phyllis, 158
Whitehead, A. N., 63
Whittaker, Martin Dewey, 110
Williams, Donna, 212
Williams, John D., 99, 107
Wodehouse, P. G., 43
Wohlstetter, Albert, 147
Wolters, Gereon, 207
Wood, Ledger, 66
Wright, G. H. von, 138

Ziegler, Howard, 104, 109, 111, 119